CUTTING INTO THE MEATPACKING LINE

DEBORAH FINK

CUTTING INTO

STUDIES IN RURAL CULTURE / JACK TEMPLE KIRBY, EDITOR

THE MEATPACKING LINE

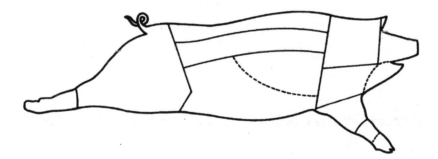

WORKERS AND CHANGE IN THE RURAL MIDWEST

THE UNIVERSITY OF NORTH CAROLINA PRESS / CHAPEL HILL AND LONDON

Manufactured in the United States of America

The paper in this book meets the guidelines

for permanence and durability of the Committee

on Production Guidelines for Book Longevity

of the Council on Library Resources.

Library of Congress Cataloging-in-Publication Data

Fink, Deborah, 1944–

Cutting into the meatpacking line: workers and

change in the rural midwest / Deborah Fink.

p.   cm.

Includes bibliographical references and index.

ISBN 978-0-8078-2388-0 (cloth: alk. paper).—

ISBN 978-0-8078-4695-7 (pbk.: alk. paper)

1. Packing-house workers—United States.   I. Title.

HD8039.P152U535   1998

331.7'6649'00973—dc21   97-22006

CIP

02 01 00 99 98 5 4 3 2 1

THIS BOOK WAS DIGITALLY PRINTED.

To the memory of Carri Archer
To the future of Lorencito Rey Quintanar

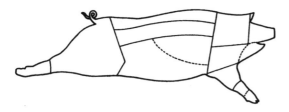

CONTENTS

A section of illustrations appears following page 112.

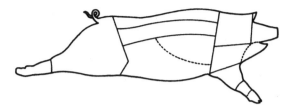

TABLES

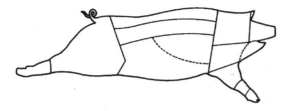

PREFACE

Having grown up in the rural Midwest, I conformed to the class inequalities laid out in this book before I knew what they were. Even as a child, I knew people who fell outside of most generalizations about the good rural life, and I knew people whose experiences confirmed the ideal of the wholesome heartland. I understood who belonged where in rural society, but I was not aware of what centered or marginalized people. Although I must have picked up something about class in my graduate studies in anthropology, leaving home taught me more than books. In the 1970s I went to Denmark, where I did dissertation fieldwork on the island of Møn.[1] Largely by chance, I entered Danish rural life through the Husmandsforening (Smallholders Union), which at that time was composed largely of wageworkers. The rules of class division are more obvious everywhere from the bottom than from the top, and in the homes of rural Danish laborers I could not escape class analysis. Approaching the study of rural Denmark through the working class, I had the ironies of unspoken class boundaries laid before me daily. In Denmark, which was supposed to have abolished class distinctions, I could discern principles of inequality that had been invisible to me in my own country.

What I learned as a foreigner in Denmark I saw with different eyes when I did fieldwork in rural Iowa and Nebraska in the 1980s. Rather than the rural working class that had guided me into Danish culture, in the United States it was middle-class farmers. The first people I knew in each area, those who introduced me to the local community, were self-employed farmers. With broad social networks and interesting caches of photographs and records, farm families had a great deal of information to share on the life of rural communities. Yet I could see wageworkers on the farms and many other wageworkers off the farms; I sensed that I would have been more intimately connected with these wageworkers had I been in Denmark than I was in the United States. Although people spoke as if rural Midwesterners in general were farmers, I was annoyingly aware of the people who were not. Eventually I toured rural manufacturing plants, drank beer with factory workers, and visited homes of rural workers and the rural jobless, but I never felt that my research did justice to the experience of the rural working class. Working-class women in particular were usually too busy to bother with me. I quilted, butchered chickens, and hoed gardens with farm women, but it was rarely possible for me to hang out with wage-earning women in the same way. Their worksites were not as accessible to me, they usually had less free time than farm women had, and they tended not to turn up in the same social settings as farm people.

I began to imagine a research project in which I would focus on rural midwestern wageworkers. Rather than centering my sights on farm people and catching glimpses of wageworkers on the periphery, I would center my sights on the rural working class and consider farm people in relation to their interaction with the world of wageworkers. What better way than to enter the belly of the whale by taking a job in a rural meatpacking plant? That was my plan. As an anthropologist, I had good models of industrial fieldwork.[2]

Meatpacking plants dot the Iowa landscape; I had choices about where to work. Both of the two leading corporations in the 1980s restructuring of the meatpacking industry had plants within forty miles of my home in Ames: ConAgra had a Monfort plant at Marshalltown and IBP had a plant at Perry. Although I had a slight preference for ConAgra, because it had been studied less than IBP, driving to Marshalltown every day on busy, two-lane US 30 was unappealing. I could take quiet backroads across the beautiful Des Moines River valley to reach Perry, and this tilted me toward IBP. I applied for a production job there, started to work on January 14, 1992, and stayed at the job through May 9. It was a random dip into the world of the modern rural midwestern meatpacker. As will become apparent in this book, it was an extraordinarily difficult process.

In addition to participant observation on the production floor of

IBP, I have drawn on interviews with 125 working-class persons and three persons whom I identified as basically middle class. These included sixty-eight women and sixty men. Characteristic of rural Iowa as a whole, the majority of those interviewed were U.S.-born and white, nine were Latino, and ten were black. I was fortunate in being able to use sixty-three interviews from the Iowa Labor History Oral Project (ILHOP) and twelve interviews from the United Packinghouse Workers of America Oral History Project (UPWAOHP). Some of the same people were interviewed in both projects, and one of the persons whom I interviewed turned out to have also been part of the Iowa project. Other primary sources included union records, company reports and brochures, manuscript census data, government reports, and newspapers.

This project has been an ethical quagmire. Anthropological ethics guidelines have been helpful as I have thought through fieldwork issues, but they have not resolved the major dilemmas that I have seen arising from my work. Indeed, the American Anthropological Association has acknowledged that conflicting values arise and that established guidelines will not apply to all situations.[3] My personal dilemmas arose as I constantly observed evil and realized that regardless of what I did I was participating in it. I lost even the option of packing my gear, going home, and reclaiming my innocence.

Essays of Judith Stacey and Daphne Patai have posed the questions, "Can there be a feminist ethnography?" and "Is ethical research possible?" In each case, they have answered with an unequivocal no.[4] Feminist anthropologists, such as myself, have sought political transformation through intimate identification with our subjects. As Stacey and Patai point out, feminist researchers are apt to buy into the illusion of an alliance with our subjects when, in fact, our position is inherently unequal to the people we are studying. We listen, sympathize, and try for solidarity, but our agendas are typically different from those of our research subjects. An acknowledgment of difference and distance is probably more honest and ethical than an identification of interests. Yet we still try hard and take ourselves seriously in our attempts to do research that answers the needs of those with whom we work. Patai suggests an attitude of "subversive humor" as an antidote.[5]

Although shedding illusions of intimacy is probably helpful, it does not release us from our ethical responsibilities. It is not a question of finding a way to make ourselves feel good in spite of everything; it is a question of coming to grips with reality. As Patai states, "However powerfully we may experience these problems on an individual basis in concrete research situations, we must not lose sight of the fact that these are not, in fact, personal problems of overly sensitive individuals. They are, rather, genuine ethical dilemmas that the broader society, built on inequalities, strategically induces us to disregard."[6] Once we rip apart the cultural conventions that shield us on a daily basis from vast injustice, the world becomes a different place.

For two years after working in the IBP plant I was unable to put together a logical sequence of words to unpack and lay out the array of physical and emotional carnage I observed or to do even intellectual justice to the people whose lives I had briefly shared. Words have come as I have reclaimed the difference and distance between myself and my subjects, and words are what I can offer to them.

My debt to my IBP coworkers is enormous. I am also grateful to the other workers interviewed for this project. Lewie Anderson, a former IBP worker, the former head of the Packinghouse Division of United Food and Commercial Workers, and a dedicated researcher of the meatpacking industry, provided background information and support. Debbie Handy, a former IBP worker from Storm Lake, Iowa, has also laid out background and years of research on IBP. Shelton Stromquist and Marvin Bergman of the University of Iowa's Center for the Study of the Recent History of the United States included me in a seminar on meatpacking workers. It was the setting for fruitful interchange with labor researchers: Paul Street, Peter Rachleff, Roger Horowitz, Wilson Warren, Bruce Fehn, Dennis Deslippe, and Mark Grey.[7] Merle Davis, who did many of the interviews for ILHOP, shared research tips and references from his extensive store of knowledge on Iowa labor. Mary Bennett and Shaner Magalhães of the Iowa State Historical Society Archives helped me navigate around ILHOP and other labor records. Mark Smith, secretary-treasurer of the Iowa Federation of Labor, graciously allowed me to use ILHOP interviews. Nancy Naples, a sociologist at the University of California in Irvine, and Brian Page, a geographer at the University of Colorado in Denver, were research allies whose parallel work enhanced mine. Stephanie Pratt of the Iowa Commission on the Status of Women did some of the interviewing for this project and shared inside reflections on Perry life as well as intriguing theoretical proposals. Clara Oleson of the University of Iowa Labor Center offered advice and support in the early stages of the research. Des Moines attorney Roxanne Conlin, whose name arose repeatedly as a longtime friend of Iowa's working people, provided information and insights. My gratitude to these workers, scholars, and activists does not imply unity in our analytical or political perspectives.

From the University of North Carolina Press, Jack Kirby, editor of the series on rural culture, and Lewis Bateman, executive editor, have been everything that an author could wish for. An anonymous manuscript reader also gave comments that tightened and clarified the text. Pamela Upton, the project editor, and Stevie Champion, the copyeditor, have worked skillfully and tactfully to smooth the rough edges of the manuscript and produce the book.

Dorothy Schwieder, of Iowa State University, the dean of Iowa history, has been a longtime friend and reality check; her open ear, vast knowledge, and broad vision season all my research and writing. As always, I have held the Danish work of Carsten Hess before me as a model of creativity and careful scholarship. The moral encouragement of Mikel Johnson, Judith McDaniel, Callie Marsh, and Nicky Mendenhall has been critical at different times.

A. M. Fink has weathered this project gracefully and has unfailingly extended his support and confidence, for which I am deeply grateful.

CUTTING INTO THE MEATPACKING LINE

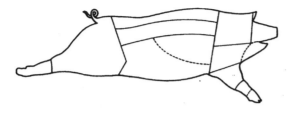

INTRODUCTION

This book is an anthropological and historical study of the working class in rural Iowa, using the porkpacking industry as a point of focus. It is a departure from the line of rural midwestern studies about family farms or about the middle class of small towns. Nearly all of these studies pick up the Jeffersonian thread of the rural virtues of independence through self-employment as epitomized in the family farm. Yet even the earliest Iowa farms had hired workers, and wage laborers built and maintained the infrastructure that undergirded Iowa's farm and small-town society. Wage labor was a central, if frequently overlooked, constituent of rural midwestern economic growth. Meatpacking, which was based on wage labor, and farming, which was based on self-employment, supported each other. Historically, meatpacking was Iowa's largest manufacturing industry, and pork was its major product.

Heartbreaking social and economic changes occurred in Iowa in the 1980s. The sudden tightening of the U.S. economy struck farms hard, forcing many farmers off the land. At the same time the restructuring of U.S. manufacturing closed down many urban factories. Corporations scattered across the globe in search of cheap labor, as communications technology surmounted barriers that had localized manufacturing in population centers. Some manufacturing functions shifted to Latin America or the Pacific rim; rural midwestern relocation was another piece of this outward movement. Like many other manufacturers, meatpackers boarded up their urban plants. By the end of the 1980s the center of gravity of the industry had shifted into the rural areas of prairie and plains states. Meatpacking workers, who had emerged as rural labor elite in the post–World War II years, saw their wages and working conditions deteriorate. Meatpacking plants rose to the position of number one among U.S. industries in both occupational injuries and occupational illnesses.[1]

Since 1960, a group of "new-breed" packers has consumed the meatpacking industry and redefined basic principles hammered out over years of struggle. Although brand names such as Swift and Armour still appear in supermarket coolers, most of the market brands are now controlled by new-breed corporations dominated by the "Big Three" meatpackers—IBP, ConAgra, and Cargill. Whereas ConAgra and Cargill are conglomerates with farflung global enterprises running the gamut of the food chain, IBP specializes in red meat production and has the world's largest red meat processing system. Taking green and white as its corporate colors because green is the color of money, IBP has come to symbolize, in the midwestern United States, the worst excesses of 1980s corporate arrogance.[2]

One goal of this book is to put this 1980s trauma in historical context. No one can dispute the significance of the 1980s as a decade of change, but *Cutting Into the Meatpacking Line* emphasizes the continuity with which these changes grew out of contradictions endemic to rural life and culture. Indeed, IBP was itself born as Iowa Beef Packers, a homegrown answer to the formidably dominant meatpacking companies of Chicago and Omaha. Yet IBP turned back on the Iowa countryside with the same weapons that it used to defeat the urban industry. Failure to recognize the realities that the rural Midwest shared with urban society left a soft underbelly inviting exploitation.

A second goal is to emphasize the rural working class as an integral constituent of Iowa's past and present. The working class is missing from the Jeffersonian vision of rural America as a land of self-employed farmers, and this vision has shaped the narrative of Iowa as a rural state. The story of Iowa as told through its political, economic, and intellectual leadership has an illustrious cast of heroes and a few heroines, but it wastes few words on the majority of the population which built the history piece by piece through ordinary lives. Social history has answered this convention with richly textured descriptions of family farm operations and small-town businesses. Yet, for Iowa, even these social histories tend to be written as if the definitive social actors were in families of small-scale entrepreneurs and to give short shrift to those who built Iowa's railroads and bridges, picked its crops, and turned its hogs into ham and sausage. Labor history, which foregrounds the institutions of the working class, provides a down-under perspective on social process. My use of anthropological research techniques adds another dimension of workers' experience, including more detail on rural and unorganized workers than is available in labor history accounts drawing on union sources.[3]

A third goal is to explore the ways that gender and ethnicity/race have shaped rural midwestern history. Scholarship in these areas in the last twenty-five years has radically altered our understandings of the world in general and the rural Midwest in particular. Studies that begin the process of integrating women and black people into Iowa history have meticulously picked up and analyzed pieces of the social fabric that had previously been left in the dusty corners. Careful attention and crafting have made these pieces important; more needs to be done. Beyond the compensatory incorporation of previously excluded social groupings, studies of gender and race examine the way that culturally constructed polarities affect the shape of daily life. How did race and gender affect the production floor and labor organizing of an Iowa meatpacking plant, even when all personnel were white men? How does the entrance of women and ethnic minorities reconfigure the reality of industrial production and working-class life? How have management and labor unions used the gender and ethnic differences that pervade U.S. society? What does "rural" add to the analysis?[4]

The title of the book, Cutting Into the Meatpacking Line, has multiple meanings. As an anthropologist, I cut into a meatpacking line by going to work at an IBP plant for almost four months, making myself part of the story of what happened to the workers both inside and outside the plant. "Cutting into the meatpacking line" also describes the painful and extended process by which women and ethnic minorities inserted themselves into the meatpacking workforce and redefined the struggle for recognition of workers' rights. Further, "cutting into the line" is a metaphor for the disorderly impertinence with which meatpacking workers as a whole insisted on claiming their dignity and their place in the social order. This claim emerged most forcefully in the forty years following the birth of the United Packinghouse Workers of America during World War II, but it also predated World War II and continues in the 1990s. Finally, the book itself cuts into the line of economic development rhetoric that privileges the viewpoints of the economic elite over those of the people who perform the physical labor that produces wealth. It follows and builds on scholarship that interprets social process in terms of the experiences of the diverse majority of common people.

Rather than one line, the story of the rural Iowa working class has a range of counterpoints and cacophonies that reflect diversity rather than uniformity of experience. Accordingly, the plan of the book involves a progressive retelling of the formation and development of the rural Iowa meatpacking workforce. Chapter 1 is a personal account of my work as a participant observer on the production floor of the IBP porkpacking plant outside of Perry, Iowa. Chapter 2 moves out from the immediacy of personal observation, placing my experience in historical and social perspective by outlining the general development of the Iowa working class and white male meatpacking workers specifically. Chapter 3 takes up the thread of gender, exploring the way that gender shaped the division of labor in rural Iowa in the early twentieth century; the impact of gender on the composition of the meatpacking workforce; and the subsequent manipulation of gender on the part of management, union leadership, and workers. Chapter 4 is about ethnicity and race as defined and developed in rural Iowa and in the changing conditions in meatpacking plants. Although rural Iowa has never been as homogeneous as sometimes pictured, it has become considerably more diverse in the 1990s. The meatpacking industry has taken advantage of long-standing ethnic and racial contradictions in rural Iowa and has in turn created new ones. Chapter 5 brings the diverse voices together and plays them in the context of the dominant strains of Iowa culture and society. The continuing reference point for the book is the rural working class of the 1990s. As I relate the study to the routine reality facing IBP workers, the overarching question is how this could happen and hence how we might turn the corner into a more humane era.

As a blend of anthropology and history, *Cutting Into the Meatpacking Line* sometimes gives real personal names and sometimes suppresses them. Having used interviews from the Iowa Labor History Oral Project and the United Packinghouse Workers of America Oral History Project,

I provide complete citations for these references. As an anthropologist, I extended anonymity to most of those whom I interviewed, a practice essential for a variety of personal and job-related reasons. I have given pseudonyms to these persons, using first names when I was on a first-name basis with the individual and full names when I did not address the person by first name.

I hope that this study contributes to progressive social change, which will necessarily entail a shift in power relations. An evil system tarnishes almost all who operate within it, but I do not intend to identify any single individual as an archvillain.

1

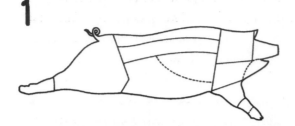

WHAT IS YOUR PROBLEM, RUTH?

AN ANTHROPOLOGIST GETS A JOB

The culture of the Perry IBP porkpacking plant is unlike that of rural Iowa outside the plant, although working in the plant radically reshapes peoples' outside lives. In January 1992, in order to study the experience of wage labor in rural Iowa, I went to work at the Perry plant, an ordeal that revealed a small part of the disjuncture between the world of IBP and orderly social life.

My fieldwork began with the application process. After driving forty miles over snowy Iowa roads from my home in Ames to Perry, I stopped first at the Iowa Job Service office in Perry, which does initial screening of IBP applicants. Once the inevitable wait and screening were done, I took the directions given by the Job Service woman, drove west of town, and turned off the highway onto the IBP road. The plant itself is set off from the rural Iowa landscape, first by an oversized parking lot that leaves a liminal space on the outer edge, and then by a fence and guardhouse. Reaching the IBP complex, I parked on the outer rim of cars, uncomfortably aware that my two-year-old Nissan did not blend into the crowd of large, sixties-era Fords and Chryslers parked close to the plant.

The people at the University of Iowa Labor Center had advised me that my hair, glasses, teeth, and clothes were all wrong for getting hired at IBP, saying that I needed a permanent in my hair and working-class glasses and clothes. Unwilling to face a permanent, I had bought two packages of tiny pink sponge rollers to curl my short straight hair, but it was a disaster. Rather than trying for a feminine look, I had moussed my hair into an Elvis Presley style and wore tight jeans and old glasses. My sister Kate told me to chew gum. Hoping that I looked normal rather than ridiculous, I walked to the guardhouse. The guard called inside to verify that Job Service had sent me and then instructed me to walk about twenty yards across the bare, paved inner yard to a side stairway, go up the stairs and through a door, and wait.

In the small waiting room were broken plastic chairs, a table, a lot of dirt, and an inside window. I waited in this room for almost two hours: my time cost IBP nothing at this point. Finally a man came out of a side door to ask what I wanted. Learning that Job Service had sent me for an interview, he went to look for the interviewer.

The interviewer—"Ricardo," he told me to call him—motioned for me to take a chair when I was finally admitted into his office. Knowing IBP's reputation as a secretive company, I had guessed that whatever else I could offer as a worker, it would not hire an anthropological researcher, so I left that part off the application form. Afraid that my residence in Ames, a university town, would flag my application, I had listed my address and telephone number as those of a Des Moines friend. I had crafted a life history that I hoped would make me seem to be a disturbed, recently divorced farm woman who had been out of the formal workforce for most of her life. Accordingly, I submitted the names of three friends who worked in the public mental health system as references. As it happened, none of this mattered. Ricardo began the interview by informing me that everyone at IBP worked sixty hours a week. As my stomach sank, I asked if I could work part-time.

"No," he stated firmly. "We all work Saturdays. That's how IBP operates. You got things to do on weekends?"

"No," I answered, looking down at my lap. "I'll do it."

"You sure?"

"I'm sure."

At least I wanted to come back and see if I could actually learn something. Ricardo informed me that the starting pay would be $6.50 an hour, gave me a medical form to fill out, and told me to come back the next day for a physical examination. The interview could not have lasted more than ten minutes, and it would have been shorter if it had not been interrupted by telephone calls.

The next day when I returned, I waited in the same room. This time I talked with a Mexican man who came in after I had been there for some time. In broken English he told me that he was thirty-two and had been with IBP for three months. Before this he had worked somewhere in Texas, at a seed nursery in Iowa, and in a tobacco plant in North Carolina. He had also worked on farms, but that wasn't "good money"; IBP was good money. He sent most of his paycheck home to his family in Mexico, he explained; between jobs he would return there for visits. On the IBP production floor, he ran a whizard and seemed to think I would know what that was; I didn't think I would understand if he explained it. Now, he had "tired fingers." He got that often and usually would just rest for several days. Staying home was lonely, because all the people he lived with would be working at IBP. He was waiting for a nurse to come and take him to the hospital. During our shared wait he talked about the impossibility of finding housing in Perry and his daily ride in the IBP bus from Des Moines, which he would miss if he didn't make it back from the hospital. He was still waiting when I finally got called for the physical.

Somehow, I had expected to walk into a clean and orderly medical office and to have a nurse's attention. This place was grimy and cluttered—more like a service station than a medical dispensary. As the nurse took my form, she warned me that any lying would be grounds for immediate dismissal. As if reciting her piece for the thousandth time, she said that this medical exam was not to determine whether or not I would work at IBP. No one failed the physical. The company wanted only to place me in the most appropriate job. All I had to do was tell the truth.

I had completed the form, which had standard medical history questions, including date of birth, illnesses, surgery, existing conditions, and childbirths. I did not think they would knowingly hire a forty-seven-year-old woman and hoped I did not look it, but I saw little point in lying about my date of birth. Maybe they couldn't subtract. Anyway, I had to provide the name of my doctor and sign a general release of all my medical records to IBP, and these would also convict me. Because I had had surgery several years before at the University of Iowa Hospitals and Clinics, where the state of Iowa sends many of its welfare patients, I wrote down the University of Iowa as my doctor. One way or another, I feared, my IBP adventure would soon be over.

Requesting a urine sample for a drug test, the nurse pointed me to a bathroom with a torn-out place where a sink might once have been. After I returned the urine sample, the main part of the medical exam, that pertaining to my back and my hands, followed. I had to bend over and try to touch my toes while the nurse probed the vertebra at the base of my spine. Then I was ordered to lie face down on a rank-smelling cot, lift my legs, hold them in the air and tell the nurse if my back hurt. It didn't. Next I was to press my palms together, bring them up to my chest, and move my fingers individually. The nurse asked if my fingers were going to sleep. They weren't. She carefully inspected my hands and wrists, pressing the insides of my wrists, my palms, and the backs of my hands with her fingers.

Then it was over. She said the drug test would take a week to ten days to process and I would be called at that time.

But the wheels of IBP turned faster than she indicated. The next evening my Des Moines friend telephoned to offer congratulations. Earlier that day Ricardo had called and left a message for me to report to work the following Tuesday at 7:30 A.M. with two pieces of identification.

That Tuesday I left my house at six-thirty to get there in plenty of time. Again I gave my name at the guardhouse and walked to the little room. This time there was standing room only. Twenty-one people in my orientation class crowded together for over two hours as we were taken two at a time for hearing tests. In the meantime, we got acquainted.

"Rosa," a Mexican, was the only other woman. I got a chance to try my bad Spanish with her, because she had just arrived from Mexico and didn't know a word of English. In spite of my distressing Spanish she smiled warmly and immediately attached herself to me. She didn't look as though she could be older than thirty-five, but she said that her children were in Mexico and were grown. Now she came to Iowa to be with her amigo, an IBP worker. She herself had never held a waged job before.

Two other Mexicans began orientation with us but were dismissed before the week was over for having trouble with their immigration papers. Four black men, all having come on the IBP bus from Des Moines, waited in the room. The rest were white men. One of them was telling about having been released from prison on December 15 with only $100 and surviving the holidays alone and broke. Three of the other white men had just returned from the Gulf War.

I found myself talking to "Guy," a smiling, sandy-haired man of about forty who had retired from a railroad job. He had been making $56,000 a year, and when he was offered $100,000 in early retirement, he took it. Guy had a wife and two daughters and had missed seeing them when he was doing his railroad runs. After taking some time off with his family, he had begun to look for a job in the area of his home in Boone, twenty-five miles northeast of Perry. His search for employment that would bring a decent income and leave him time for his family had been futile. He assured me that after job hunting in central Iowa for several months, the IBP starting pay of $6.50 an hour seemed good. Like me, Guy had worried about his appearance and his record and had shaved off his full beard and downplayed his work experience and union membership when applying at IBP. Friendly and thoughtful, he was easy to like. I was soon discussing my research with him.

Finally the long and cramped wait was over, and our orientation leader—"Archie," as he told us to call him—led us into the building and upstairs to our orientation classroom, where we would spend two days being initiated into IBP. First we filled out various forms, had our pictures taken, and got our green plastic identification cards and lockers. Orientation involved a series of lessons on IBP procedures. As we completed each lesson, we signed a form confirming our having been instructed on the given topics.

The safety director came to the classroom to review the plant's safety rules: no horsing around, no running, be sure to use the stair rails. She warned us that we could be written up or fired for violating safety rules. For the purposes of safety, she explained, IBP would make certain that each person's worksite was the proper height and had the proper space. A short worker would have a special platform to stand on as he worked; a tall worker might need a higher worktable. All equipment must be in good repair for maximum safety. Whatever could be done to ensure a safe workplace was done. Safety was imperative and was everyone's responsibility. No one should ever overlook an unsafe situation. To reinforce the safety message we saw a video called "The Convincer," with gory pictures of injuries caused by industrial accidents.

The safety director also showed a diagram of the plant with the various emergency exit paths, although this was hard to process. We had yet to see the actual workfloor, we didn't know where we would be working, we couldn't make out the writing on the map, and we weren't given maps to study. In fact, as one accustomed to a lot of paper, I was struck by the absence of lists of rules and procedures that we could keep for reference. The company collected the forms for our files as we signed them, and even those of us quick enough to read them before signing and returning them would have been hard-pressed to remember precisely what they said.

Throughout orientation we repeatedly heard about IBP's commitment to safety. The other watchword was attendance. When asked what two words we had to know to keep our IBP jobs, we would dutifully answer in unison, "Safety and Attendance."

Our fellow workers would be annoyed, Archie said, if we missed work. If we called in sick, however, we were to call by 6:00 A.M. On the days when we called in sick, a supervisor might phone us or materialize at our homes at any time. Anyone who had called in sick and was not home would be summarily fired. Anyone sick for three or more days had to have a physician's signature to return. It would have been impudent to ask how I was going to get a physician to come to my home to certify my illness.

So central was the issue of attendance that our only orientation handout was called "Probationary Employee Attendance Policy." It was hopelessly complicated and contradictory. Two unexcused absences in our ninety-day probationary period and we were fired; four absences in our probationary period would result in termination, only unexcused absences being considered for disciplinary purposes. Three days sick and we needed a doctor's signature to return; four days and we were fired. What did they mean by two absences and we were fired, four absences and we were terminated?

Being confused and generally afraid of not reaching the plant on winter roads, I asked Archie to explain. He shook his head and said, "Look,

we're not trying to fire anyone. It costs us money to hire you people."
That was my answer.

The list of additional rules was lengthy but not hard to retain, because a rule existed for almost everything. Anyone caught leaving the
plant with stolen equipment would be fired. Anyone bringing a camera
or tape recorder into the plant would be fired. Anyone criticizing IBP or
any of its employees would be fired. Anyone caught with liquor or drugs
in the plant would be fired. Anyone caught stealing someone's lunch
would be fired. Anyone caught fighting would be fired. No swearing or
obscenity was allowed. We were responsible for all equipment checked
out to us; having it stolen was no excuse for losing it. No food or drink
was allowed in the locker rooms or on the production floor. We were to
wash our hands before and after going to the bathroom and to remove
all equipment from our persons before going to the bathroom. Our employer could request breath or urine tests at any time. In fact, IBP had
the right to search our bodies, clothing, possessions, or lockers at any
time. We initialed the separate categories of rules and signed each form
affirming that we had been told.

The president of the United Food and Commercial Workers Local
1149 was given ten minutes to speak, and he came in quickly and distributed union cards. He reported that union representation in the
plant was 82 percent, but the biggest problem was the twenty to thirty
new workers that came in each week. The union was waiving its $30
initiation fee, and we would pay only $5.30 weekly, which would be
subtracted from our check. I was one of the few to fill out a card, and
he smiled at me, read my name, and said, "Thanks, Deb."

"Ruth," I corrected. I went by my middle name in the plant as a minor
effort to thwart identification.

When Archie returned, he concluded with a video and a talk on IBP as
an innovative and public-spirited corporation and on the benefits that
its plants had brought to various communities. As Archie was elaborat-
ing on how eager we all were to work for a company as great as IBP,
"Dean," one of the black men, got restive and started to interrupt.

"Our bus is gonna go."

Then, "Are you watching the time?"

"We gotta go."

The rest of us were trying our best to pay attention and work our way into the system. Dean's interruptions of Archie's performance spoke my mind better than I was willing to do, and I was thankful for his spirit.

I was thankful for all of my cohorts, even though they smoked so much that my throat burned raw and my eyelids felt as if they were sandpapered on the inside. Rosa ate with me at breaks during those days. Because the plant's Spanish interpreter came in only sporadically, I was left to help her with her locker combination and her food. Much of the orientation must have been a blur for her, and I could be important for knowing slightly more than she did about what was going on. Except for Guy, who was an instant comrade, the men were earthy and outrageous.

At seven-thirty on Thursday morning we gathered in the classroom again, this time to begin lessons on knives and meat. Three trainers came and showed a video on sharpening knives. With enlarged drawings of the sharpening steel, the video included microscopic detail on how to prepare steels to produce the minute lengthwise striations that would give the knives a razor-sharp edge. The procedure involved roughing the steel surface with varying textures of sandpaper, carefully working it in only one direction, keeping the strokes straight, and not using too much pressure. The knife edge then fit into the striations as the knife was drawn over the steel—if we did it right. We also saw drawings of how our knives would be dulled if we grated the sandpaper across the steel rather than drawing it lengthwise or if we tilted our knives at the wrong angle as we sharpened them.

After we had studied the drawings and listened to the video explanation, the trainers passed out steels and sandpaper. Each of us got to try working a steel. I attempted to follow the procedure carefully. The trainers then brought knives around to each person and spent time with each individually, demonstrating how to handle the steels and knives. Although I had been working my steel for about fifteen minutes by the time a trainer reached me, he found nothing to praise. After examining my steel, he took the sandpaper and spent a couple of minutes on it. Although he did not use the exact technique shown on the video, he prepared the steel sufficiently so that I could try to sharpen a knife with it. I did not do this well either, but after some coaching I was able to draw the knife over the steel somewhat correctly a couple of times.

Notwithstanding this knife sharpening introduction, none of the new hires was prepared to move forward independently to practice the skills. I was clumsy and inept. The rest were not much better. The process was sufficiently complicated and demanding that we would each need much more time and instruction before we could work on our own. Later, maybe.

Then Archie brought in our work clothes. Although we could have supplied our own work clothing, provided it met safety and sanitation standards, all of us bought our work clothes from IBP. For most of us, this included rubber boots with steel toes and white jackets called "frocks," which by federal regulation we were to wear when on the cut and converting floors. Kill floor workers would get white trousers and shirts. The costs of these items were to be deducted from our paychecks. In addition to what we purchased for ourselves, IBP issued a hairnet, earplugs, and hard hat to each of us.

Wearing these new uniforms, we took our first walk through the three main production areas—kill, cut, and converting (also called boning). Moving from the smoky, overheated classroom on the second floor of the office wing to the production area plunged us into the chaotic interior of the plant. Machines of all sizes clanked and churned, huge metal tubs groaned as they were shoved and dropped, and the air control system roared at us from above. The noise surrounded and engulfed us. The production area was a labyrinth of large windowless rooms, and I immediately lost all sense of orientation. Starting on the cut floor, Archie shouted explanations as we walked through the production areas, but mostly it was a lost cause. We heard little above the packing din as we filed through the upper and lower cut floors and into converting.

Cut and converting constituted the cold side of the plant. Meat moved on conveyor belts, and workers stood on platforms, wholly absorbed in cutting meat as it moved by them. Forklifts maneuvered around the floors transporting big tubs of meat and loads of packing materials. Giant blending and processing machines scraped and banged as they dug up, digested, and expelled tubs of meat.

We quickly moved onto the kill floor. The meat in cut and converting looked like meat and the rooms were cold. They seemed clean, if
frenzied. The kill floor, in contrast, was hot and humid. The reality of
dead pigs saturated the air. The smell was staggering. In kill, the campaign was tangibly more intense than in cut and converting. As the
heavy, warm, suspended animals moved down the line, the workers
sliced forcefully through the necks, split open the bellies, pulled the intestines, and executed other maneuvers before each pig swung into the
cooler. As in the cold rooms, the workers stood on platforms and drove
fiercely; but here the work was more raw and more brutal. Dressed in
blood-covered white cotton shirts, the sweating workers wielded their
knives and saws in broad yet precise motions as they attacked the
bodies of the pigs and wrenched them apart.

Then we walked out, shutting the door, and the din receded. Off
the production floor and again set to absorb the mundane protocol of
having a job, we walked to the knife room to check out our equipment.
We waited in the hall as the three trainers—one each from cut, kill, and
converting—took us individually to get knives and other equipment
and led us to our places on the production floor.

Assigned to work in the "cellar," the lower part of the cut floor, on
the belly line, I would use a whizard, which was what my Mexican confi-
dant had used before he got tired fingers. For this job, I signed for a pile
of equipment and the trainer helped me dress. Already wearing my new
steel-toed boots, hairnet, earplugs, and hard hat, I added a long, knife-
resistant mesh sleeve on my left arm under my frock. On my hands I
first put on a pair of nylon gloves, followed by a pair of cotton gloves.
Over my cotton glove on my left hand I wore a steel mesh glove that
fastened at my wrist, and this was covered with a rubber glove. I wore a
knife resistant nylon mesh glove over my right cotton glove, which was
also covered with a rubber glove. On my left arm, over my mesh sleeve
and my frock, I wore a hard plastic arm protector. To protect the front
of my body, I strapped a thick, hard synthetic apron around my middle.
I also was issued a steel with which to sharpen the whizard. I was curious to see how this would work.

We walked down to the cellar, and again I was overcome by noise as
we approached a work station that was particularly chaotic. One of the
workers looked at us with curious, wild eyes and boomed out in a voice

that carried above the clamor, "We're gonna get shut down if we don't get this shit cleaned up!"

The trainer turned to me and yelled, "Change of plans. You're going to be a janitor."

He directed me to take off my equipment and white frock and leave them on some hooks in the production area. My janitor outfit was a blue frock together with the rubber boots, rubber gloves, hairnet, ear-plugs, and hard hat that everyone had to wear on the production floor. The trainer instructed me quickly: While wearing a blue frock I was not to touch any equipment or meat on the line. Several big yellow plastic barrels were the only ones that I was permitted to touch. He showed me how to use shovels and squeegees to clean out the scraps under the scaffolding platforms that the workers were standing on. None of my cleaning equipment was to touch any container of edible meat. Meat scraps from the floor went into the yellow barrels. Scraps of wood, plastic, and paper also littered the floor, and I had to keep these picked up and to put them into large pasteboard boxes — "combos" — in the corners of the room.

Then the trainer disappeared.

Picking up trash and shoveling meat kept me busy. I soon discovered a few unused muscles that got sore as I shoveled, but mostly it was just tedious, and I could handle tedium. More discomfiting was the cold that penetrated inward as the morning wore on. I had only my rubber gloves on my hands, my jeans, a sweater under my cotton frock, and my rubber boots. My fingers and toes became disconnected chunks of ice. My nose was running. How long until lunch?

After awhile the worker who had yelled at the trainer when we came in walked over to me. "Mike" was his name, according to the tape on the front of his hard hat. He was in his mid-twenties, a white man with a strong, handsome face and curly black hair under his hairnet. His eyes, however, still conveyed something curious and disconcerting, and his voice had a menacing and hollow sound as he bellowed, "What's your name?"

"Ruth," I shouted. Archie had given each of us a tape printed with our names to put on our hard hats, but I had thrown mine away because it said "Deborah Fink."

"Ruth. You don't go to lunch until this place gets cleaned up!" Then he pitched in and helped me for a few minutes, showing me how to work under the platforms and how to use the squeegees to pull the meat. " 'Clyde's' sick," he clarified.

I continued. The floor was perhaps seventy-five feet across, with seven different production or packing areas and a long conveyer belt of boxes coming from the cut floor above and going into a separate room to be sealed. The enormous room was mine to clean. No one else from my orientation class had been assigned to the cellar, and no one but Mike seemed to notice I was there.

Around twelve-fifteen the rest of the workers cleared out and Mike came over, ordering me to get moving with the cleaning so it would be done when they returned. Before leaving home at six-thirty that morning I had eaten a bowl of cereal; now my stomach was empty and churning. Shaking with hunger, exhaustion, and cold, I began to pick scraps of meat from the latticed scaffolding where the workers had stood. Presently I felt a tug on my frock from behind and turned around to see someone motioning me to get down. It was Clyde, my supervisor, wearing the identifying yellow hard hat with his name taped on the front. Suffering from a cold and with almost no voice, he showed me how to climb under the scaffolding. Although the space was cramped and awkward, the work went faster from underneath. When all the pieces of fallen meat were thrown on the floor, we hosed it down with hot water and squeegeed and shoveled the pile of waste. The hot water and steam rising around me was a gift from God. We finished by one o'clock.

I made my way to the locker room to go to the bathroom and washed my hands in hot water until I could move them. I then retrieved my lunch from my locker. After reciting the rule about never taking food into the locker rooms, Archie had suggested that we put our lunches in our lockers, because lunches often got stolen. Our food had a negligible effect on the locker room, anyway. Armies of cockroaches invaded our lockers, marched up and down the walls, and lurked around the pipes, but their main diet was the fat and bits of meat that we left from our boots. Our lunches were merely lagniappe. My sandwich was in a plastic bag tied tight with a twistie, and I carried it up to the cafeteria to eat.

My first day I had eaten the inexpensive and adequate fast food from the cafeteria line, but I wanted my own food, as did many of the other workers. We had only thirty minutes for lunch, and break time was counted from when we were working on the floor to when we were again back at work. With the minutes spent taking off and putting on equipment, walking out, around, and back through the plant, and going to the bathroom and washing our hands, we had at most twenty minutes in the cafeteria. I didn't want to spend it standing in line. Most of the workers smoked three or four cigarettes during lunch, and although there was a rule against it, they smoked as they went through the food line.

Workers from converting ate lunch after the cut floor workers, and Guy had been assigned to converting. As I was eating later than the other cellar workers, I ate with him. Rosa was nowhere to be seen.

After finishing lunch I put on my nylon and cotton gloves under my rubber gloves before taking up my work again, and the afternoon was not bad. With everything cleaned up once, it wasn't hard to keep up. In fact, the whole area seemed loose and relaxed compared with the morning. Several of the men on the line started hooting as quitting time approached. When the line stopped at about three o'clock, Mike came over and ordered me to get everything cleaned up before I left, but he helped out and showed me what I had to do. We were through in a half hour, and I was home before five.

The next morning my orientation group started in the classroom again. Archie gave a pep talk. Now we were learning to be real workers —we had been on the production floor. The trainers were going to take over the class now. Listen up, because this was what work at IBP was about. The three trainers filed in and Archie left. They pulled out chairs, sat down, put their feet up, lit cigarettes, and meditated for forty-five minutes. The new hires knew what to do. They too lit up.

"Well, time to get off our butts," said one as he pulled himself up. We performed a round of arm and hand exercises to ward off carpal tunnel syndrome, and then we were ready to go back to the production floor.

I still had my whizard outfit in my locker and I asked if I was a whizard or a janitor. The cellar trainer told me to get on my whizard gear, and we went down to the belly line.

Bellies came down a belt from the cut floor above us. In the mornings, when processing sows, the upper floor cut workers trimmed off the sides, squaring the flat slabs of belly so that strips of scraps, includ-

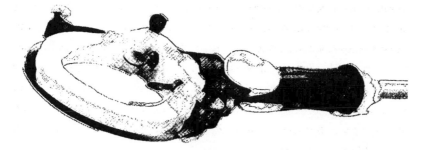

The circular electric knife used on the cut floor to make horizontal, scraping cuts, commonly called a whizard.

ing the long teat line,[1] would move along the belt with the bellies. A worker stood at a T on the belt as the bellies and scraps reached the cellar, shunting the bellies in one direction and the scraps and teat lines in another. The scraps and teat lines then went through a skinning machine, landing on a table. My job was on the teat line table.

The whizard is an O-shaped electric knife that you strap to your hand to make horizontal, scraping cuts.[2] My knife was about four inches in diameter and hung from an electric line overhead. My assignment was to grab a piece of teat line or other scrap, lay it flat on the table in front of me, trim all remaining skin and teats and throw them into a barrel on my left side; flip the slab over, trim off the lean meat, and push that into another barrel next to the table on my right; and then throw the mostly fat remainder into a large metal tub at the foot of the table.

"This barrel is mostly skin, that barrel is mostly lean, and here is mostly fat," the trainer said.

He showed me how to use the safety strap to bind the whizard onto my hand and how to turn on the electricity. If I dropped the whizard, I was not to try to catch it, but to let it drop and then turn off the electricity. My instructions were to steel the whizard blade, but not too much because I would have problems if I steeled it too much. Presumably, I would learn how much was too much. Unlike the straight knife steels we had worked on in the orientation classroom, whizard steels did not need to be worked. Only minimal skill was required to maintain a whizard. The trainer told me to take time off to do the hand exercises we had learned. If I had any questions I could ask my partner across the table.

Two of us handled the teat line, one on each side of the table. Across the table was a short, bespectacled black man about twenty years old with the name "Owen" taped on his hard hat. He set his jaw and glared at me. Talking was impossible with the noise, but I tried some smiles before giving up. Owen did not like me.

The work was not hard, but as time passed my arms got exhausted. With my right hand holding the whizard, I used the muscles of my left arm to flip the teat lines and toss them into the tub after I had cut off the skin and meat. With the weight of my steel glove and the rigidity of the plastic arm guard, my left biceps ached and burned within an hour. My right arm and shoulder were also fairly sore from holding the knife, but it was my right hand that was making me increasingly uneasy. Wrapped around the whizard, it caught the vibration of the moving knife. This was worse when I had to use pressure to cut into a hard piece of fat, which occurred in about one out of ten pieces of belly. For awhile my hand hurt, and then it didn't exactly hurt but I didn't think I could move my fingers. Although I didn't need to move my right fingers to do my work, I needed the strength of my hand to maintain my grip. I wasn't sure I could continue to use my hand effectively.

When we stopped for the morning break, I lifted my hands to do the hand exercises we had learned and my right hand went to sleep. But there was no one in particular to tell, so I took up my work on the teat line after break.

By about 11:45 Mike ordered me to get my blue frock and clean up the floor. Someone else had worked the floor that morning and it was manageable. As I was walking behind the platforms pulling down meat and cleaning up, one of the workers turned around, leaned down toward me, and flashed a broad smile. Under the hard hat was a young Asian face with the first sign of human warmth I saw on the production floor.

"How do you like your job?" he shouted.

"Okay, I guess. How's your work?"

"Awful. This job is awful." And then he turned back to his work.

I finished cleaning up, so Mike told me I could go to lunch with the others. I found the worker who had talked to me sitting alone and I joined him at lunch.

His name was "Chang" and he seemed to be about twenty. Although Chinese, he had lived in Vietnam before coming to the United States.

He said that he spoke Vietnamese and Chinese in addition to English, which was rudimentary, but we could communicate. Without a family, he had worked in a factory in San Francisco before finding his Iowa job. He showed me a picture of his girlfriend and said that she was going to school and that they were going to be married when he had enough money. Like me, he came to work at IBP without a group of friends. Perhaps 10 percent of the packinghouse workers were Asian, yet Chang, being the only Asian American in the cellar, ate separately. We finished our lunch, and Chang caught a final smoke as we walked back to the floor.

I served as janitor for the rest of the day, but janitor work was never as hard in the afternoon as in the morning. In the morning the cut floor processed sows, and they were harder and more complicated than the butchers that came later. Butchers had no teat line. After the switchover to butchers, between eleven and twelve o'clock, Owen climbed onto the production scaffolding, where he weighed and sorted butcher bellies; I stayed below and cleaned up under the scaffolding. After the initial late morning cleanup, being a janitor was boring and cold, but that did not approach the repetitive pain of the whizard. When the cut floor stopped at three-fifteen, I stayed a half hour to pick the meat out of the scaffolding, hose down the floor, and shovel the scraps into the yellow barrels.

On Saturday, the last day of orientation, we met again in the classroom before being sent to our jobs. Mike waved me over to the teat line. He was trimming bellies and Clyde was nowhere to be found.

I found my spot at the table, but my whizard had no safety strap to hold it onto my hand. The table was piling up with meat and Owen was working alone. I shouted across to him that I didn't have a safety strap. He looked at me with cold disinterest. Not knowing what to do, I kept trying to reach Owen. In exasperation, he shrugged his shoulders and went on with his work. I asked him where I could get a safety strap and he motioned toward the exit. When I didn't quit asking, he relented and said to go to the nurses' station. That seemed strange, but I walked back off the floor and up to the dispensary and told a nurse that I didn't have a safety strap for my whizard. She handed me one, which I took back to the table without knowing what to do with it. I have never been adept at figuring out how to put things together, and with four layers of gloves strapped on my hands I was even more inept.

I tried asking Owen to help me again, but I wasn't surprised when he ignored me. I pulled off my gloves and started to work on it. Studying Owen's whizard as he worked, I was able to attach it. But it was inside out; the velcro closing was on the wrong side. I took it off and tried again, to no avail; it was wrong side out again. Owen looked at me with more disgust than usual as he pushed through the pile of meat alone. On the third try I got it on and threw myself into doing my job.

Not long after I had been working, a trainer and a supervisor approached Owen and yelled at him. For people with average voices, communication on the floor involved shouting or getting within inches of the other person's face. They were doing both. Their anger seemed vicious, and I felt the uncomfortable pounding in my chest and stomach that transported me back to my terror of some forty years before when a grade school teacher would lose her temper. Although I didn't catch much of what was said, I heard, "You keep your two feet on the floor," whatever that was about.

Then Mike called over and directed me to get on the blue frock and get things cleaned up. After going to my locker to leave my gear, I washed my hands long and slow with hot water before returning to the floor. The floor was a mess, and I didn't find my way to the cafeteria for lunch until one o'clock.

It was after five when I got home that Saturday afternoon, and I was exhausted and stiff with cold. With a sore throat and aches all over my body, I feared that I was coming down with something. I had just enough energy to ride to a restaurant to eat in my smelly packinghouse jeans and shirt. Once home, I soaked in a hot bath to warm up and ease my aches, falling asleep there before I could make it to bed.

I had endured five days of IBP.

Although all workers had to be available to work six days a week, when the work was slack we didn't go in on Mondays. Every Friday afternoon after lunch the company posted a list of which production lines were free and which lines had to work the following Monday. Cut had been working on Mondays, but that Friday the announcement had said that only the ham line in converting would work on Monday. That gave me two days to collect myself before the next week, and I needed them. On Sunday I slept all day with a heating pad on my neck.

On Monday I felt better and knew that I wasn't sick, just tired with an irritated throat from the cold and the dense smoke of the classroom, cafeteria, and locker room.

Because we would no longer be in the classroom, I abandoned my first week's hairstyle and clothes and put together an outfit that would keep me warm. I began with a cotton turtleneck; over this I wore a set of long thermal underwear. Over the underwear I wore jeans and a quilted jacket. On Monday after the first week at IBP I bought three used non-collegiate sweatshirts at the Salvation Army store, and I would wear one of these on top of my jacket. My IBP equipment and frock went on top of all this. Cotton socks and sweatsocks under my steel-toed rubber boots kept some of the cold away from my toes. Because I would be wearing my hairnet and hard hat all day, I stopped moussing my hair and it reverted to its unkempt nature.

Cold plagued me the entire time I worked at IBP, the cellar being one of the coldest work areas in the plant. Although the temperature was supposed to be around forty-seven degrees, we frequently had trouble with ice on the floors. On some days enormous icicles formed where water and blood dripped off the production areas. It seemed as though the temperature in the cellar varied with the outside temperature; on the coldest days we had the most trouble with ice. Varying temperatures in adjacent rooms caused drafts, and closing the doors made the forklift drivers mad. My work as a janitor allowed me to move around, but the workers on the line stood still in the cold. On the other hand, as a janitor I usually managed to get wet, which added to my chills. My nose dripped constantly.

With orientation over, I clocked in with the other cut floor workers at 7:00 A.M., which meant that my days began at 5:15. I would dress, eat breakfast, and try to be on the road by 5:45. By the time I went through security and reached the locker room, it would be 6:45. I would put on my work clothes and boots and clock in on the production floor by 7:00.

The Tuesday after orientation I met "Susan," whose locker was next to mine. Susan was a black woman, a single mother, who rode the IBP bus from Des Moines. She worked in converting, which didn't start until seven-thirty, but coming on the bus she was there before seven.

Although Des Moines is only forty-five minutes by car from Perry, the bus made several stops and took longer. Susan had to catch it at five-thirty in order to begin work at seven-thirty. Sometimes she would go to the cafeteria to eat breakfast before starting work, but usually she sat on the bench in front of our lockers smoking and putting on makeup.

"This is the craziest place I've ever worked," said Susan quietly as I dressed. She had worked in nursing homes but had tired of taking care of sick people. At IBP she made more money, although the work was terrible.

In the minutes before I went onto the floor we would talk about people and about our lives. When I complained about something that happened on the floor, Susan would respond as simply as "That's too bad." I have not understood her charisma, but other women, white and black, felt it just as I did. Susan would listen to countless stories about problems with work, husbands, and children as women came to talk. I got in on them because I was lucky enough to have a locker by Susan's.

Susan and I met off and on at our lockers throughout the day, but this was unpredictable. Only in the morning could I count on her being there. As long as I worked for IBP, hoping for a few minutes with Susan every morning would be enough to make me look forward to going to work and to miss being there when I didn't go.

I worked the whizard on the teat line in the morning and became a janitor as soon as the cut floor switched from sows to butchers. Owen did not like me any better the second week. One morning when my whizard started to vibrate violently so that I couldn't cut with it, he eventually told me to tighten a screw to adjust it, but mostly he was silently hostile. At one point he threw several uncut pieces of teat line in the tub where I threw my finished pieces, which would have put me in trouble if I hadn't seen them and dug them out. At times Mike came over and watched me work, adding to the tension.

Clyde, who had been out sick most of the first week that I had been there, returned the following Tuesday. He was not even as helpful as Mike.

"Speed, Ruth, work for speed!" he shouted as he stood over me. "One cut! One cut! One cut for the skin; one cut for the meat. Get those pieces through!"

There wasn't much more I could do. I was taller than most of the other workers, and I towered over the worktable. In fact, my stomach guard did not even reach down to the worktable, making it useless as a safety measure as well as unwieldy. Remembering the safety director's lecture on how IBP tailored each work area individually, I showed my trainer the difficulty I had. He told me to strap the guard around my butt, which didn't work at all. Oh well.

That concern was minor compared to my growing panic about my right hand, which hurt fiercely. When Clyde asked how my hand was, I told him it hurt. When my trainer asked how my hand was, I told him it hurt. "Well, that's part of it," he said, "it'll be okay once it's broke in." By the middle of the second week I couldn't hold a pencil to write. My hand was constantly asleep as I drove or slept. I repeatedly awakened in the night with my hand clenched in a tight, painful knot and had to use my left hand to straighten the fingers one by one. Something would have to happen soon.

The fatigue of work was all-consuming, and at first I was only intermittently aware that I had no friends to hang around with during breaks. Being a janitor, my noon breaks were irregular, and I never knew who would be in the cafeteria when I was there. The social groups were fairly well defined in terms of ethnicity, gender, and work area. I wasn't part of any of these groups. Several times I joined tables of workers and introduced myself, only to be ignored. I seldom ran across anyone from my orientation group. In the cafeteria I once saw Rosa and went over to join her. She was with her *amigo*, and I asked to meet him. Without smiling, Rosa positioned herself on the other side of "Jose" and did not speak to me. I got to know his name but that was it. I discovered that although I could be Rosa's friend when he was not around, she was not interested in me when she was with him.

One day as I was eating by myself, a group of young white women sat down at my table. I tried introducing myself again, and a short, red-haired woman looked at me, smiled, and said she knew me. Her ex-husband—"Buck"—was in my orientation group and had told her all about me. I was pleased, even as I wondered what he had to tell all about me. Her name was "Annie" and she talked. She and Buck were divorced, but they had a five-year-old daughter and he had come back to live with them. She was twenty-five and had been remarried and divorced since Buck had previously left. She had been working for IBP for nine months.

Annie smoked rapidly as she ate and talked. Like me, she was a cut floor janitor, but she worked up on the main cut floor and was a janitor all day. Buck came through the line and sat with us, and the three of us discussed IBP and our jobs until it was time to get back to the floor.

When I got back I found that my whizard steel had been stolen. I didn't need it in the afternoon, so I put off having to face this problem. But the next morning I had to go to the knife room to check out another steel. A thirty-something white woman was working there. She glared at me and asked if I was new.

"Yes."

"Well, here's another one. This time take care of it," she said without cracking a smile.

Other workers left their equipment at their work stations when they took breaks, but that did not work for me. My janitor supplies disappeared constantly. Once two men came and asked me if I had any squeegees. I showed them my squeegees and they took them. I never learned who they were or where they went, but the squeegees were gone.

Mike had a fit. "Don't tell no one where anything is!" he roared. "They ask, you say you ain't got no squeegees." Then he went out to scout around the other floors and bring back a squeegee. Every night when I finished I would hide the squeegees where Mike told me to, and I could usually keep one for about a week before someone would find and take it. It remained a challenge to find someplace to hide the equipment that I couldn't put in my locker so it wouldn't get stolen. Not only my equipment, but any equipment I used. Later I managed to talk the quality control workers out of a screwdriver that I needed by promising to guard it with my life and return it when I was through. Then in the midst of my work I forgot and put it down, leaving it to be stolen. The quality control workers were philosophical about it, but I never asked to borrow their tools again.

Mike was an ordinary production worker, but Clyde leaned on him heavily because he knew the operation. Informally, he was Clyde's second-in-command. When Clyde was back, though, he added considerably to my janitor duties. Why wasn't I taking out the trash?

The combos used for meat and trash were hexagonal pasteboard boxes about five feet in diameter and four feet high. Showing me what to do, Clyde yanked a combo of trash along the floor into converting and up an incline to a freight elevator. He closed the door, pulled down the overhead latch that locked it, and ran the elevator up to the first floor. The inside safety door on the elevator never closed, and to run the elevator he had to stand in the doorway and trip a safety switch with one hand and reach over to press the elevator button with the other. On the upper floor Clyde pulled the combo out the door, down the floor, and over to the compacting machine.

The trash compactor was a small room with a hole in the floor about four feet by five feet—just a little bit smaller than a combo with trash sticking out the top. Clyde dumped the trash in, stood back, and pressed a button to compact it. Mostly the compactor pushed the trash back up to floor level when it operated. Clyde told me to work on it and he left.

If my nonfunctional hand was a nagging worry, this compactor was blunt terror. Getting the trash to compact meant working it into the hole and compacting it into a pancake by pushing the button that ran the machine. I had once seen a James Bond movie where it looked as though Sean Connery got squashed in a car as it compacted. Now that scene came back vividly. My rubber boots slickened with pork fat, I imagined a dozen ways of sliding into the hole with the trash. (Another janitor later told me that someone had actually gotten compressed in the trash compactor, but I am not positive this was true.)

I was also scared of the elevator. I envisioned my arm or leg caught between the elevator and the shaft as I tripped the safety switch.

The next day I tried to ignore the trash, but it seemed to pile up faster than before. By noon Clyde ordered me to pull the trash upstairs. I managed to trip the safety switch and get the trash upstairs, but I piled it on top of the compactor and did not try to compact it. When I was lucky "Francisco," a Mexican janitor from converting, would come up with me to help. A heater in the area just off the elevator on the upper floor blew warm air, providing limited compensation for both of us.

In the middle of my second week at IBP the cut floor general supervisor—called the general—came down from upstairs and looked through

Owen's barrels of skin and into the tub holding the belly fat. He was angry. Owen had been cutting off fat and meat along with the skin that went into the skin barrel; he was leaving lean meat on the pieces going into the fat tub. He had to cut closer; he had to cut more carefully.

The general then came to look at my work and raised hell with me, too.

"Only skin in this barrel! I don't want to see no fat in there and I don't want to see no meat!" He picked out scraps from my tub and said I was throwing too much meat into the fat tub.

The only way we could trim closer was to slow down. That seemed as though it might also save my hand, so I was all for it. I reasoned that Clyde could not badger me or Owen about speed after the general had told us to trim closer. The next day the teat lines piled up on our table as Owen and I neatly and carefully trimmed away the skin and meat the way the general had ordered.

At the rate we were going, Owen and I would still be working teat line after the switchover to butchers. Clyde blew up. He directed Owen to take his place on the butcher belly line, and he stood over me throwing meat and yelling, "Speed! Speed! You can't stand here all day!" He sent Mike upstairs to bring my trainer down. The trainer took my whizard but worked no faster than I, and his trimming was less precise. Still, Clyde kept yelling at me.

The trainer finally turned to me and said, "Get this shit cleaned up." Then he left.

I started to work again, but Clyde pushed the rest of the meat onto the floor in disgust and ordered me to get on my blue frock and clean the floor.

That afternoon Clyde told me that I would want to work late so I could get in some extra hours. It wasn't an offer or a question. I had folded some box tops one afternoon when I had nothing else to do, and now he needed boxes made. They had to fill a big order of shoulders, and several of us were tapped to stay late to fold boxes and fill, weigh, and label them.

The boxes IBP used for meat came in various sizes and shapes. The ones we used in the cellar most frequently came as flat pasteboard sheets that we folded and assembled by putting tabs together. The box tops, which I had folded before, were made of lighter material than the box bottoms and were easier to handle. By the time I had folded twenty of them I was good at it. The box bottoms were different. Made of heavier material, they required considerable strength and agility to put together.

Clyde told me to make box bottoms and constructed one of them while I watched. When I tried to do it myself, I found that it was much harder than folding tops. Moreover, if I yanked the tabs slightly askew they tore, making the box unusable. Clyde showed me again. "Shirley," a white woman of about my age, was also assigned to make boxes, and she was having at least as much trouble as I.

"I ain't doing no more of that shit!" she announced as she stalked over to the scale to pull the boxes away and cover them after they were weighed. Clyde accepted her authority.

That left me folding the boxes and Clyde in a rage. I would start to fold a box and he would wrench it away from me, finish folding it himself, and scream, "What is your *problem*, Ruth? What is your *problem*?"

About eight people were working late to fill this order, and the work degenerated into chaos. Several people folded tops, but the box bottoms were a bottleneck and I was working on them alone. Meat was coming down faster than we could handle, and the floor was getting slippery with meat. Clyde almost fell as he strode around barking orders. Moreover, it was Ruth's job to keep the floor clear.

"Go get a bucket of one-eighty for this floor!" Clyde shouted at me.

I went. It didn't seem like the right time to mention that I had no idea what one-eighty was. I knew what a bucket was and so I got that first. Then I went to the area where we washed our boots with hot water, filled the bucket with this water, and presented it to Clyde. He seemed satisfied and managed a "thank you."

"Don't pay any attention to Clyde; he's always like that," came a friendly voice at my shoulder. I looked into the face of a white man I had never seen before. I appreciated his kindness, but I didn't like feeling like a basket case. As I worked in the cold through Clyde's haranguing, I thought over and over how much I wanted a glass—or two—of brandy. I had never before turned to alcohol for comfort.

Finally Clyde turned to me in disgust and told me to clean up the rest of the floor and go home.

I had failed to make the grade twice that day and thought I would probably be fired. How ironic, I reflected, that I had worried so much about my identity being discovered and now I would be fired because of my work performance. I was discouraged and humiliated, even as I knew that this was not the final test of my life and that the operation had disintegrated under the weight of its own absurdity, apart from my incompetence. But I was also dead tired and cold.

Shirley was changing her clothes in the locker room when I got there. I had tried to talk to her before, but she had her set of friends and had offered only perfunctory replies. Now she talked. "Clyde is a shit!" she spat out contemptuously in an incongruously high-pitched and proper voice. "Why don't you tell him what he can do?"

I didn't tell him because I was a probationary employee with no right to appeal any disciplinary action and because any sign of life from me would have further inflamed him. No woman reaches my age without knowing how these things work.

But I was learning what it took to make friends on the production floor. I went home happy, if fearful of losing my job and seeing my research fall apart just as it was starting.

The next morning when I arrived on the production floor, a Laotian man stood at my place on the teat line. Clyde ordered me to put on my blue frock; he needed an all-day janitor. That was the end of my regular work on the line. Plant jobs were graded from zero to four, each grade adding twenty cents an hour to the paycheck after qualifying—usually at the end of probation. I went from a grade one to a grade zero job. It solved the problem of my hand; I would have had to quit if I had stayed on the whizard. Nevertheless, I was mad at Clyde.

Shirley looked at me in surprise when I saw her. "We thought you quit!"

"No, I'm hanging in."

But most of my orientation group weren't. On January 30, barely two weeks after we had started, I stopped to talk to Buck in the hall by the cafeteria. I hadn't been where I could see anyone in our group regularly. Now Buck told me that everyone had quit or been fired. Well, not quite everyone. Eight of the twenty-one of us were left. Three irreverent black men had run afoul of their supervisors shortly after starting. Guy had left along with most of the others. Buck was there; Rosa was running a whizard on the upper cut floor; "Fred," a black man, was hanging onto a knife job in converting; and four other white men were also staying on. Thinking over the differences between the stayers and leavers, I concluded that those with insubordinate mouths did not stay long at IBP, nor did those like Guy who had experience and expectations of decent employment. Otherwise, I didn't know.

Clyde had tried to make me quit. I was going to make him fire me if he wanted to get rid of me badly enough. He wasn't prepared to do that, and when he saw me coming back he accepted my presence. I am convinced that it was not by chance that almost no women worked in the cellar.

As a janitor I had long stretches with nothing to do. The place was scrubbed down nightly by the cleaning service—the real janitors—so I had a clean room at seven o'clock each morning. It wasn't until around nine, when the line speed was turned up, that the meat started flying. It took time to try to locate my squeegees, which were constantly being stolen or broken, but basically I stood around. For a period I had the job of sponging down the overhead pipes that were dripping unsanitary water on the meat. That was diversion, and I was sorry when a maintenance crew came in to fix the pipes. I had about three hours of actual work between ten and one o'clock, but when I got the sow mess cleaned I would sometimes settle into unbroken standing around until quitting time, when the butchers had gone through the line and I would clean up and pack things away.

One morning as I was shoveling meat off the floor, Annie came down from the upstairs cut floor. "Come on. I'm going to get you some metal handles."

I didn't know what metal handles were or why I would want them, but I didn't mind going with Annie. I said I'd have to find Clyde and ask him.

"Oh, Clyde," Annie groaned in disgust as she walked off, "Clyde can't even fix his own car."

That being as logical as most of what I heard at IBP, I followed her.

"I fuck off when I'm caught up," she called over her shoulder. "Clyde can't do anything. Me, I got friends."

She took me up the stairs, through the cut floor, down the hall, and to the window at the knife room.

"I want two squeegees with metal handles," she ordered. "Metal handles."

"Okay, honey. We got 'em."

"Annie, Ann-ee, An E!" she corrected him.

The knife room man handed us the squeegees and we walked back to the cellar.

"You can't pull nothing with plastic handles," said Annie. For the next several days Annie was around when I worked. "Those pricks, they think just because we're women we know how to clean," she said as she showed me how to stuff the trash into the compactor.

I savored every minute that Annie was around, but I never knew when I would see her. Like mine, her work was unpredictable, and the upper cut floor was larger and busier than the cellar. Her mouth got her into trouble, which cramped her style at times. She moved out of being a janitor into a maintenance job after a couple of months and then I ran into her even less at work, although I came to hang out with her whenever possible outside the plant.

The two new squeegee handles did, in fact, make my work much easier, but they didn't last long. Clyde wanted to use them after I left one afternoon, and he didn't hide them when he was through. They were stolen. I was glad he had done it and not me. Still, I was surprised that he didn't blame me.

One morning as I stood around waiting for something to clean up, Clyde yelled and waved at me from across the room, and I went over to him. Standing behind a conveyor belt that was broken, he was lifting and pushing boxes of meat over the five-foot stretch that wasn't moving. He shouted, "You can do this. Get off your blue frock."

I changed into my white frock and spent an hour and a half pushing boxes of meat over the broken conveyor. This warmed me up. Some of the boxes weighed as much as fifty pounds, and I was soon sweating profusely as I thrust each one along the line. I felt as though my arms were going to be pulled out of their sockets. Then the conveyor was fixed, and I went back to my shovel and squeegee with sore arms but no lasting damage. This was typical of the pattern of my work at IBP— stretches of idleness punctuated with explosive orgies of heavy work. I came to look forward to the times when I had something to do, even as

I knew I was lucky not to have to strain the same set of muscles continuously day in and day out.

Before long I was wearing my white frock under my blue frock and pitching in with various jobs. I could turn from a polluted janitor, prohibited from touching any meat product, into a hygienic production worker just by taking off my blue frock. I did learn how to fold box tops and bottoms well, and at times when there was a big order or when someone didn't come in I made boxes. I would also pick up and wash the salvageable meat that went onto the floor, and for this I needed my white frock. I did odd jobs for Clyde and learned to use the dry ice machine. Clyde called me his "gal." These jobs made the time go faster, and I learned that by finding my own chores I could partially avoid Clyde and his assignments.

"We got blacks working, we got Laotians, we got Mexicans, and we got this guy," the white belly line forklift operator joked to me, pointing to a tall white worker on the platform who was weighing bellies. The forklift driver was "Pete," and I didn't know whether or not there was a nuance in his joke that I didn't catch.

Pete and I worked in the same space around the belly line. He, more than anyone else, became my work partner. He carted off the combos of bellies, meat, skins, and fatback that came off the belly line. He would use his forklift to push my heavy combos of trash into the elevator, and he would push my full barrels of meat or dry ice across the floor for me. I would watch his combos of skins fill, strip off my blue frock, and keep them from spilling over when the machine was not working.

Pete was about forty and something of a bad boy on the floor. Some of the workers refused to talk to him, but usually he took his breaks with a line of older male workers who would sit together on a bench against the wall of the cafeteria smoking and wisecracking. Like Pete and Mike, most of this core group of white men had worked for Oscar Mayer before IBP.

During my sixth week at IBP Mike yelled at me from the scaffolding where he was working and asked if I was signing out with "n.b." What was that? Each day the line workers clocked out by running their identification cards through the time machine when they left. Because management always knew when the production line shut down, the time the workers clocked out would be within a few minutes of the time the line stopped; there was little chance to adjust this. Those like me who stayed to work after the line stopped were supposed to report to the office of the general and sign out by hand before we clocked out. Apparently, this procedure was to prevent a worker leaving the plant and handing his card to someone else to punch out at a later time. I had been signing out daily in the office.

Mike explained that by union contract we were entitled to a paid fifteen-minute break if we worked past three-fifteen, which I always did. Rather than take the break, which I knew nothing about, workers who stayed late would usually work straight through to four-thirty or five. By writing "n.b." for "no break" beside their names, they collected their pay for these fifteen minutes. During the quarter I worked for it, IBP made a record profit of $35,496,000 from its production operations, and almost $50 of this came from not paying me for my afternoon breaks in the first six weeks I worked there.

After I figured out what I was doing, I never took my breaks with the cellar crew. Neither of the two other women in the cellar talked to me very often, and I didn't want to get in the habit of eating with the men on the belly line. I had to clean up the floor while the rest of the workers were gone, but even when I managed to have the floor in good shape before the cellar workers left, I tried to find something to do so I didn't leave when the others did. When I went out on my own, Clyde didn't keep track of my time and I enjoyed more relaxed breaks than did most of the workers.

One afternoon I was complaining about the cold as Pete and I stood around watching the others work. "Well, why don't you go to the locker room?" asked Pete.

"What?"

"Just go to your locker and get some gloves or something. Clyde can't find you in the locker. That's the one place he can't go. If he comes around I'll cover for you."

It sounded like a good idea, and I went and washed my hands in warm water, blew my nose, and stood around awhile. Several women were there smoking, and we chatted before having to return to the floor. The quiet of the locker room gave us a warm respite from the production campaign.

I had a new survival secret.

I gradually realized that Pete covered for a number of workers. On some afternoons three or four of us who weren't on the production line would be standing around. "Try and look busy," Clyde cautioned me once, and I would walk across the floor as if I were going somewhere.[3] But it was hard. Most of the other idlers were smokers who would duck out for cigarettes, and Pete would tell Clyde they had gone to the bathroom if he happened to come around looking for them. With the irregularity of work, we probably served a useful function. Every once in a while we had frenzied days in which everyone worked at full tilt all day. Other days it seemed as though none of us who weren't on the line had anything to do. The upper cut floor, where the supervisors ran a tighter operation, would sometimes send excess workers down to help us, and then it would be even harder to find something to do. It was perhaps to IBP's credit that they would keep workers on the job as long as possible before sending them home or laying them off, but my observation was that nowhere besides the cellar were there so many extra hands so frequently. I think the plant manager and cut floor general supervisor suspected that the cellar was pretty relaxed for favored workers, but it was not until after I left that they reassigned Clyde and lowered the boom. The company also decreed that no one could go to the bathroom more than twice a week outside of scheduled breaks.

Some of the workers smoked marijuana as well as cigarettes. In addition, one of the line workers explained to me that by doing cocaine they could avert hand injuries, because their hands would stay loose and flexible. Drugs were exchanged and consumed fairly openly in the plant, in the parking lot, and in the bar next to the plant. I asked Pete how people passed their drug tests. He sighed at my naïveté and said that a basic drug test cost $80; a complete analysis cost $300. With all the workers IBP took in, they didn't spend that money; they flushed the urine samples.

"But you can bet if I got in a fight or had an accident they'd do a test," he said.

Recalling being hired before my drug test could have cleared, I thought what he said seemed logical. Besides saving money by not doing the drug tests, the lax enforcement of drug rules held a further advantage for IBP. For those who took drugs, the threat of an actual drug test would keep them from reporting injuries and thereby improve the plant's safety record.

The people who maneuvered around the cellar floor included Clyde, Mike, me, Pete and four other forklift drivers, and often one or two other workers who were off the line for some reason. We had one obvious thing in common: we were all white. Although at least half of the plant population consisted of Latino, Asian American, or black workers, these workers were poorly represented among the group that walked or rode around the floor. I had a grade zero job, and there were other women and nonwhite men in janitor jobs around the plant— although probably none with as much freedom as I enjoyed.

Of all the jobs in the cellar, the most punishing were whizards; very few people could stay at those jobs for long. No one, for example, was ever able to keep my whizard position as long as a week after I left. Owen, as will be discussed later, was fired. Mike would sometimes pick up my teat line whizard and help out, but never for more than a half hour. The workers who had morning and afternoon whizard jobs on the belly line were almost all Mexican, and few of them spoke English.

My work at IBP was nowhere near as physically brutal as that of many others, and my being white was a major factor in deciding this. I could not have stayed in the plant for four months on the whizard—and probably not in many other positions on the production line. My mobility allowed observation and passing acquaintance with a larger number of workers than I would have known had I stayed on the line. Only when I talked with persons of color did Clyde object to my wandering. Yet the stress of my work was palpable and all-consuming.

Surveillance cameras combed the IBP building, yard, and parking lot. The eerie sense of being watched from a distance at any time added to the nagging foreboding that grew in me almost imperceptibly as I plunged every day more deeply into the IBP world. Indeed, IBP surveillance cameras followed some workers outside of IBP property and to their homes. Would I ever again be safe from IBP?

I had never done the monotonous, repetitive motions that I did in cleaning out the latticework in the scaffolding, shoveling meat scraps, folding stacks of boxes, or pushing boxes along the conveyor. With commuting, the job consumed nearly twelve hours of my day—sometimes more—and I would reach home stiff with cold and totally exhausted every evening. Large purple, yellow, and green bruises covered the front of my thighs as long as I was at IBP, although I never figured out what I did to cause this injury. I was lucky if I could enter notes in my computer at the end of the day, and I dozed whenever I tried to read or watch television. I even dozed off one evening when my spouse and I were trying to visit with friends.

Bit by bit work at IBP engulfed my life and pushed everything else into the margins. Details like getting my hair cut or going to the post office were hard to negotiate, and I shuddered when I imagined trying to do the job and cope with children at home. Actually, I shuddered often as I learned what some of my coworkers faced with second jobs, dangerous cars, broken furnaces, racial harassment, inadequate child care, and unpaid bills. Before I left the plant I was carrying heavy depression and thoughts of suicide that were more real than any I had known before. My lifelong habit of lying awake nights and sorting through issues failed me. Even though I slept poorly while working at IBP, I found that my mind would fill with grotesque flashbacks, and I was unable to process events or emotions as I had before. I dreamed about looking into a combo of meat and seeing detached arms and tormented faces reaching up to me to be saved—or to pull me in. My ears have rung constantly since working in the plant.

But I was a fake meatpacker. My world was different from that of my coworkers, even though we spent most of our waking hours together. As a researcher, I came to the job with a different agenda, which reached beyond IBP. As perplexing as my work became for me, both my immediate and long-term concerns profiled a privileged position unlike that of other IBP workers. When I finished work each day, I put on a down parka and L. L. Bean boots to brace myself for the Iowa cold. My Nissan never failed me, even in the coldest Iowa weather. My sons were grown and living in other states, which largely insulated them from the effects of my job. I could buy whatever food I wanted to eat. My university-tenured spouse had flexibility and resources unknown to IBP workers, as did I.

Only forty miles from my home in Ames, this fieldwork in some ways took me as far from my own culture as I had ever been. Exploring differences between the lives of my coworkers and mine drove my search for who they were and how they came to be working at IBP.

2

WHAT MORE BETTER WORK COULD YOU ASK FOR?

PERRY WORKING MEN AND MEATPACKING

"Pete's" roots were in the countryside surrounding Perry; his appearance in the IBP plant was a piece of the development of the rural Iowa working class. Born in 1952, he had grown up on an eighty-acre family farm twenty miles north of Perry. In the early years of the twentieth century a farm of this size in central Iowa provided a home for a family in return for steadfast labor and acceptance of minimal consumer comforts and conveniences. After 1960, better prospects for nonfarm jobs and more expensive farm technology transformed both the economic and social climates in rural Iowa, making it less likely that children such as Pete who were raised on such small farms would be satisfied with the prospect of making a living on the land or, for that matter, able to afford it if they wanted to.[1]

Neither Pete nor his older sister had seriously considered taking over the farm operation in the 1970s; both had stayed in the area as wage workers. Pete found his job in the 1970s in what was then the Oscar Mayer porkpacking plant in Perry. He married in 1978 and took up residence in an old farmhouse a few miles away from the plant, commuting to Perry by car each day.

By the time Oscar Mayer closed in 1989 Pete was no longer married. He had a stint selling machine oil from farm to farm, but the income was low. He coupled with another ex–packing worker and for a time lived in her Perry apartment. Both of them were more than ready to sign on when IBP opened for production later the same year in the former Oscar Mayer plant. The wages were nothing compared to what they had been in the happy years of Oscar Mayer, but they were good compared to the income from almost any other jobs Pete and his companion could find in the Perry area. To live more cheaply, they moved into an apartment in a small town ten miles away.

A number of IBP workers, like Pete, came from family farms that were no longer viable in the changing agricultural economy; others came from generations of farm laborers. Family farming, which had dominated the rural Iowa landscape since European settlement, was not incompatible with hired labor. In 1920 in the Dallas County townships of Spring Valley and Beaver, just east of Perry, approximately one-third of those recorded as being employed in agriculture were hired workers rather than family farmers. These workers gravitated toward the nonfarm labor force as farms mechanized and eliminated hired hands.[2]

Although Iowa historically has been a major farm state, since 1920 the farm population has dropped steadily, particularly since 1940. By 1990 only 9 percent of Iowans lived on farms. On the other hand, Iowa's nonfarm rural population has increased steadily over the years, claiming nearly a third of the state's residents in 1990. But even within the small remaining farm population, growing numbers of workers have been turning to nonagricultural employment (see Table 1). Tracking industrial change in terms of the weight of the agricultural and manufacturing industry workforce in rural Iowa and the state as a whole shows the decline in the percentage of persons recorded as working in agriculture. Since 1930, even among those living on Iowa farms, farm employment has decreased from 90 percent of the total number of persons reported as being employed to 49 percent. In the state as a whole, farm employment has decreased from 36 percent of the workforce to 8 percent in the same period. A growing number of manufacturing industries, like the meatpacking plant near Perry, have located in rural Iowa and drawn their employees from the rural population base. In fact,

Table 1. Percentage of Iowans Employed in Agriculture and
Manufacturing, 1930–1990

	1930	1940	1950	1960	1970	1980	1990
Rural farm population							
Agriculture	90	94	87	77	63	57	49
Manufacturing	2	1	2	5	9	9	10
Rural nonfarm population							
Agriculture	10	8	10	9	7	7	8
Manufacturing	17	8	12	17	21	23	20
Iowa population							
Agriculture	36	36	29	21	13	10	8
Manufacturing	17	11	15	19	20	20	17

Source: U.S. census, various years.

in terms of the percentage of employed workers in manufacturing industries, rural Iowa since 1970 has been more industrialized than urban
Iowa. Furthermore, even within the Iowa population officially classified
as urban in 1990, the greatest concentration of manufacturing workers
has been in towns like Perry, which are under 10,000 population.[3]

Pete was part of this rural factory workforce. He lived in the same
countryside as his parents and grandparents, but he encountered a
rural Iowa unlike what his parents and grandparents had known as
small-scale farmers. For Pete, the Oscar Mayer plant of the 1970s had
promised security and income beyond anything he could have fore-
seen on the family farm. This promise dissolved in the restructuring of
the 1980s.

The story of how conditions changed for rural workers has complicated and interweaving threads. To begin, it includes the Dallas County
economic community, with Perry as its biggest town. A local meatpacking industry developed out of the capital and labor resources in place in
the community, but over time it became less and less local in character
as it folded into the national meatpacking industry structure. Yet local
autonomy may have been more illusory than real. How things worked

at the local level was always contingent on national political and economic developments, although the intensity and visibility of the contingencies shifted.

AGRO-INDUSTRY IN DALLAS COUNTY

Brian Page and Richard Walker draw attention to the centrality of
manufacturing in building the economic strength of the rural Midwest,
identifying "agro-industrialization" as a distinctively midwestern phenomenon. Rather than a model of development in which a manufacturing system grew out of an agricultural base, they show that historically
the midwestern economy emerged from the simultaneous and interlocking growth of farms and factories. This gave rise to a more dispersed industrial distribution than existed in the northeastern United
States, where factories were concentrated in giant metropolitan centers. The vigorous economic growth that occurred in the Midwest was
rooted in the interconnection of farm and factory.[4]

Iowa has been a unique example of this phenomenon even in the
Midwest. With no large cities on the order of St. Louis, Chicago, Minneapolis, or even Omaha, Iowa has had a dispersed distribution of a
few small cities and many towns such as Perry with less than 10,000
population. In the early twentieth century these towns were supporting
a robust small manufacturing system that provided both forward and
backward linkages with agriculture. In addition to factories for processing the grains, dairy products, and meats that farmers produced,
farm implement and supply factories provided farm production needs.
Iowa had a lumber and furniture industry that further stocked the farm
operations. The Maytag and Amana Companies, major home appliance
manufacturers, were also born and headquartered in rural Iowa.

A look at Dallas County in the early years of the twentieth century
reveals a local manifestation of the economic diversity that Page and
Walker presented. Dallas County lies just west of the centrally located
state capital city of Des Moines. Although the east of the county is presently considered part of the Des Moines metropolitan area, it was well
outside the city limits before World War II. With central Iowa's fertile
soil and profitable corn-hog farming pattern, Perry drew on the wealth
of the surrounding countryside, while the surrounding farms drew on

Table 2. Distribution of Dallas County
Workforce by Industry, 1915

Industry	Number of Workers
Agriculture	3,211
Trade and transportation	2,592
Manufacturing	997
Professional services	529
Domestic and personal services	510
Other	742
Total	8,581

Source: Iowa Census of 1915 (1916), 556–57.

the resources of the town. Occupational statistics from the 1915 state census show that although more Dallas County people were working in agriculture than in any other industry classification, agriculturalists nevertheless accounted for less than 40 percent of the workforce (see Table 2). Those employed in manufacturing or "other labor" accounted for approximately 20 percent of the workforce. Perry, with a population of 4,234, was the largest town in the county, but twelve other farm towns combined to bring the number of town dwellers in Dallas County to 9,692, which was just under half the population of the county as a whole.[5]

Perry had been founded when the Des Moines and Fort Dodge Railroad built its line through the site in 1869. When the Milwaukee Railroad placed a division point in Perry in 1881, the town boomed. In 1906 an interurban electric line was added, connecting Perry to Des Moines and other towns. By 1910 railroads employed approximately one-third of the town's workers. It was Perry's position as a railroad center that made it a magnet for the surrounding countryside. Perry railroads shipped out grains, poultry, dairy products, cattle, and hogs; they brought in farm equipment and supplies as well as building materials, home furnishings, and clothing. Although the early years of Perry's development showed a variety of minor farm production lines that gradually disappeared, corn and hogs stood as a consistent cornerstone of the local economy.[6]

In its early days Perry had a variety of manufacturing plants, but they were all small; the typical ones moved in and out quickly. Only about 5 percent of the recorded workers were employed in manufacturing in the 1910 and 1920 censuses. Short-lived factories made spring beds, washing machines, cigars, ironing boards, or chalk channels; even an auto manufacturer materialized and turned out exactly one car. The plants that stayed long enough to cast a shadow anchored themselves in the agricultural economy. Two factories made plow and cultivator parts, and a dairy processing plant, tomato and corn canneries, and a grain mill handled farm produce in Perry before 1920.[7]

Perry was a rural town, organically connected to the farms surrounding it. Not only did Perry businesses process and ship farm produce and help to supply the surrounding farms, the town's rural character came through in the many town households that kept poultry, pigs, or cows along with gardens and orchards. Many of these enterprises added cash as well as food to town households. Women, children, retired persons, or those who had other jobs and would not have reported their occupations as farmers or gardeners often did this work, but eighty-three Perry residents reported being engaged in the business of farming or gardening at the time of the 1910 census. These included both owner-operators and hired workers, some living and working within the borders of the town and others living in Perry and working outside. Conversely, some persons residing close to Perry in the surrounding farm townships commuted to work in town.[8]

Further evidence of the bonding of rural town and countryside was people's movement between them at different stages of life. With no high schools outside of town, most of the few country youths who attended high school roomed in town. Farm boys would often forego high school and remain on the farms as workers until they married or otherwise succeeded to their own farming operations, whereas farm women were more likely to spend some of their unmarried years in town. A small normal college and commercial school in Perry trained women for teaching or secretarial work, and this and the similar high school program brought some young farm women to Perry. Other unmarried farm women were drawn to town to take jobs in domestic service, shops, or other businesses. Some of these women returned to farms as wives, but many did not. The chronic shortage of women on the farm was one factor in the declining farm population. In addition to the young women who came off the farms and into the town, retired farmers commonly moved to town. Country people also came into Perry for shorter excursions to buy groceries, clothing, furniture, or farm machinery, or to sell their grain and livestock. Many also went to church or visited relatives in Perry.[9]

"We are all farmers," wrote the *Perry Daily Chief* in 1940. "When farmers are on the up-up, the rest of us are sitting pretty, and when they are in the depths, our meat barrel becomes low."[10] Even when U.S. farm and nonfarm economic curves diverged, Perry's fortunes followed those of farmers rather than city dwellers. The farm depression following World War I snared Perry as well as the surrounding countryside.[11] The "roaring twenties" veneer of prosperity, which distracted urban America from its underlying economic weakness, was too thin to hide the economic disarray in Perry, where three of the four city banks failed in 1925, along with thousands of other rural banks across the Midwest. Local jobs were scarce and the whole town seemed to be in a weary and tense mood, made palpable in the news stories of the thinning local newspaper. One after another of Perry's businesses went bankrupt, leaving workers with only day labor. A 1922 newspaper story reviewing the year's work of the Perry Bureau of Commerce in fostering industrial development stated: "The past year has been a trying one for many Perry industries, and the organization has whenever possible given what assistance it could while they have been handicapped at times for lack of money yet the officers and members as well have given a great deal of their time and money whenever it was possible to do so. In spite of all the handicaps Perry has industries of which they may well be proud."[12]

One of the industries of which the Perry Bureau of Commerce could be proud was Hausserman Packing Company, a meatpacking plant that emerged out of a local butcher shop in 1920.

EARLY MEATPACKING

Iowa's meatpacking was a natural adjunct to its corn-hog agriculture. The nineteenth-century packing industry, which developed on the Mississippi River as a means of marketing hogs, tapped seasonally idled farm labor. Hogs, which represented a more efficient feed conversion than did cattle, complemented the abundant corn production. By feeding some of their corn to hogs rather than marketing it directly, Iowa farmers had a homegrown means of enhancing the value of their field crop. Hogs were known as "mortgage burners" because of their high potential profits, and the Iowa packing industry grew around hog processing and marketing. Nineteenth-century Iowa hogs were fat, being bred to maximize lard production. In the nineteenth century some Iowa farmers walked hogs to market from as far away as one hundred miles, but this was costly for fat hogs. The physiological makeup as well as the temperament of Iowa pigs precluded the long-distance drives that cattlemen used to get their livestock to market. The most practical system involved slaughtering hogs close to where they were raised. Whereas beef was preferably eaten fresh, more than half of a slaughtered hog was processed in the form of such products as bacon, ham, sausage, or lard; and this created a more local geographic network of hog packinghouses. The term *packing* came from the procedure of layering pork and salt in barrels for shipping down the river.[13]

With the latter nineteenth-century development of refrigerated railroad cars and the extension of the railroad network into the interior of Iowa, the meatpacking industry also spread to small towns across the state. However, the panic of 1893 decimated the pattern of small-town packing plants, driving the majority of them into bankruptcy. Following this shakeout, Iowa came to be dominated by the large packing companies that controlled the industry nationally. Sioux City, which lies on the state's western border on the Missouri River, adjacent to Nebraska and South Dakota, emerged as the state's major packing center. Its Cudahy plant had been strong enough to survive the panic. In 1901 Armour established a plant in Sioux City, and Swift entered in 1917. Cudahy, Armour, and Swift were leading packing companies, and their presence stabilized the Sioux City economy with thousands of jobs. The south-central Iowa town of Ottumwa, with the U.S. general offices and a large production plant of the John Morrell Company, became the state's second largest packing center.[14]

In addition to the continuing growth of the big packing companies, the early decades of the twentieth century were again expansive years for small Iowa packing companies, as plants reappeared across the countryside. In terms of product value, meatpacking was Iowa's number one industry, with pork the major commodity. In 1929 the meatpacking industry employed one-tenth of all Iowa factory workers.[15]

The Perry packing industry opened as a community effort in 1920. At the end of World War I local farmers and businessmen, seeking an outlet for area hog production as well as an investment opportunity, had a packing plant on the drawing board. A German immigrant, Charles Hausserman, had come to Perry and opened a butcher shop in 1894. By 1919, having been in business for twenty-five years, he had demonstrated his character and abilities. Technical skills, capital, and enterprise converged to form the Hausserman Packing Company, with Charles Hausserman the president and general manager. Proudly billed as "one of the most modern and complete small packing plants in the central west," [16] the plant butchered hogs as its main operation, but also slaughtered cattle and sheep and marketed sausage under the Pros-PERRY-ty label. This was a mark of pride for the town as well as for Charles Hausserman.[17]

Bad luck clouded the venture immediately after the bold and spirited opening. Between 1920 and 1921 the price of a bushel of corn dropped from $1.50 to $0.35, sending farmers and other investors into a tailspin as the rural depression descended.[18] Nineteen-twenty was arguably the worst year of the century to have inaugurated a rural business. In 1921, while making a meat delivery, Charles Hausserman was struck by a train and killed, but the company limped along as a small operation. The investment having been made, the local backers struggled to keep it going and protect their capital. In 1922 the Hausserman Packing Company employed fifty production workers and eight traveling salesmen. Automotive transportation was replacing trains for most distribution, and Hausserman sent three truckloads of meat to Des Moines each day and two truckloads weekly to Ames and to Boone, all lying within a forty-mile radius of the plant.[19]

A financial community losing three banks could not continue to put its money into a sinking packing plant. With no bank able to provide Hausserman with working capital in 1925, it was forced into bankruptcy. Employing forty men in the production force at that time, the plant had swallowed $147,000 of local capital. As the *Perry Daily Chief* explained the failure, "Trade conditions throughout the country commenced to be demoralized within a few months after the plant started operation some five years ago, and although the officers of the company have been loyal in every way to it, adding their own credit to that of the organization and seeking to maintain it on a solid financial basis, the conditions of the past few months brought on a situation which could not be longer maintained." [20]

The court appointed a receiver, and in 1926 the Hausserman Packing Company was sold at a sheriff's sale. Two Omaha investors stepped in to buy the plant, expanding its capital base with money from outside the distressed town. The reopened plant was named the Perry Packing Company. Widening its market range across west-central Iowa, the new owners added six trucks and ten salesmen. They also enlarged the distribution and product line, selling fish and canned fruit from California and canned vegetables from a Perry cannery, along with cheese, butter, margarine, honey, and an assortment of condiments. The plant's forty-two workers themselves turned out a variety of products, including pork, beef, veal, mutton, lard, ham, and an array of luncheon meats. The investors again upgraded and expanded the plant in 1929.[21]

The 1930s proved to be even harder for small rural manufacturers than the 1920s had been, and the regional marketing system became impossible to continue. (Note in Table 1 the decade's precipitous drop in rural manufacturing in the 1930s.) In 1930 the plant investors and workers again faced bankruptcy and closure, but after four months of being shut the local backers raised more capital, and a new business, the Perry Packing and Provision Company, opened in the ten-year-old building. This firm struggled for three years, until Arnold Brothers Packing Company of Chicago bought it and turned it back into an expanded meat production facility. Arnold Brothers tripled the hog kill to 100,000 a year, arranged for fresh pork to be sent to its Chicago processing facilities, and began to market Perry's locally produced poultry in Chicago. In contrast to the early appreciation of Hausserman Packing as a small, local business, this time the Perry newspaper found optimism in size: "The importance of the new project to this city and vicinity cannot be over-estimated and may mean one of the largest industrial concerns of its type to be organized here." [22] Besides being the largest, it was the only packing plant. It managed to employ additional workers by contracting to process beef and pork for federal relief programs.[23]

Arnold Brothers lasted three years before it was forced to secure more capital by becoming a subsidiary of the Swift Packing Company, which was one of the national industry leaders known as the "Big Five." Although the sale allowed the plant to survive and more workers to be employed, in sixteen years it had undergone transformation from a locally developed enterprise to a subsidiary of a huge corporation that had little concern for or involvement in the town or the workers.

Swift was able to run Arnold Brothers as a relatively small packing plant for the next seventeen years, lasting out the Great Depression and taking advantage of the economic reprieve afforded by government contracts secured during World War II. In 1953 Arnold Brothers folded into Swift, and the plant came to be called Swift rather than Arnold Brothers. In 1956 it was employing only sixty workers when it definitively closed, the aged facility being beset with water and sewage problems that the company was unwilling to remedy.[24]

Although a hog-buying and processing business employing sixty workers had cut a wide swath in the Perry economy and in the economy of Dallas County as a whole, the Swift plant in Perry was a midget by twentieth-century industrial standards. Other Iowa packing plants were employing thousands of workers. Such small businesses as Hausserman/Perry/Arnold Brothers have been periodic casualties of boom-and-bust economic cycles. The support of Swift, with its deeper pockets, prolonged the life of Perry's packing plant, but it could not capture the economies of scale that provided the margins of profit in larger packing plants. The blow of the plant closing to the local farm economy was softened when Swift maintained its hog-buying station and sent area hogs to its larger processing plants in Marshalltown or Sioux City, all within 120 miles. Perry remained without a porkpacking plant for six years.[25]

THE BIG PACKERS

Perry moved into a new era of packing history with the construction of a modern plant west of town in 1962. The old plant had been a bit player in the larger industry, bouncing in and out of crises according to national economic conditions. Since 1936 it had been a subsidiary of a major company, but with the coming of Iowa Beef Packers to rural Iowa, Perry was drawn into the high drama of industry restructuring.

From their early years, the great meatpacking companies that emerged after the Civil War were paragons of ruthless capitalism. By the 1880s the "Big Four Packers"—Swift, Armour, Morris, and Hammond—had divided up the industry among themselves, controlling livestock prices, retail outlets, and profit margins before laws could begin to keep pace with their practices. The Sherman Antitrust Act of 1890 was a response, in part, to these excesses, although it had little effect on industry practices. The Jungle, a novel written by Upton Sinclair in 1906, was an exposé of the squalor that Chicago packinghouse workers faced, but its immediate effect was the passage of the Pure Food and Drug Act in 1906, which addressed the sanitation and meat quality problems brought out in the book rather than ameliorating the gruesome conditions that confronted packinghouse production workers. Labor, although organized in the Amalgamated Meat Cutters and Butcher Workmen of North America (Amalgamated) in 1896, was largely ineffective in confronting the companies.[26]

World War I brought higher wages and improved conditions for packing workers nationally, but it also broadened and consolidated the power of what were then called the "Big Five" packing companies: Armour, Cudahy, Morris, Swift, and Wilson. The interwar years saw legislative reforms but little change in the power of labor. In 1920, to avoid antitrust prosecution, the Big Five signed a consent decree by which they "agreed to divest themselves within two years of holdings in public stockyards, terminal railroads and facilities, private railroad cars, cold-storage warehouses, and market newspapers."[27] The Packers and Stockyards Act of 1921 set a code of fair practices, although there were continuing infractions. The passage of the Wagner Act of 1935 protected labor organizing and resulted in the formation of the Packinghouse Workers Organizing Committee (PWOC) under the CIO. The goal of PWOC was to organize the entire range of skilled and unskilled packinghouse workers rather than following the practice of the Amalgamated in organizing by skill. Although such an effort held potential for a larger and more powerful union, the depression was not a propitious time for labor organizing in the meatpacking industry. The masses of job seekers were daily reminders of workers' well-grounded fears of losing their jobs. This compounded the logistical problems and limited resources of organizers, neutralizing the power of the labor legislation.[28]

It was the labor scarcity and the government regulation of industry during World War II that laid the ground for the success of packing union organizing efforts. In 1943 the United Packinghouse Workers of America (UPWA) was born out of PWOC as a CIO union that effectively organized the industry in the Midwest. After World War II the Amalgamated, an AFL union, and the UPWA represented the majority of the packinghouse workforce and coordinated its bargaining. However, the power of its organizing was weakened with the federal passage of the Taft-Hartley Act in 1947, Iowa's passage of a right-to-work law, packing workers' subsequent defeat in a major strike in 1948, and the descent of the McCarthy period of red-baiting, which was most damaging to the more radical UPWA union.[29]

In the 1950s, with these adjustments, the major companies and the major unions settled into a conflictual but mutual acceptance of each other. The unions engaged in pattern bargaining, using a master contract that effected a measure of uniformity and control across the industry. The growth of the U.S. economy and the dietary preference for large amounts of meat helped to cushion the transition away from the wartime high level of government demand.[30]

Notwithstanding the comparative stability of the 1950s, continuing mechanization in the pork industry affected Iowa workers. The meatpacking industry in general has remained relatively labor-intensive because the irregular sizes and shapes of livestock have necessitated human handling and cutting. But pork has been more susceptible to mechanization than has beef, because it involves more processing and packaging after the initial kill and cut operations. Making sausage, handling ground meat, slicing and packaging bacon, and skinning wieners were jobs that could be given over to machines, given the company incentive of substantial labor costs. The industry continued to evolve with management-union confrontations over these jobs and over wages and benefits.[31]

The 1960s fractured the industry production curve and in a short time radically changed the production equations. In 1960 Iowa Beef

Packers was chartered, and in 1961 it opened its first operation, a beef-packing plant, in the town of Denison, ninety miles from Perry. Started with a loan from the Small Business Administration, Iowa Beef Packers must have looked to the major players like one more small, rural operation that would soon be bankrupt or absorbed by a larger company. But Iowa Beef had a heretical plan to specialize in the kill operation, to mechanize and rationalize, and to save money by buying cattle in the countryside rather than going through the stockyards of the major packing centers. By centering its operations in rural Iowa and bypassing urban stockyards, it intended to avoid union wage standards. Although companies such as Swift had long maintained smaller subsidiary plants across Iowa, their nerve centers had been in the major meatpacking cities of Chicago, Omaha, or Kansas City, where they were well watched both by organized labor and by each other. Iowa Beef Packers was attempting to write its own rules rather than competing on the terms of the established industry.

Back in Perry in 1961, a group of businessmen had formed an organization called "Perry Industries" in hopes of scouting out industrial development such as a new packing plant for the town. Legend has it that an Iowa Beef Packers official happened to stop at a Perry gas station on his way through town, when a chance encounter ignited the spark that set the wheels of progress in motion. Perry Industries then took the helm, clearing the sale of stock, selling one million dollars in shares locally, and shepherding the construction that launched Perry's industrial future.[32] According to the solicitation for local investment in the Perry plant, to be called the Iowa Pork Company, the stream-lined hog kill operation would be modeled on the production system of Iowa Beef: "The trend the past several years in the meat processing industry has been to decentralize from large cities and central markets to smaller and more efficient operations. The efficiency gained and the savings in transportation of live hogs for long distances have proved that this has been a very successful trend which is likely to continue in the coming years."[33]

The new plant, which would employ two hundred workers immediately on the kill floor, was sold to the people of Perry in terms of increased retail sales and as a purchase outlet for hogs produced by local farmers. The proposed kill rate of three thousand hogs daily would be an impetus to increased hog production and greater profits for farmers.[34]

As explained by "John Kramer," a Perry worker who got one of the first jobs in the plant,

> Andy Anderson, the originator of IBP industry, or empire, had come from Denison. He'd opened a plant in Denison. He came down here and he talked the townsfolks into backing him. . . . He had $10,000 of his own money. That's it. . . . But anyway, he opened the plant and the businessmen all got together and bought the first stock and got it off the ground. And those who wished to work in construction had seniority when the plant opened—the promise of a job. So when the plant was finished they had an old gentleman named Pete Peterson, who was an old Norwegian or Swede. He was very uneducated, but he knew the construction business. . . . Anyway, he ramrodded the construction. Then when the plant opened he brought in some people from the Denison plant who knew how to process the carcasses, et cetera, you know.

The Iowa Pork Company started operations in December 1962.[35]

The original link between Iowa Pork and Iowa Beef of Denison was informal, but within months of the opening of Iowa Pork a merger between the two companies was proposed. The merger would bring Iowa Beef capital into Perry, enlarging the plant to include a cut floor in addition to the existing kill floor. The editor of the local daily, the Chief, owned to a "fairly substantial investment in the Iowa Pork Company" as he promoted the merger: "Getting a new cutting and packaging plant built and equipped at a cost of something like a million dollars without any additional local capital sounded good. . . . Pulling back has never made the wagon roll. If it is good we want it."[36] By August 1963 the merger was complete and the addition was begun. The number of production workers was set to increase from 150 to 350.[37]

Union talk arose almost as soon as the plant opened. John Kramer, whose wife had been raised near Perry, had been a member of the UPWA when he worked for Armour in Omaha in the 1950s. He moved to Perry to join his wife's community and signed on as one of the first hires at Iowa Pork. Receiving $1.40 per hour in Perry as opposed to the $2.20 he had made in Omaha was an instant lesson on the benefits of a union. As he remembered, "The wages were so, you know, unfair. We didn't have any contract. We didn't have anything, see?" With the help of UPWA officers in Des Moines, John Kramer pushed the collection of signatures for a representation vote. A tooth-and-nail fight with Iowa Beef ensued, but the weight of the Democratic administration's enforcement of federal labor law tilted the balance toward the union organizers. Before it was over, the workers had secured National Labor Relations Board (NLRB) decisions to invalidate the first two elections—which they had lost—because of company infractions of voting regulations and intimidation of workers. In the third election, held in December 1964, the workers voted overwhelmingly in favor of representation by UPWA. [38]

Negotiations for a contract started in January 1965 and were immediately deadlocked. John Kramer, as a negotiator for UPWA, seems to have accepted that Iowa Beef Packers wages would be less than those in the master contract, but the company and the union remained at odds over how much less. To add to Iowa Beef's troubles, it had a second packing plant that had also voted to be represented by the UPWA and was also bargaining for a contract in 1965. This was a beef operation, purchased in 1961, in Fort Dodge, forty-five miles north of Perry. Iowa Beef was paying the workers in its Denison plant, which voted to accept a company-sponsored union, more than it paid its UPWA-organized Fort Dodge or Perry workers. The Fort Dodge plant struck on March 6, 1965, and the Perry plant followed suit on March 10. [39]

Iowa Beef shouldered a vulnerability in the pork business operated in Perry that it did not have when producing beef in its Fort Dodge or Denison plants. The company could sell its beef to supermarkets, where it would be retailed directly as generic fresh meat. With hogs, where the major part of the carcass was further processed rather than being retailed as fresh meat, the processed meat was usually sold under a brand name. Over the decades processors spent large sums of advertising money in establishing loyalty to branded product names, and Iowa Beef Packers was outside of this loop. Specializing in kill and cut, it fed most of its pork back into the industry system, where it would be further processed by other companies before being distributed to retailers to be sold under the brand names owned by the companies. On May 1, 1965, the Armour Company, which had been buying all of the pork killed in the Perry plant, announced that it was canceling its purchase contract. As a unionized company it had the backing of workers who did not want to handle Iowa Beef Packers meat. On May 20 Iowa Beef Packers settled its dispute with its Perry workers with a compromise that leaned heavily toward the workers' demands, although the wages remained below the industry standard. Following this, Armour negotiated a new contract to buy the pork from the plant.[40]

But Iowa Beef faced too many problems in the pork industry, and it was ready to leave. Its original plan had been to specialize, and its beef operations were its main line. After negotiating a contract with the Perry workers, it sold the plant to Oscar Mayer and left the pork business. By 1969, Iowa Beef Packers had effected a revolution in the beef industry and was slaughtering more beef than any other company in the world. Intransigence of UPWA workers gave the pork industry a reprieve.[41]

Tensions relaxed dramatically when Oscar Mayer bought the Perry plant. Unlike the upstart Iowa Beef Packers, which had no interest in the rules worked out through the post–World War II packing union negotiations, Oscar Mayer was well within the fold of the old-line meatpackers. Founded in 1883 by a Bavarian immigrant, Oscar Mayer was a family business whose high-quality wieners and luncheon meats had made it an industry leader in processed meat sales.[42] It had plants organized with both UPWA and Amalgamated, and it carried no burning anti-union agenda. Moreover, it had invested in public relations, putting its good name on the products that consumers would select when they wanted the best. Its interest was in stability, orderly growth, and quality.

Oscar Mayer immediately enlarged and upgraded the Perry plant to employ over six hundred workers. Although at times the company experimented with curing meat in the plant, the basic function remained pork kill and cut. Its product was raw pork. It marketed the loins fresh and trucked much of the remaining pork to its other plants for processing. As John Kramer remembered the transition from Iowa Beef to Oscar Mayer, "When Oscar Mayer bought it (the plant), it was quite a change. They were a decent company, and they . . . had past patterns to follow, and they had contracts . . . in whatever plants they had, you know. So they bought our labor contract right along with the purchase of the plant."

"Albert Schroeder," who worked in plant maintenance, said that Oscar Mayer's ongoing advances made the plant run more smoothly:

They started making gradual improvements in the place over there. It was long hours, long days. It was still six and seven days a week. As time went on . . . things got better. We used to have a lot of break-downs. You know, when IBP built that place over there, they put in all this junk machinery, and stuff like that that they'd gotten out of another old packinghouse. And it was nothing but trouble from day one, and it was just usually run, run, run all day long. After Oscar Mayer bought it things started getting better, because they started bringing in newer stuff and converting the different things that was problems for IBP—just started making my job easier all the time. . . . We'd still have breakdowns all the time—quite a few of them—but like I say, as time went on it started getting better.

In 1968 the UPWA merged with Amalgamated, the two unions having worked in close coordination since World War II. The Perry local, which became Amalgamated Local 1149, negotiated contracts with Oscar Mayer every two to three years through the 1970s. These con-tracts attest to a steady improvement in wages, benefits, and working conditions. In 1970 the break period was lengthened from fifteen to twenty minutes, Veteran's Day was added as a paid holiday, a section dealing with first aid appeared, and a specified procedure for bidding on jobs was laid out. In successive contracts workers got improve-ments in their medical, disability, and life insurance coverage; extended vacation and holiday time; more explicit grievance procedures; clothes-changing allowances; more equipment to be provided by the company; and cost-of-living allowances. With seniority, workers could ascend to higher-pay brackets, and in many of the higher-pay brackets the com-pany offered incentive pay, which further rewarded those who produced above a set standard. Oscar Mayer paid its employees well. Packing workers built some of the most expensive houses in and around Perry; late-model cars and recreational vehicles stood beside them as further signs of prosperity.[43]

Oscar Mayer controlled its workforce by providing high-quality jobs. The plant was a magnet for farmers in the surrounding countryside who wanted to supplement their incomes, and it gave summer work to college students and to teachers in the Perry school system. Hiring workers was never a problem, even given the relatively large workforce and the rural setting. Only rarely did Oscar Mayer bring a new cohort of permanent workers into the plant, and when it did it had a ready waiting list of applicants. It was this environment in which Pete started his packing career. Having been a marginal high school student and being basically untrained, he could bless his luck at finding a high-paying job without leaving the place where he grew up.

Perry people reminisce about the "Oscar" days and the generosity of the company. Those who were children in the 1970s remember Christmas parties at the plant, stuffing themselves with hot dogs and taking home balloons. It is not hard to elicit warm testimonials from Oscar workers: "I felt that the job—the person I worked for—was really nice," said one. John Kramer summed up the general sentiment: "I was there twenty-eight and a half years. What more better work could you ask for?"

But even as the packing workers, and indeed the town of Perry in general, basked in Oscar's glow, the industry was changing. Iowa Beef Packers, which changed its name to Iowa Beef Processors in 1970, continued to ride roughshod over the beef industry, moving its headquarters out of the state to the more corporation-friendly Dakota City, Nebraska, just across the Missouri River from Iowa. It continued to open new rural plants. As the same unions represented both beef- and porkpacking workers and as the old-line companies handled beef and pork in the same plants, the collapse of the beef industry put pressure on the pork industry. In 1976 Iowa Beef bought a Madison, Nebraska, pork plant that had been started by Robert Peterson, who joined Iowa Beef to become its president. From that point Iowa Beef would be aggressively pushing on the pork industry, but since it did not take up curing meats or developing branded products, the old-line companies retained their control on a critical step in pork production.

The business climate of the 1980s turned to the advantage of Iowa Beef and to the disadvantage of the workers. In 1980 Ronald Reagan was elected U.S. president on promises to curtail regulation of business and to halt inflation. His leanings toward business interests resulted in appointments of NLRB members who provided corporate management

with the conditions needed to sidestep the demands of workers. A recession in 1981 created hardships for businesses, especially small businesses, but in tightening the supply of jobs, the recession strengthened
the hand of management in dealing with workers. The simultaneous
reduction of public services and public employment made workers even
more nervous about losing jobs, and a rising number of unemployed
persons grew more desperate to take jobs on any terms. In Iowa, the
farm economy, which had ridden high with the inflation of the 1970s,
collapsed under the suddenly tightened money policies of the Reagan
administration, putting more rural workers in the job market. The at-
tractiveness of the rural labor market was luring large-scale manufacturers in increasing numbers.[44]

A wave of business mergers and buyouts in the eighties transformed
the meatpacking industry. In 1980 Oscar Mayer augmented its meat
processing operation with the purchase of the Louis Rich Company,
a family-owned turkey processor, and it expanded its Perry rendering
works to coordinate the processing of by-products with the Louis Rich
turkey plant in West Liberty, Iowa. It was a step in the direction of
adapting by enlarging and easing itself away from dependence on pork
kill, which Iowa Beef was undercutting. But in 1981 General Foods, a
Minneapolis-based conglomerate, acquired the Oscar Mayer Company
as it struggled to reach one hundred years of age.[45]

Iowa Beef itself had been acquired by Armand Hammer's Occidental
Petroleum in 1981 and had signaled its continuing designs on the pork
industry by dropping its Iowa Beef Processors name and becoming
simply IBP. Even more disturbing was the fact that IBP acquired its first
1980s Iowa pork facility in 1982, when it purchased the closed Hygrade
facility in Storm Lake, which had previously operated as a unionized
plant, and reopened it as a nonunionized plant. Iowa had long been the
leading state in hog production, and a movement into Iowa porkpacking attacked the heart of the industry.[46]

Corporate raids were a major factor in weakening the old-line packing companies. Wages at IBP were substantially lower than those at
the other porkpackers, and the other companies were pressing their
workers to take cuts that would allow them to compete. This press
was intensified as IBP's production practices were reinforced by two
other burgeoning corporations. In 1983 ConAgra, an agribusiness con-

glomerate based in Omaha, entered the arena with its purchase of the meatpacking concerns of Armour, an industry leader that was currently owned by Greyhound. Swift, which had been the largest packer in the country for many years, was spun off from its parent company and then acquired by ConAgra. ConAgra followed this with a merger with Monfort of Colorado, another large packing company. Wilson, an old-line packing leader, filed for bankruptcy in 1983. The Excel Packing Company emerged as a division of the privately held Cargill Company of Minneapolis. ConAgra, IBP, and Cargill were the foundation of what came to be called the "new-breed" packers.[47]

ConAgra and Cargill, with their vast and diversified operations, dwarfed IBP, although their red meatpacking operations were not as large as those of IBP, which was the point player in the beef- and porkpacking industry reorganization. ConAgra and Cargill coasted in IBP's wake, taking advantage of the low wages, rural relocation, and anti-union patterns for which IBP struggled.[48] ConAgra's description of its Armour purchase acknowledged IBP's leadership in meatpacking and explained the competitive edge in the new industry: "(The) new, smaller, more efficient facilities were located out in rural communities, close to the farmers who supplied their animals. . . . The new meat-packers could also pay lower wages to their rural, generally non-unionized employees. The Big Four, with nationwide union 'master contracts,' could not compete."[49] In the major packing cities the stockyards and plants turned to rust and rat infestation as the urban packing industry died. ConAgra took over Swift plants in Des Moines and Marshalltown, giving them the Monfort name. Excel operated a pork plant in Ottumwa, which had been the former site of Morrell and Hormel plants.[50]

ConAgra purchased brand names with its acquisitions, but the core of the new-breed packing companies was in kill and cut. Although IBP did not invent boxed meat, it brought the technique into wide use in the packing industry. With the old system of handling meat, packers would sell carcasses, called hanging or swinging meat, to retail outlets, where skilled butchers would cut and sell them. The practice of the new-breed packers was to do much of the cutting and packaging in the packing plants and to sell boxes of loins, ribs, rumps, or other popular cuts that could be readily packaged and sold in supermarkets or served in restaurants with minimal further cutting. By buying boxed meat, merchants could avoid having to sell or dispose of hard-to-market parts of a carcass and could save money by not having to hire butchers with the level of skill needed to handle hanging meat. By packing beef and pork in small, easy-to-handle boxes, the costs of shipping and handling were lessened. In addition to trimming the costs of moving meat within the United States, the companies were able to take advantage of their packaging along with improved refrigeration and freezing techniques to increase their export of fresh meat. Boxed meat became the standard for the industry.[51]

In keeping with the move toward bigger and more powerful companies, the Amalgamated packing union merged with the Retail Clerks union in 1979 to become the United Food and Commercial Workers (UFCW). The logic of the merger was that if workers were to face larger and more determined anti-union companies, they needed a larger base of power and deeper pockets. The other side of such a merger was that meatpacking workers became one corner of a larger organization, and they could not necessarily count on their agenda becoming a priority of the entire union.[52] The UFCW began to promote mergers among its packing locals, a strategy that held the promise of building a wider and more solid front to face the companies but the disadvantage of lessening grassroots participation. In addition, old conflicts between former UPWA members and those who had identified with the more accommodating Amalgamated organization played out in union politics.[53]

Under General Foods, speed and intensity at the Oscar Mayer plant in Perry were stepped up. In the three-year contract they signed in April 1982, workers agreed to a wage cut and then a wage freeze. But such measures did not bring them into line with the IBP system. In February 1983 each Oscar worker received a letter from the company stating that if workers would not accept a mid-contract wage-and-benefit cut, the plant would close. According to the company, Perry workers were receiving $5.00 to $7.00 per hour more than those working for the new industry leaders, the new-breed competitors. The union's Local 1149 responded by negotiating a $2.50 hourly pay cut, which was softened by each employee's receiving a lump sum in "severance" pay, based on the number of years in the plant. Such a bonus was not contingent on the worker leaving the plant at that time, but was understood to be in lieu of any severance pay due at a future time. It amounted to as much as $11,000 for long-term workers. The base rate of the master contract of the UFCW was $10.69 per hour, and Perry workers were accepting an $8.19-per-hour base with a promise of twenty-five-cent raises in 1984 and 1985. Dental, optical, and prescription provisions were cut from the insurance package, and the medical deductible was increased.[54]

The Perry workers were not the first in the industry to agree to wage concessions that placed them below the level of the master contract, and IBP was hiring packing workers in its Storm Lake pork plant for considerably less than the Oscar Mayer workers would make in Perry. But the international UFCW officials ordered the local not to submit the revised contract to a vote. The local president went ahead with the vote in defiance of the international, and it was approved. The plant would stay open. "Max," a worker who opposed the concessions, said that the local officers "got in bed with the company" and spent more than $28,000 negotiating a contract that sold the workers down the river. The international then placed the local in receivership, dismissed its elected officers, and appointed new officers.[55]

From the perspective of another plant worker, the Perry folks were casualties of President Reagan's assault on labor. As John Kramer reflected on the concessions: "That was right after the Reagan deal with the ground controllers and the airplane deal. That, kind of, was the start of the downfall of all labor negotiations. . . . Oscar Mayer kept harping that we can't be competitive: 'We can't be competitive. We got IBP out there working people for nothing. . . . We've got all these other places that aren't paying up to standard, up to par, and we've got to have concessions.'" Some of the old-time Oscar workers left rather than accept the concessions, but in the 1980s there were plenty of new recruits who would take jobs at $8.19 an hour.

Oscar Mayer workers got a new set of top executives when Philip Morris, an overgrown cigarette manufacturing company, acquired General Foods in 1985, but it made little local impact. In the 1986 contract Perry workers' base pay was raised to $9.00 per hour, which was still substantially below the $10.69 industry standard. This time the contract was negotiated by the international union's own appointees, and it no longer looked as bad as it would have in 1983.

Just as telling as the wage level was the myriad of minor concessions that the workers accepted by the time of the 1986 contract. Some of them were largely symbolic, but they were nevertheless stark reminders that workers were no longer calling the shots. The earlier contracts had all contained a union shop clause stating that when Iowa repealed its right-to-work law, all production workers would immediately be required to belong to the union. Although it was already largely moot because the Iowa legislature was nowhere near repealing its right-to-work law, this clause disappeared in 1986. (Union membership nevertheless remained at 100 percent through the Oscar Mayer period.) The 1986 contract had no provisions for a cost-of-living raise or for paid clothes-changing time. Whereas employees had previously been considered terminated if they were off the job through injuries or layoffs for two years, the 1986 contract shortened this to eighteen months. Workers lost their Easter Monday holiday. And the probation period for new workers, during which time they had only minimal rights to union protection, was lengthened from thirty to ninety days.[56]

In October 1988 Oscar Mayer gave notice that it was really closing the plant on February 3, 1989. Although workers who had already received "severance" pay in 1983 were not entitled to anything at that point, the company offered a bonus, based on a worker's length of service, to those who would stay on the job until the plant closed.[57]

IBP RETURNS TO PERRY

The bad news was that Oscar Mayer was leaving. The good news came two months later, just before Christmas, when IBP announced that it was going to buy the plant, remodel it, and reopen it in the summer of 1989 as a specialty sow kill and boning facility. John Chrystal, a prominent Iowa Democrat with business interests in Perry, declared the sale to be "a wonderful Christmas present for central Iowa hog farmers, grain producers, businesses and labor."[58]

For all the odious history of the company, including its brief interlude in Perry as Iowa Beef Packers in the 1960s, some workers were not sorry at the prospect of having IBP as their new boss. The last few years with Oscar had been stressful. The line speed had increased, and workers were getting repetitive motion disorders along with every kind of shoulder, back, foot, and leg pain imaginable. The anger of betrayal clung to them like the odors of the plant. With IBP, they would be working for a rising star rather than a relic of the past. Just one year before, in 1987, IBP had succeeded in reducing $5.7 million in Occupational Safety and Health Administration (OSHA) fines through reconciliation with the UFCW and the government. By the terms of the deal, they had agreed to institute a costly safety program based on ergonomics. Surely that boded well for future labor relations. Although some Oscar workers, as a point of honor, would never work for IBP, most of the workers hoped for the best in a new job.[59]

An Oscar worker recalled the mood of 1988–89: "Before Oscar closed they were down on it—called it every name in the book. The great IBP was going to take over. Those guys came in and, boy, they were IBP 100 percent." The president of the Perry Chamber of Commerce attempted to assuage the lingering queasiness of those who remembered the bad IBP days in Perry by declaring, "They're changing their reputations."[60]

Some Oscar workers hired onto the construction crew that remodeled the plant. The majority waited nervously until July 1989, when they could go to the Perry National Guard Armory building and put in their applications for IBP work.

The IBP starting wage of $5.80 was jarring, considering the 1988 Oscar base wage of $9.50. In fact, it was the lowest starting wage of sixteen regional porkpacking plants surveyed by the Cedar Rapids UFCW local in 1990 (see Table 3). The drop was partially cushioned by a two-tier system in which IBP started workers who had been at Oscar Mayer for eighteen months at $7.00 per hour. It was not great pay, but not many alternatives existed in the rural Iowa of the 1980s.[61]

The lowered wages of meatpacking workers occurred despite increased production per worker. In terms of their share of industry profits, Iowa packing workers reached a maximum in the 1970s (see Table 4). Workers' share of meatpacking revenues, low in the early years of the twentieth century before successful labor organizing, had risen dramatically with the successes of the UPWA and had held strong until the 1980s. The steep wage drops of the 1980s cut workers' slice of the revenue below the levels of the early years, when the notorious company giants had run roughshod over their workers.

When Oscar Mayer sold the Perry plant, it got out of the kill busi-

Table 3. Comparison of Starting Hourly
Wages for Production Workers in Porkpacking
Plants, 1990

Plant	Wage ($)
IBP—Perry	5.80
Dakota Pork—Sioux City	6.50
Excel—Ottumwa	7.00
IBP—Columbus Junction	7.20
Hormel—Austin	7.50
IBP—Council Bluffs	7.50
IBP—Storm Lake	8.00
ConAgra—Marshalltown	8.25
ConAgra—Worthington	8.25
Morrell—Sioux City	8.25
Farmstead—Albert Lea	8.92
Farmstead—Cedar Rapids	8.92
Farmland—Denison	9.00
FDL—Dubuque	9.25
IBP—Waterloo	na
Supreme Pack—Sioux City	na

Source: P-3 Pacer (newsletter of UFCW Local), Cedar
Rapids, Iowa, April–May 1990.

ness and became a specialized pork processor. One of the trends in the
meatpacking restructuring was a separation of slaughter and processing operations. Unlike the old-line packers that had the entire production chain from livestock delivery to packaged wiener loadout in one
plant, the new plants cut up the chain, with different companies taking
over different segments of it. In 1963, for example, only three Iowa
meat processors did not have kill operations; by 1992 the number had
risen to seventeen (see Table 5). The increasing number of Iowa production workers recorded as working in meat processing plants were,
in fact, workers who previously would have been working in integrated
kill, cut, and processing plants, referred to at that time as simply packing plants. Initially IBP specialized in kill, and later it did more cut and
boning.[62]

Table 4. Meatpacking Production Workers'
Wages as a Percentage of Value Added in
Manufacturing, 1919–1992

Year	U.S.	Iowa
1919	45	40
1929	36	38
1958	44	48
1963	44	48
1972	39	48
1977	41	50
1982	34	41
1987	31	36
1992	28	31

Source: U.S. Bureau of the Census, Census of Manufactures:
Industry Series: Meat Products, various years.

Table 5. Trends in the Iowa Meatpacking and Processing Industry,
1958–1992

Year	NUMBER OF PLANTS			NUMBER OF PRODUCTION WORKERS		
	Packers	Processors	Total	Packers	Processors	Total
1958	29	4	33	19,058	288	19,346
1963	36	3	39	18,496	157	18,653
1972	43	7	50	19,500	1,100	20,600
1977	40	12	52	16,300	2,000	18,300
1982	38	14	52	14,500	1,800	16,300
1987	27	12	39	10,900	2,700	13,600
1992	30	17	47	14,900	3,600	18,500

Source: U.S. Bureau of the Census, Census of Manufactures: Industry Series: Meat Products,
various years.

Note: According to terminology used in the census reports, "packers" included the
operations that had both kill and processing; "processors" had no kill operation.

In 1987 Occidental Petroleum sold off 49 percent of IBP and totally spun it off in 1991, making it once again an independent company. In recent years it has been inching over into processing functions, albeit without a brand name of its own.[63]

Most of the pork produced at Perry's IBP plant was sold to processors, including Oscar Mayer. A former Oscar Mayer worker explained to me that the company now has a twenty-year contract with IBP for the supply of its raw pork. Although neither company has published such a contract, it would be a logical surmise. Oscar Mayer needs a dependable supply of raw pork for its processing operations. Unless it wants to risk a nasty labor incident, it cannot kill hogs as cheaply as it can buy IBP pork. For its part, IBP needs dependable buyers. Such an arrangement was tested and failed in the 1960s; its success in the 1980s suggests a rapprochement between IBP and the packing union.

To John Kramer, who worked in the Oscar Mayer plant, it was obvious that IBP and UFCW had reached a deal before the Perry plant was opened, because IBP was not known as a union-friendly company; it was reportedly threatening workers with dismissal for signing union cards at another plant, where it forced new employees to watch anti-union videos. In 1988 Maurice McGill, an executive vice president of IBP, was quoted as saying that, as an incentive for plants to stay non-unionized, the company kept its hourly pay higher in its nonunionized plants than in its unionized plants.[64] Yet such actions and statements, which would seem to impede workers' right to organize, were not contested in the 1980s as they might have been earlier.

Anticipating, for whatever reason, that it would represent the workers of the Perry IBP plant, the UFCW kept its locally appointed president on salary during the time that the plant was closed. John Kramer recounted a conversation he had with "Max," the local president appointed by the international UFCW: " 'Max,' I said, 'I'm going to tell you right now. When IBP bought the plant from Oscar there was a sweetheart deal put in there.' I said, 'They're keeping you on full time, Max. You got nothing to do. The reason they're keeping you is there's been a deal cut already, and I know there has—without proof, but I know there has—that they are going to let you organize and UFCW is going to be their representation.' "

Increasingly the UFCW saw its best hope for survival in the meatpacking industry in accommodation with new-breed packers. The UFCW and IBP had come a long way toward a peaceful coexistence that would have been impossible in the context of the 1960s, when the scrappy UPWA had faced the company down. Incredibly, even the international UFCW stepped in to pull IBP out of legal trouble in the late 1980s. In 1987 IBP president Robert Peterson was facing the possibility of perjury charges for lying to a U.S. House of Representatives committee hearing on the documentation of injuries at the Dakota City plant. William Olwell, executive vice president and international director of collective bargaining for the UFCW, pulled rank on the director of the UFCW packinghouse division, who had brought a complaint against IBP for having two sets of injury and illness records and for not reporting major injuries. Olwell testified: "IBP officials did not make false statements before Chairman Lantos' Subcommittee on Employment and Housing. Rather, it appears to me that was an unfortunate misunderstanding and not an attempt to mislead the Congress."[65] The UFCW then helped to get IBP's $5.7 million fine reduced to $975,000.[66] In short, the UFCW was kinder to IBP than was President Reagan's OSHA.

In Perry, IBP recognized the UFCW local with its internationally appointed president without a representation election. Recognition of Perry's Local 1149 came in a chain of UFCW-IBP agreements that included a recognition of the IBP beef plant at Joslin, Illinois, also without a representation election, and the calling off of organizing drives at pork plants in Columbus Junction and Storm Lake. According to UFCW official Al Zack, the union would stop criticizing IBP, take a less confrontational approach, and concentrate on organizing its new-breed competitor, ConAgra.[67]

The cooperation between UFCW and IBP was not, however, apparent in the terms of the labor contract or in the $7.00 or $5.80 starting wage rates. The workers got a sixty-hour workweek, the seniority system was largely scrapped, and the chain speed increased. One of my IBP coworkers who had been five years away from retirement with Oscar claimed that IBP moved four to five times as much meat as Oscar did. He could not imagine spending his working life under the pressure that he experienced in the IBP plant.

Chris Lauritsen, a meatpacker and union activist who worked in Spencer, Mason City, and Denison, described some of the changes that he had seen since IBP took over:

> We always thought that . . . if you were a lucky enough guy to get hired at the pack, you were set for life. You bought a house, you bought your car, you started your savings account, you looked forward to sending your kids to college, everything. Your life was set because you were a union man, you had your life. . . . Iowa Beef destroyed that and they destroyed it mostly with a lot of predatory ways. . . .
>
> [E]very worker, I think, has a right to a certain amount of dignity on the job, to be treated with respect and dignity. I mean that certainly no one has a right to curse you, to swear at you, to call you stupid or ignorant or a lot of other things, okay? It doesn't make any difference what they pay you, they don't have that right. Iowa Beef does that. They talk to their workers like a dog. . . . And Iowa Beef has a tendency to believe because we pay you less and we work you harder you're stupid enough so we're not gonna show you any kind of respect. And that's the way they treat 'em. They treat 'em badly in that respect. They work 'em at speeds that are unbelievable and incomprehensible to somebody that's never tried it. And through their high speed work they cause all kinds of afflictions like tendinitis, carpal tunnel syndrome, arthritic joints. The floors are slippery so they slip on the floors constantly and get dislocated discs in their back, they get all kinds of disorders. They're treated badly in that respect. In a lot of cases for on-the-job injuries they don't have any workman's compensation. They tell 'em, 'No, we're not gonna pay you workman's comp. You go ahead and get that taken care of on the regular insurance.' "[68]

By the 1990s mainstream U.S. newspapers from the *Wall Street Journal* to the *Los Angeles Times* had joined the progressive labor press in a chorus of criticism of IBP. In Iowa, Bruce Babbitt, stumping the state for the 1988 Democratic presidential caucuses, had called IBP a "corporate outlaw." Farm groups believed that the large share of the market controlled by the three new-breed leaders was depressing livestock prices. The *Des Moines Register* labeled IBP "fiercely anti-union" and reported deals that IBP had made with organized crime in the New York City meat market. The local environmental group Citizens against River Pollution (CARP) in Louisa County, the site of IBP's Columbus Junction plant, pressed complaints against IBP for polluting the Iowa and Cedar Rivers in southeastern Iowa. Religious and community leaders decried the community breakdown associated with IBP's high turnover and low wages and the consequent heavy call on social services. A candidate for county attorney in Buena Vista County, site of the IBP Storm Lake plant, defeated a long-term incumbent in a campaign in which he accused IBP of "social pollution."[69]

Iowa critics also pointed out that IBP had considerable local, state, and federal subsidies in its assault on the packing industry. Starting with its initial Small Business Administration loan, IBP had pressed into rural communities with the promise of jobs in exchange for various job training funds and economic development grants. It is difficult to put an exact figure on these payments, because some of them, such as Perry's offer to help widen a highway, would not necessarily be added up in IBP's column. The Republican state administration's Iowa Department of Economic Development sent me information in 1992 that indicated IBP had received $4,738,000 in loans ($738,000 forgivable) and $7,055,000 in job training funds from bonds sold by community colleges to private investors. On the other hand, in 1990 the Iowa House of Representatives Democratic Research Staff totaled $14,262,965 in public assistance to IBP over a seven-year period. Whereas Republicans generally tallied the jobs that IBP brought to distressed communities, Democrats more frequently tallied the well-paid, unionized employment that was lost with the dissolution of the old-line packing companies.[70]

But IBP's defenders have been quieter in the 1990s. No other Iowa company has been so popularly caricatured as a villain as has IBP. ConAgra, with its Monfort meatpacking division, and Cargill, with Excel meatpacking, though larger, more powerful, and arguably as ruthless as IBP, have been more skilled in staying in the background and keeping themselves out of trouble. They have done nothing as flamboyantly ideological as IBP's open support of long-shot Republican conservative candidate Phil Gramm in the 1996 Iowa presidential caucuses, a move that embarrassed the Gramm campaign. Yet growing numbers of books and articles have assailed the political background of the 1980s growth of ConAgra and Cargill. Despite unemployment and the closure of Spencer Pack in northwestern Iowa, in 1995 a group of concerned citizens successfully pressured the city council of Spencer not to provide rezoning that would allow the establishment of a Monfort plant in town.[71]

Pete and I worked at the Perry IBP plant in 1992 along with nearly seven hundred other production workers. But not everyone had this chance. Some sixty Oscar Mayer workers were turned down when they applied for jobs at IBP. Because union membership under Oscar Mayer had been 100 percent, all of them had belonged to the UFCW local, but some of them were quiet and inactive members. John Kramer was among those who did not apply, but he found himself on a company list of persons not permitted on IBP plant premises, so he would probably have been turned down.

Perry's meatpacking story continued its rocky course after I left the plant. In January 1994 IBP announced that it was closing its Perry plant. Citing failure of workers to ratify the 1993 union contract, the attempt of the town of Perry to annex the plant, and meanness on the part of U.S. Department of Agriculture (USDA) meat inspectors, IBP claimed that it had never made a profit in Perry. In response, the town dropped its annexation plans, the USDA transferred out all of its meat inspectors, and workers ratified the contract at the eleventh hour. And IBP stayed. Forming a partnership with Nippon, a Japanese firm, it expanded the plant, specialized its production for the Japanese market, and added two hundred new jobs, bringing the total number of workers to one thousand.[72]

Perry had a small, locally operated packing industry in the early twentieth century. As such, it connected organically with the corn-hog agriculture of central Iowa and provided jobs for a modest number of rural wage laborers. Although the local operation expanded in size and was taken over by a large corporation in the 1960s, the presence of a union, together with the benign intervention of the government, made guardedly favorable conditions for a rural blue-collar workforce. This changed most dramatically for Perry in the 1980s, when the government eased its regulation of business and threw its weight more decisively on the side of management, consolidating the control of new-breed packers. Unions were smashed or co-opted. Perry's story in this respect was not that different from many others coming out of the 1980s. John Kramer summed up his disdain for IBP and the changes he saw with industry restructuring: "When you base your livelihood, your profits, on human misery, something's wrong."

Corporate greed came in and enveloped a rural hamlet. It is true. Pete and his coworkers felt the sting of the corporate whip in a way that his parents, grandparents, and great-grandparents had not. In the following chapter, which focuses on "Annie" and other rural women wage earners, we find that the inclusion of gender opens another story.

3

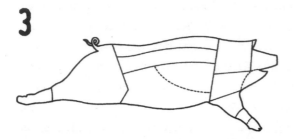

FRANKLY, SHE'S NOT WORTH IT

WORKING THROUGH GENDER

Toward the end of my employment at IBP, "Jake," the plant manager, called me in for an earnest talk about what he had learned I was doing. As it happened, we conversed more about him and his work in meatpacking than about me. A post–World War II Polish immigrant, he went to work at a packing plant when he was faced with supporting his widowed mother and siblings after high school graduation in 1961. Eventually he married and had four children. Working hard, he made good money, moved up through the ranks of the packing union, and only recently had shifted from labor to management. I asked him how he felt, knowing that the people who worked for him would never have the opportunity that he had to make enough money to support their families. He responded that it was because so many women were now working.[1]

This apparent non sequitur picked up a piece of the gender contradiction running through meatpacking work at least since World War II. Women did and did not cause the drop in wages. Working women were and were not treated the same as men in the IBP plant. Gender conditioned the structural changes in meatpacking. It has a history and a presence that refocuses the picture of rural labor in general and meatpacking in particular.

Gender concerns the relationship between what is held to be true, characteristic, appropriate, and just for men and what is held to be true, characteristic, appropriate, and just for women. Men and women have always been defined differently, although the differences change over time and vary by class, race, and ethnicity. Definitions of women and men are complementary, even though they are frequently contested and in tension. Moreover, statements about gender seldom coincide with what is acted out in daily life. Gender constructions, though subject to change, are grounded in primal experience: they are basic to the way people see, understand, and live in the world.

An impressive body of scholarship on gender and labor studies demonstrates that work has been different for men and women. Men and women factory workers have had different reasons for going to work. The social and emotional costs exacted from them as workers have differed. Once on the production floor, men and women have had different job assignments and different pay scales. Their skills have been differentially evaluated. Seniority systems have functioned in different ways for men and women. Their collective voices have differed. Without taking gender into account we cannot know what is involved in the formation of the working class.[2]

Support for gender division in the workplace has been broad. The historical differences in men's and women's work in rural Iowa provided a structural precedent for meatpacking work, and discriminatory policies and laws of the government both reflected and reinforced gender inequality in work.[3] The norms and values of rural Iowa have further channeled the way both men and women think about men's and women's experiences of work.[4] As Jake indicated, corporate managers have used the logic of gender to their advantage.[5] In their turn, unions have used gender constructions to challenge corporate power.[6] Both men and women on the production floor have used and validated gender divisions for their own purposes, even as these divisions have generated workplace conflict.[7]

This chapter deals with the way that gender—as expressed in laws, in rural culture, in plant management policies, in packing unions, and in everyday life—shaped and was shaped by the ongoing reorganization of the meatpacking industry. Although a range of cultural, social, legal, and political factors continuously reinforced gender division, separate

pieces emerged forcefully at different points. Rural women's historical position in the informal or hidden labor force conditioned their
entry into factory jobs, and the question of "decency" was a deeply
rooted theme with variations that played through the decades. Major
challenges to existing gender division came during World War II, when
plant managers sought female workers to fill places left by departing male workers; and during the 1960s, when legal changes, feminist
discourse, and industrial restructuring converged to create a clash between some women workers on one side and union and management
on the other. The definition of "skill" and its link to gender became
critical as new-breed companies "deskilled" their production lines.
Meatpacking companies could manipulate gender to lower labor costs
and raise profits, while packing unions, by declining to act on gender contradictions, became the (at times unwitting) ally of new-breed
packers.

Too often gender has been construed as being only about women.
The second chapter can be read as an account of economic restructuring—which it is—but more specifically it is an account of male experience of economic restructuring. If male experience is taken as norma-
tive, then recognizing the significance of gender entails bringing in at
least the possibility of women in order to perceive the significance of
maleness. Gender is present with or without women, although it may
be invisible and unspoken. As expressed by Alice Kessler-Harris, to recognize gender we need to make men the "other." By problematizing
masculinity and complicating the male-centered account, we deepen
the understanding of the process. No one is a generic worker; one is a
male worker or a female worker.[8]

Although the focus in this chapter is on meatpacking companies' exploitation of the economic and social vulnerability of women, they have
also exploited men's vulnerabilities, including their concerns about
their manhood. Work is a central element of manhood, and men's
status as workers has been increasingly eroded with new-breed packers
in control of the industry. Besieged men might define their opponents
and allies in a variety of ways as they seek to reclaim their manhood.
Although men might join with women to oppose their employer's practices, they might also turn against women and attempt to bond with
powerful male managers. Or they might do both.[9]

Power is embedded in gender relations. As Joan Scott writes, without seriously engaging the concept of gender we run the risk of either isolating women workers in male terrain or making them honorary males.[10] In either case, women workers are perplexing and without agency. As isolates in male space, they constitute a special case to be explained in terms of the particular economic, social, and cultural conditions required to accommodate the dissonant presence of women. On the other hand, if we try to discard gender markers and make women workers into simply (male) workers, they are measured against norms established by male experience, norms that never play out the same way for women. In injecting gender into analysis, the fact that meatpacking is among the occupations historically shaped by male workers and managers becomes something to be analyzed in terms of the way in which it has shaped the lives of women and men.[11]

All of workers' struggles occur in a gendered context. Gender shapes struggles not by determining the outcome but by bringing its complex reality to the playing table. Gender poses thorny questions that do not go away, although the parameters shift. By looking at the multiple twists that brought Jake to the assertion that working women lowered packing wages, we see the significance of gender in the history of the packing industry.

RURAL WORKING-CLASS WOMEN BEFORE 1940

A 1936 editorial in the Perry Daily Chief declared that although it might be necessary for a woman to work, it was "unnatural." Any man would instinctively resent it.[12] In the 1930s common wisdom recognized women as outsiders to the business of making a living. Yet the reality of daily life placed them in the world of work, whether it was in the informal sector, in domestic service, or in manufacturing. In seeking pay for their work, women found themselves outside of society's norms, which tempered potential claims to equitable compensation. But money itself was different for men and women. Even small amounts proved an incentive for women, not just to provide what they could for themselves and their households but also to relinquish the identity and respect conceded to "decent" women.

Jake implied that women began to work in the 1980s. This was consistent with a general and long-term denial of the fact of rural women's work, a denial that both confirmed and flew in the face of my years of study and fieldwork with rural women. While interviewing women in rural Iowa in 1982, I formulated "Elsa's hypothesis" when I first faced this contradiction. "Elsa," an eighty-one-year-old rural woman, spent an afternoon reminiscing about a lifetime of solid, productive work on the farm, yet at the end of the interview she claimed that she had never worked after her marriage in 1921. She explained that no "decent" woman would work. Well, maybe if she worked for someone she knew, like a family member, then it would be okay; otherwise not. With "Elsa's hypothesis" I posited that a woman could do any task as long as she did it within the context of the family; if she moved outside the care and protection of the family, her work became disgraceful—"indecent." Women could "help" within a family farm or a family business, but they did not actually "work." What I considered work—scrubbing a chickenhouse, digging potatoes, stocking dry goods in a general store—was not called work if done within a family business. Hence, a woman could do these activities and remain "decent." [13]

But for a rural working-class woman, the possibility of working in a family economy diminished because her family did not own a general store or a large farm. She was more likely to be forced into "indecency" than was a middle-class woman. Indeed, the lack of family property of women who were pressed to work outside the household probably contributed to the sense of their "indecency." During wartime, for example, when middle-class women took paid jobs, they were less "indecent." Nevertheless, the concern for "decency," the shame associated with women's wage labor, runs through the texts of women workers in rural Iowa. "Decency" was gendered.

The matter of "decency" constrained working-class women in a different way than it did middle-class women. In households of the rural working class, the necessity and value of women's work was never in question. Their work was important, valued, and required. Their dilemma concerned the kind of work, the pay, and whether they might associate and organize beyond the household or extended family. The shadow of social disapproval, the suspicion of "indecency," lay over their work and led them and their families to deny its significance even—or especially—as they depended on it for their survival. Both middle-class and working-class women tended to work informally in the 1920s. The 1930s depression reinforced this tendency as women were pressured to cede their formal jobs to male breadwinners.[14]

The "Harvey" family history illustrates the centrality of women's labor for the household economy in rural Iowa before 1940. "Martha Harvey," born in Dallas County in 1906, taught country school as a teenager. At age nineteen she gave up teaching to marry "Carl Harvey," a car salesman. Although she may well have hoped to live on his income, her status as "nonworking" wife disintegrated abruptly in 1929, when Carl lost his job. The economy of Dallas County was already in the doldrums after World War I, and it further deteriorated in the 1930s. Carl was lucky enough to get a job at the Perry meatpacking plant, but his income was too low to support the family. Three small children added to the stress. In response to their crisis, they negotiated a move to a farmhouse, their rent consisting of care of the farm's livestock. Carl commuted to the packing plant. Living on the farm, Martha raised chickens, supplying a small amount of money and food for the family. A further blow fell in 1931, when Carl strained a muscle and suffered temporary paralysis. Unable to work, his small income disappeared. At the same time Martha had a fourth baby. She took care of her family, kept a garden that provided a major share of their food, and maintained the poultry and livestock. Her sister moved in to help, and the two of them pulled the household through.

Martha and her sister did not have recognized jobs, hourly incomes, or salaries, but their work was in every way critical for the survival of the Harvey family. Contrary to the belief in the norm of the male breadwinner, the reality was that working-class men provided the primary household support for limited periods of time at most.[15]

Because of family positions, Martha Harvey and her sister handled livestock and did other farm chores without being defined as workers. The inclusion of a woman as an appendage to her husband helped to hide and deny her work. Before 1940, a farmer seeking hired help often advertised for a married man. This meant that the worker would presumably be older and more experienced than a teenaged boy, but it also meant that the farmer expected the labor of the wife as part of the package. Incidental to the man's employment, but fully expected to work, the wife of the farmhand did farm and household chores for her husband's employer.[16] Although this did not entail a culturally recognized job, the household economy depended on it.

Even rural women who lived in town did a great deal of informal subsistence production. Before 1940, people kept milk cows, pigs, and poultry in rural towns and raised most of their own fruits and vege-tables. In Perry, the daily newspaper published a standard April re-minder that chickens had to be penned up in order to protect gardens.[17] Some women earned money doing laundry and housecleaning with-out having what they called jobs. At the time of the 1920 census, 53 of the 1,491 households in Perry had roomers living in them, which was another way for "nonworking" women to produce income.[18] Although not listed as workers on the census forms, women and children of these households provided economic support.[19]

In addition to aboveboard informal work, some rural women en-gaged in illegal work when the alternative to not doing it was worse than the work itself. "Agnes Brown," who lived in Perry as a child dur-ing the 1920s, recalled an economically and socially marginal neigh-borhood: "There was a west side area where most of the gamblers and hookers lived, . . . 'Mrs. George' had this place, way out, and lots of the lawyers would go out there on weekends and booze it up. You know what I mean. She ran a bootleg joint. . . . The businessmen put blind-ers on and didn't question it, because a lot of them participated in the gambling and the drinking and the whoring that was going on."[20]

This undoubtedly confirmed the worst fears of those who con-demned the "indecency" of working women, but it may also have pro-duced more money and financial independence for women than did more respectable choices of work. According to Thomas Morain's study of Jefferson, a town just northwest of Perry, drinking became a popu-lar form of middle-class recreation during Prohibition. Some drinking money got redistributed downward into the working class. Although we cannot know how much money women made in their clandestine activities, even a little money was significant in working-class house-holds. It had to be balanced against continuing personal and legal jeop-ardy and the social unacceptability of the work.[21]

Rural culture simultaneously denied and required women's work, a contradiction that conditioned their movement into the formal labor market.[22] Although a majority of rural women worked informally be-

Table 6. Percentage of Manufacturing Jobs
in Rural Iowa Held by Women, 1930–1990

Year	Factory Jobs	Percentage Held by Women
1930	34,820	9.4
1940	15,664	14.4
1950	30,739	17.0
1960	49,180	21.1
1970	68,630	24.7
1980	92,929	29.5
1990	92,444	24.7

Source: U.S. census, various years.

fore 1940, a few of them edged into the formal labor market.[23] Factories had some of the best-paying jobs for women, even though factory jobs properly belonged to men. Only a minority of the minority of women with formal employment were working in factories (see Table 6).[24] Most women not driven by extreme economic need shunned factory work, but for every factory job open to women, there were crowds of applicants attracted by the hope of income.[25]

Getting a factory job often entailed indirect entry or a tainted association with a nonfamily male. In the thirties women as well as men waited around factory doors for months to get manufacturing jobs, but women nearly always required a personal benefactor to open the door. Jeanette Haymond, a divorced mother with two children in the 1930s, told about getting a job at the Wilson packing plant in Cedar Rapids after what was probably a layoff:

Every morning they'd come in [to apply for work]. It seems like it was around six o'clock we'd all get there. You'd sit on benches in there, and then they would come out and pick out some if they wanted them. You turned in an application, of course. You filled out an application and that, but every morning they wanted you to come down there anyhow. You come down there and sat and waited to see if you were going to be called. Every morning. . . .

Now this is the way it worked back then. I met a fellow that went around to dances when I did. I knew him real well and that, and he was working in the beef department there. He asked me what I was doing down there.

I said, "Well, I'm trying to get back on again. . . ."

He says, "Well, that'll be a problem, won't it?"

I said, "It might be. I don't know. So far, nothing."

You know, you go down there in the morning, and you sit and wait, and they say, "Well, that's all. We're through hiring."

And he told me that he was a good friend of the fellow that did the hiring. He says, "I'll talk to him for you. You come back tomorrow morning."

And I did, and the next morning the guy that did the hiring called my name. I went in there and talked to him, and he says, "Well, I've got an opening this morning, a couple of openings, but it's on the killing floor. I don't think you'd like that very well, but you come back day after tomorrow and I think I can get you on in the trimming floor. It's cleaner there, and I think you'd like that better."

I says, "I think I would too."

So I went back. If you know somebody and they pull the strings a little bit for you you can get on.[26]

Although there was no suggestion of any sexual exchange in Haymond's getting her job, other women reported intrusive sexual demands connected with their packinghouse work. No woman could exercise comparable control by requisitioning sexual services in exchange for work favors. This control of the work setting through a double sexual standard rested on, and in turn buttressed, gender inequality. The presumption of immorality and "indecency" when unrelated men and women worked together was part of the dynamics of power on the production floor. It kept most women out of the packinghouses, and it circumscribed the movement of the few women inside them.[27]

The imbalance between the work expectations of men and women altered the structure of packinghouse employment. A 1937 report placed the average hourly packinghouse pay of women at 54.3 cents as compared to 75.2 cents for men. Although statistical data are incomplete, women's hourly wages seem to have been approximately two-thirds of

Table 7. Gender of Iowans Employed in the
Manufacture of "Food and Kindred Products,"
1930–1990

| Year | NUMBER | | Percentage Women |
	Men	Women	
1930	21,216	3,284	15
1940	27,703	5,406	16
1950	34,270	9,507	22
1960	44,629	10,995	20
1970	37,644	9,143	20
1980	37,340	10,503	22
1990	30,037	10,880	27

Source: U.S. census, various years.

men's in the early twentieth century. However, women had shorter and more unpredictable hours of work and more frequent layoffs, further widening the income gap.[28] Men's higher wages and better treatment provided an incentive for manufacturers to hire women. As can be seen in Table 7, in the category of employment in the manufacture of food and kindred products, approximately half of which was in meatpacking plants, the number of Iowa women increased by 65 percent between 1930 and 1940 as the percentage of food manufacturing workers who were women increased from 15 to 16 percent.[29]

Women worked in the larger packing plants such as those in Sioux City, Waterloo, or Ottumwa. Smaller plants, those employing less than one hundred workers, including those in Perry and Storm Lake, did not hire women. In small towns women remained in low-paying seasonal jobs in small poultry processing plants rather than working in cattle or hog slaughtering operations. The poultry plants, which tended to be locally owned, were often no more than overgrown farm or basement operations that popped up and operated for a few years before disappearing.[30]

In the 1930s gender lines in manufacturing shifted to include more women workers, but gender segregation remained, even as the zigzags in the structure betrayed its arbitrariness. Women could work in brickyards but not in lumber mills; they could haul bricks, but they could not fire a kiln; they could do hard manual labor, but they could not run a machine; they could cut chickens but not pigs. "They'd get muscles like a man," according to one man.[31] But they got women's pay. In fact, it was not unusual for women to report that they were required to work fifteen to thirty minutes each day without pay in exchange for the privilege of having a job.[32]

Gender inequality structured the distribution of jobs within meatpacking plants. In simple terms, the meatpacking production line was a disassembly chain running from the receiving of livestock, through the kill floor, onto the cut floor, into the curing operations, and from there to weighing, packaging, and shipping out wieners and bacon. Retail butchers bought hanging carcasses, but the final operations for the meat that carried the company name took place in the plants. The prevailing gender division dictated that men work in the first part of the chain with the handling of live animals and killing. As the pieces of meat got smaller and cleaner, women appeared on the line. Women predominated in the final slicing, weighing, and packing. Although women sometimes had minor, tedious trimming jobs such as cutting meat off animals' heads, most of their work entailed tasks such as twisting sausages or packing bacon that did not involve the use of a knife. Men held virtually all of the supervisory jobs, they designed the production systems, and they ran the machinery.

Besides saving meatpackers money, women were considered more dexterous and meticulous and hence better suited to the careful work of producing a clean and attractive final product. Whereas men wore overalls and boots, women wore white dresses similar to nurses' uniforms. Although men's work was graded according to the strength and skill required to do it, women's wages were generally the same for any of the women's jobs they performed. Women accepted these gender disadvantages within packinghouses because even the discriminatory packinghouse pay was higher than they could anticipate in other jobs.[33]

1940–1960

The trickle of Iowa women entering the factory workforce broadened in World War II as many men left for the military, and government demands for a wide range of products intensified industrial production. Government meat purchase contracts specified cost plus 10 percent, and this changed the parameters of the production equation from the 1930s. Some packing plants hired two women to replace each departing man. Reports that managers would encourage workers to loaf around rather than clock out are understandable in terms of the government price formula, which may also have been a factor in easing potential resistance to hiring women. Moreover, women's work came to be seen as more patriotic and "decent" in the context of the war. Even the writers of women's pulp fiction were advised by the Magazine Bureau of the Office of War Information to lay off stories of working women having affairs on the job.[34]

The image and reality of Rosie the Riveter reworked, rather than obliterated, gender divisions. Both Rosie and GI Joe were gendered. Although a number of meatpacking plants across Iowa opened their doors to women, some of them—including the Arnolds Brothers/Swift plant in Perry—declined to hire women. Rather than working in meatpacking, Perry women found work in the poultry plant, which dried eggs in addition to processing chicken during the war. The women in other locations who were able to take advantage of the higher wages in meatpacking plants did so with the understanding that returning soldiers would have first claim to the jobs they left.[35]

Only a minority of the women who went into Iowa meatpacking plants during World War II actually took men's jobs. With government contracts calling for boxed, canned, and cured meat, the greatest increase in jobs was in processing and packaging. The majority of the new women hires worked in these women's departments during the war.[36] Male packing workers who became soldiers accrued seniority in their absence.[37] After the war some women were laid off or quit, but others who had taken men's jobs moved into cured meat departments where the majority of their coworkers were women. By and large, equal pay for equal work, supported in principle by labor, was moot. Jobs were gendered.[38] Both men and women believed that women's jobs were worth less than men's.[39]

The clearest gender division in meatpacking production occurred between those who did and did not use knives. Making the large cuts on a beef or pork carcass calls on complex skills. A skilled cutter runs his knife through precisely the right contours of the carcass, feeling the tendons and sinews and cutting cleanly and carefully so that the loins, hams, shoulders, and other major cuts emerge in good form. Anyone without the knowledge and feel for the work has a slow and perplexing task and produces mangled cuts of meat. Moreover, an expert cutter constantly sharpens his knives. With his sharpening steel hung on a chain around his waist, he draws his knife over the steel at precisely the right angle, with precisely the right arc and the right pressure. Further, the sharpening steel must be carefully prepared with varying textures of sandpaper so that its minute striations provide the proper sharpening surface. Working the steel in itself is an exacting skill.

A worker learned knife skills only on the production floor with instruction from an experienced worker. A new worker would never be expected to do as much as a skilled cutter before slowly easing into the job. It might be months before he would master even one cut. Cutting meat, especially making the critical large cuts that initially disassemble a carcass, took time to learn. A dull knife necessitated more hand pressure. Increased hand pressure caused cramping and blisters, making it yet more difficult to pick up the feel of the work. An unskilled worker trying to work through pain and keep up the pace was easily injured and often passed along a messier cutting job to workers down the line.

In short, any new knife worker tapped the patience and indulgence of the veterans. As a result, the existing workers could, in practice, determine who succeeded on the line. Women trying to enter men's departments commonly met resistance, typically not being taught how to sharpen knives. Vida Morrison, a woman who worked for the Armour Company in Omaha from the 1930s, said, "Usually the boss would assign some person to show you a job and most of them were pretty good at not telling you all the points."[40]

Few women worked with knives in the 1940s and 1950s. Some women trimmed heads or did other trimming tasks, but they did not become expert knife workers. Some plants had men sharpening knives for women, who would generally admit that they never felt competent in handling knives. One woman with a knife job in the forties recalled that women themselves would pay men two dollars a week to sharpen their knives, but men often refused, even for extra money. Most women

remained in, or gravitated to, the bacon, sausage, or canning departments. Except for male supervisors and machinery operators in these
departments, the workers were women. They made less money than
the men in cut and kill, but the advantages of having their own space
and their own jobs seemed to outweigh pay differentials. They spoke of
having close, all-women work groups and talking the hours away with
topics of children, recipes, vacations, and clothes. I have no report of
any Iowa woman complaining about either the division of labor or the
unequal pay in packing plants in the 1940s and 1950s.[41]

However, ongoing mechanization of the weighing and packaging
processes meant that over time fewer women were needed. A major
impediment to the mechanization of the meatpacking industry, the
reason why it remains to this day labor-intensive, is that physical variations in livestock require human rather than machine handling. But
this limitation does not apply to the final stages of the chain where
meat has been ground or otherwise standardized. Women's jobs in
weighing, packaging, and other end-of-the-chain operations could be
done by machine; increasingly in the 1950s and 1960s they were. Some
plants that hired women workers in the 1940s phased them out after
the war. A woman hired in 1950 at the Hormel plant in Austin, Minnesota, said that no more women were hired in that plant through the
1950s and early 1960s because women's departments were automated.
A core of the World War II cohort of women workers remained, but
with men available for kill and cut jobs, managers had no interest in
hiring women.[42]

If women were to stay in meatpacking in the 1960s, they needed to
make a collective response, either to contest the ongoing elimination
of their jobs or to contest the gender division that prevented them from
moving into different jobs. One recourse would be to go to the unions.
As many of the women had been union members since World War II,
when unions won their battle for collective bargaining, they could draw
on twenty or more years invested in union building.

Both the Amalgamated Meat Cutters and Butcher Workmen of North
America (Amalgamated), the older packing union, and the United
Packinghouse Workers of America (UPWA), which dominated midwest-
ern packinghouse organization in the 1940s, were ambivalent with re-

spect to women. Although it would have been counterproductive for unions to ignore the many women who entered the industry during World War II, women were an appendage to men's struggle rather than being what the organizing was about. Bruce Fehn, in his study of the UPWA, has written that men and women were steadfast allies in the union and on the shop floor and that the international worked hard to do away with the gender discrimination instituted by meatpacking companies.[43] Dennis Deslippe, on the other hand, processed the same data and presents a more skeptical perspective. He points out that the roots of packinghouse union successes in the 1930s and 1940s were in a period of retrenchment of the family wage ideal and the consequent muting of women's concerns as workers. Women were in the packinghouse union movement from the 1930s through the 1950s, but they were not the leaders; they lived the ironies and contradictions of the times.[44]

Women packinghouse workers, particularly those from pro-union families, had worked hard to bring their coworkers into the UPWA in the 1930s and 1940s. Some women initially were afraid of losing their jobs and were reluctant to sign up. "They were scared and they ran" when a union man would approach them, according to Vida Morrison, the wife of a meatpacking local president in Omaha and herself a union worker.[45] Yet after the initial hesitance, women came to be among the stalwarts and they worked to dispel coworkers' fears. Mary St. John, who worked with her husband to organize packing workers in Fort Dodge, said that women got men to go along with the union by serving coffee and doughnuts at meetings. As Sylvester Ames, whose wife Martha worked with him to organize Rath workers in Waterloo, recalled, "When you get a bunch of women started on something, they go!" [46]

Men set women in motion as union members, and men retained central roles. Women like Martha Ames who took leadership often acquired their roles by virtue of their relationships to male leaders. Velma Otterman, for example, was vice president of the Waterloo Rath local when her husband went into the service in 1942; she recalls that she was treated with the respect and oversight due to her as the wife of a union brother. Louise Mann, who was a steward in the Sioux City Armour plant for a short time in 1946, said that without her husband she never would have even tried to fulfill the duties: "He'd tell me what was right and what was wrong, because he'd been in from the ground floor."[47] Rachel Maerschalk, who worked at Dubuque Pack and was active in that local, remembered that for years she was the only woman at seminars and study sessions, the only woman steward, the only woman on the pension board, and the only woman on negotiating committees. She operated in a low-key manner to avoid male resistance. If she had issues to bring up, she would go to one or two men outside of the union meeting and they would present them for her.[48]

Family roles constrained women's union participation. Some women said that their husbands were jealous when they attended union meetings. Many women said that the responsibilities of housekeeping and child care made it impossible for them to go to meetings—although this did not keep them from serving soup, doughnuts, and coffee during strikes. Unmarried women who were supporting children found union dues as well as time demands of union participation to be a challenge. With the formation of women's committees and women's auxiliaries, women found a structural arrangement that matched their supportive and noninterfering stance. A Fort Dodge woman reported that except for an inactive women's committee and a woman secretary, her local was "strictly male" before 1960.[49]

What were the gender-specific benefits of packing unions? Women did not get the kind of money and potential leadership status that men might anticipate, but they did see their wages increase through union negotiating. Packing locals won pregnancy leave in the 1940s, although the terms of the leave differed from plant to plant. Some women received only minimal paid leave and sustained years of unpaid unemployment before being recalled after taking pregnancy leave. Rather than pregnancy leave or higher wages, women identified the greatest union benefit as the seniority system, because it relieved women of the necessity of flattering and placating bosses in order to keep their jobs or move to better ones.[50] Until the 1960s the UPWA sidestepped issues of the gender division of labor and pay equity.

But the separation between men's and women's jobs was tenuous at best. The memory of the women who did men's jobs during World

War II provided a lingering sense of the contingency of gendered job assignments. A few women remained in men's jobs as ongoing testimony. In addition, men worked in women's departments. Typically these men had special jobs such as operating machinery, hauling boxes, or being in charge of a work area. These tasks gave them their own job titles, but sometimes the work of men was almost indistinguishable from that of women. Nevertheless, men's pay scale remained above women's even when job titles were the same. An Armour worker from Omaha said that in the 1950s the UPWA negotiated a difference of eight cents per hour for men and women doing the same work. One union contract in the fifties specified that if a woman were assigned to a male job, she must be paid the male rate. On the other hand, if a man were assigned to a female job, he would continue to be paid the male rate. Requiring these (obviously inferior) workers to be paid as much as men nullified the danger of using women as cheap substitutes for men. The contract protected men from the lower wages of women, which might have prevailed by virtue of women being there and working at a lower scale. The possibility of demanding higher wages for both men and women and removing gender sorting was not high on the union agenda.[51]

RENEGOTIATION OF GENDER, 1960S

The amicable gender division dissolved in the 1960s as increasing numbers of women's jobs were eliminated. Because of the dual system of job placement and seniority, women with years of experience were laid off as new male hires came in. Rather than unequal pay for segregated jobs, which most women accepted, women faced no jobs and no pay. What had been for many a personally and economically comfortable situation dissolved. Ethel Jerred, who worked in the Morrell plant in Ottumwa, recalled that for ten or fifteen years after World War II she felt that her job was secure, but after 1960 this security vanished.[52] The companies had incentive to mechanize, given postwar union contracts awarding women higher wages.[53]

Then in 1964, by a fluke that had nothing to do with the packing industry (and almost nothing to do with women), Congress passed the long-awaited Civil Rights Act, with a ban on sex discrimination added shortly before the final House vote.[54] Gender bias in employment became illegal by federal law. Suddenly packinghouse women had a legal basis for contesting their layoffs. As male UPWA officer Virgil Bankson said in a 1978 interview, "That's when we had trouble with women." [55]

The legal fight over the implementation of Title VII of the 1964 Civil Rights Act in Iowa packinghouses is laid out in detail in the writings of Dennis Deslippe and Bruce Fehn.[56] District 3 of the UPWA, which included Iowa and Nebraska, had a weaker record of women's participation and weaker support for gender equity than did District 1, which was centered in Chicago. In 1966, responding to the lack of interest in their deteriorating work status, Iowa women packinghouse workers brought suits against both the companies and the UPWA. Both the UPWA and the companies stood accused of gender discrimination, as the women bolstered their cause with the power of federal law. What emerged was an interim solution, also gendered, called the ABC system. Rather than having male and female jobs, the packing plants classified jobs into three categories. An A job was generally fit to the strength and ability of a man, a B job was generally suited to a woman, and a C job might be done by either. The agreement abolished the dual seniority system, specifying that jobs would be awarded on the basis of a single seniority list, with each person who got a job being required to demonstrate the ability to do it within a given time.

The effect of the litigation and the instituting of the ABC system was to heighten gender tension and conflict. Ethel Jerred, who supported the litigation against the UPWA and the Morrell Company but was not herself a litigant, had her house broken into and vandalized. Men with considerable seniority would intrude on women's space by bidding on B and C jobs, displacing women. Women who tried to do A jobs found themselves harassed and sometimes in physical danger. Because few new women were hired in the 1950s, the women with greater seniority were older and physically challenged in adjusting to A jobs. These jobs themselves got redefined to involve heavier lifting and more strenuous labor when women took them. As new workers still depended on existing workers for training, they were vulnerable to the resistance of men who tried to make them fail.[57]

Nadine Klaner, who went to work in the Wilson plant in Cedar Rapids in 1963, reported that women were monitored more closely than men and were subject to more pressure.[58] Viola Jones, a Fort Dodge Hormel worker during the 1960s and 1970s, related:

> The company was responsible, I think, for [our] not learning [our jobs], but I think the fellows kind of ganged up on some of the jobs and decided this was for them. . . .
>
> Anybody could bid on a job. You had so long to learn it, and if you didn't learn it you could be fired. . . . [I]f the boys didn't want you on it, you never learned how to do that job. Believe me, they can make it very rough for you if they want to. . . .
>
> I went down, and I had my Senator make an appointment for me with Roxanne Conlin who was in there. They got together and talked to me and she explained just exactly to me what the law meant, and it didn't mean that a woman had to do the things we were doing. It didn't mean when you went in a department you had to take the hardest man's job in the department. But they had us believing that, and so did management.[59]

Nor was it only men who resisted the change. Although women's jobs were disappearing before the litigation, they disappeared faster as men came into their work areas and took over. Women who had developed camaraderie over the years saw their circles of friendship ripped apart. The men they had to work with were more belligerent and less cooperative than they had been when gender divided the work areas. Women who did not endorse the changes blamed "women's libbers" for destroying their work environments. Age also divided women. Women who had had packing jobs for decades were loathe to accept men's jobs, whereas young women who came into the plants after the Civil Rights Act believed that they should be able to do men's work.[60]

RESTRUCTURING

As workers and companies renegotiated gender divisions and adjusted to change, a new force shook the system, annihilating understandings developed over decades of struggle. Iowa Beef Packers (IBP), established in Denison in 1960, was gathering strength. Gender contradiction became a cornerstone of its strategy.

The near total absence of women in packinghouse production in Perry had averted gender conflict before 1960. As in other small packing plants, the overwhelming majority of the production workers were male in Perry's Arnold Brothers/Swift plant. Work in egg and poultry processing remained an off-and-on-again job possibility for Perry women through the 1960s, and few women encroached on male space. One exception was "Alice Anderson." A poultry worker in the 1950s, she got a job at the Swift plant through a supervisor who made the same move shortly before the plant closed in 1956. Alice Anderson worked briefly on the production floor, but this did not effect a shift in the gender identity of workers.

Gender division in the new Iowa Pork Company, which opened in Perry in 1962, continued the established pattern. The developers were men, as were the new managers and the board of directors. News stories about Iowa Pork discussed the number of men who would work in the plant. Some collateral news items featured wives of the directors and managers, but the only mention of women working in the plant was about secretaries. With the heading "Darlene, Marlene Add Charm to the Pork Plant," a newspaper story portrayed unmarried Marlene, a secretary, as "the attractive five foot, three inch blue-eyed blond" who "enthusiastically described the appointments of the new office which will be paneled in walnut with desks of light green with dark green trim. . . . She was quite happy to be given the responsibility of choosing the paneling and colors."[61]

Iowa Beef, which acquired the plant through a merger several months after it opened, was not yet producing the boxed meat for which it would become well known in a few years. It was a specialized kill operation, with minimal processing. Thus, by the nature of its business as a truncated production line and its opening before the Civil Rights Act of 1964, it avoided the gender conflict that occurred in older Iowa packing plants, where livestock was killed, cut, and processed. Iowa Beef had no bacon or cold cuts to slice, weigh, and wrap. By the prevailing gender consensus, production workers would be men. News reports of the plant opening missed the three women hired as production workers. Alice Anderson was one of them. Two other women joined her but they lasted only a short time. Alice Anderson, a single mother, remained as the only woman among several hundred men.

Workers in the Perry pork plant and Fort Dodge Iowa Beef plant handed the company its first union problems when they elected to be represented by the UPWA and demanded a wage increase. (Iowa Beef had been paying substantially below the union standard.) Iowa Beef's reply was that as a new-breed company, it did not come under the master contract of old-line packers. It ran kill operations, not processing operations. The two kinds of plants were different and did not compete with each other. The Perry plant, for example, routed its pork back into the processing system by selling it to Armour rather than selling it directly to retail markets.

The presumptive response would be that the kill floor represented the high end of wage costs for the old-line packers; accordingly, Iowa Beef could be held to an even higher wage standard than the existing industry. Instead, it was allowed to make the opposite argument, contending that the kill floors of old-line packinghouses lost money and that the companies balanced this loss with the profitability of cured meat operations. Because new-breed packers produced no cured meat to offset losses in kill, they could not be held to the same standard. Indeed, the fact that Armour purchased hog carcasses from Iowa Beef was an indication that this might be true. The question was whether Iowa Beef competed by its streamlined and specialized kill system or by unfair wages.

The implied resolution was that both technology and low wages were factors. The union negotiation brought Iowa Beef closer to the industry standard while accepting that it was to some extent a different animal and therefore not subject to the same terms as the other companies.[62]

We do not have the numbers behind Iowa Beef's argument that the profits of processing operations of old-line packers allowed them to run their kill floors at a loss. In terms of gender, they were in effect claiming that the low wages of women workers subsidized men's high wages. Because Iowa Beef had no low-paid women workers to balance the wages of the men in kill, they could not operate by the same accounting formulae. If the contention were true—and the union conceded that it had some validity—the phasing out of the women's departments may have signaled the end of the old-line packers, as they surrendered the industry to the new breed over the next twenty-five years. But as of 1965, Iowa Beef left Perry, selling the plant to Oscar Mayer, which struggled in Iowa Beef's wake.

Elsewhere, Iowa Beef was aggressively hiring rural women to work on its cut and boning floors by the latter 1960s. Although Iowa Beef did, in fact, maintain gender segregation inside its plants by keeping women off the kill floor for years, it marketed itself as a company that stood for women's rights by giving them jobs. Later it would even open a child care center at its Lexington, Nebraska, plant to attract women workers.[63] By breaking down the production operations the company simplified each worker's task to one basic cut. The meat moved continuously down the line at the speed set by the company, and the jobs were defined as unskilled.[64] One effect of this practice was to make the worker less mobile and more dependent on the company's production design. A worker knew even less of the full cutting process than before and required less training. Such a worker—often a young rural woman—usually had no background in union life, either.

Again the packing union, now the Amalgamated, protested. In 1969 a wave of strikes and work stoppages occurred. The center of the action was at Iowa Beef headquarters, which by then had moved across the Missouri River to Dakota City, Nebraska. The Dakota City Iowa Beef plant voted to be represented by the Amalgamated, and strikes and violence erupted there and in the company's Iowa plants in Fort Dodge, Denison, Le Mars, and Mason City. Once again Iowa Beef claimed that it could not be held to the industry standard because it was not the same kind of operation as the old-line packers.[65]

As before, the fact that Iowa Beef did not encompass the full production chain arose; Iowa Beef did not produce the bacon and cold cuts that provided profits for the other companies. It did not even produce pork, another reason it was not the same. But its major claim was that it had transformed the production chain so that it no longer hired the skilled workers that the other plants required. Its advantage was its technology, not its wage scale. Iowa Beef paid its Dakota City workers a base of $2.73 per hour for kill, compared to the $3.53 that kill workers got across the river in Sioux City; in cut, the Iowa Beef workers got $2.42 as compared to $3.53 in Sioux City.[66]

Iowa Beef buttressed its arguments for its lower wage scale by alluding to the absurdity of paying women workers the wages for which only men could qualify. Skill belonged to men. Iowa Beef vice president Arden Walker stated, "We can hire a woman at eight o'clock in the morning and have her doing her job at ten o'clock. She shouldn't be paid the same as a butcher who spent years learning his trade. Frankly, she's not worth it."[67]

Everyone knew that a woman could not do the demanding jobs of a skilled meatcutter. The union vehemently protested the Iowa Beef pay scale and charged that it discriminated against women by paying them $2.12 per hour for the same job that they paid men $2.73 per hour. Yet the company argument was only a slight variant of what workers had implicitly accepted since the end of World War II. A woman could not do a real (male) job; if a woman could do it, it was not the same job that a man had done.[68]

Iowa Beef prevailed in the 1969 strike. Ronald E. Miller, an Iowa Beef management employee who subsequently went to the University of Iowa to get a master's degree in business administration, wrote an analysis of the wage system of Iowa Beef as his master's thesis. He described the company as "the experiment of two men who have not been blinded by past traditional concepts of meat packing. They have taken their experience and disillusionment with the old and built a new and more efficient beef slaughter and fabricating complex."[69] As he laid out the strategy of Iowa Beef, the use of women workers was fundamental to deskilling jobs and thereby breaking out of the grip of the packing unions. Miller argued that the use of women demonstrated that the work was unskilled: "Another factor which IBP feels supports the unskilled theory which they propose is that within their processing divisions they have introduced the use of women who are the majority of workers in these areas. Iowa Beef claims that if they can do parts of jobs, which in their former skilled forms were physically too demanding for women and took years to learn, they should not have to pay the Amalgamated skilled rate."[70] Although claiming that Iowa Beef understood the implications of Title VII of the 1964 Civil Rights Act, he defended the use of women at lower wages: "It should be noted that the factor of women generally relates to their relative lack of mobility, training, and types of economic behavior leading to the general finding that the greater number of women used within an industry or company will result in a lesser overall average of wages." [71] Miller concluded that, in general, companies would be advised to lower labor costs by following Iowa Beef's example of deskilling jobs and employing women: "Firms can reduce wage levels and forestall union bargaining gains by employing a greater percentage of women." [72]

Although the UPWA and later the Amalgamated remained locked in an extended and frequently violent struggle with IBP over the years, the unions never effectively contested the company's frank gendering of skill as a means of lowering wages.[73]

The new-breed and old-line packers existed alongside each other in the 1970s, but neither looked like they had ten years before. Iowa Beef, joined by other new-breed packers, took over the beef industry, becoming the new industry giant. The old-line packers, still operating under the union's master contracts, were largely limited to pork. Within the fragments of this besieged industry the gender structure was shaken; as the industry disintegrated, that gender conflict became moot. One after another, women employed in old-line companies retired or lost their jobs as plants closed. Iowa Beef lowered labor costs by aggressively recruiting women workers, but not the older women workers with experience in the women's departments.

The Perry plant, which Oscar Mayer bought in 1965, was a hybrid. Although a hog facility, it was designed for the specialized kill of Iowa Beef; its later curing operations were short-lived. Yet Oscar Mayer was an old-line company and operated under the union's master contract. On the other hand, unlike most other old-line companies, it did not have the history of women's departments. It did not have a critical mass of older women who had gone to work in the packing industry in the 1940s.

Women workers, as they came into the Oscar Mayer plant in the 1970s, expected no special treatment and found no separate worksites. Unlike women who went into packing plants in the patriotic and male-centered context of World War II, the 1970s women entered with popular feminist assumptions. Although few called themselves feminists, they had a defiant sense of their right to equal employment opportunity. Using women's movement language, they expressed their espousal of gender equality on the job: "I wanted to prove that a woman could do it," said one. Another declared: "I believed in people's rights. I believed in good working conditions. I believed in women being able to work there. I was a ground-breaker, more or less. . . . I believed in what I was doing." [74]

In spite of these women's expectations of equal treatment on the job, gender division continued on the production floor, perhaps more contentiously than before. The Perry women who went to work at Oscar Mayer in the 1970s entered a space where men had staked out their territory. Men had struggled and organized against Iowa Beef in the 1960s. Even though they appreciated working for Oscar Mayer, their experience with Iowa Beef was a close-up view of its siege on the industry. These workers knew that Iowa Beef was on the move and would be continuing its assault on the wages and benefits built up over years of bargaining. Women's appearance signaled change. Women represented low wages, shifting economic roles, and a trivialization of men's skill. Overall, their arrival promised diminishment. Not having themselves experienced Iowa Beef, women could only partially appreciate the enormity of the threat they presented to men. For them, the pay was better than any they had seen before, and men's carrying on about wages made little sense. Even Alice Anderson, who endured the early tumultuous years of the plant, did not complain; this was the only period in her life when she was able to support her family comfortably.

"Trudy Wright" applied at Oscar Mayer in 1972. There were four women out of a total of approximately six hundred workers when she started; five more women began at about the same time that she did. A young wife with three children born from 1969 to 1972, Trudy had worked as a nurse's aide in a nursing home at $1.75 an hour with no benefits. The Oscar $4.85 hourly wage with benefits looked good. Although she had little idea of what to expect, she decided to give it a try.

During her job interview Trudy was asked how long she planned to work at Oscar. Although she had not given it much thought, she answered, "one year," and was hired. In retrospect she concluded that her "promise" to be gone after a year was why she was one of five additional women chosen. She believed that the company was hiring women to improve its employment statistics in order to avoid charges of discrimination. Otherwise, an Oscar job was hard to get. "Bonnie Howard," another new woman hire, said: "Like, they thought it was a big joke. It wasn't going to last. It was a fad. They were going to get the government off their butt by hiring these women. They were going to comply, but if we couldn't hack it and couldn't stay, too bad."[75]

From the first day in the plant the women felt the stress of male workers' belligerent rejection, much of it dressed in lewd humor and crude slapstick. Trudy told about her first foray onto the production floor:

> I'll never forget that day. Ever. . . . I was very young and very naive and very trusting, and I walked in there. The kill floor was the worst. I walked through there, and the whole floor, it was still moving, but you'd never have known it. There was so much noise. They were banging their knives, their steel, anything they had, and they were yelling. . . . It was just me alone, and I thought then, "How am I ever going to make this?" . . .
>
> "We got fresh meat here! Let's show her what this place is like!"
>
> And my face was immediately red and I just wanted to find a place to crawl into and die. . . .
>
> It was like that every day when I walked on the floor. I walked out for a break, it was the same thing . . . and it was the same for the other women.

Describing her reaction to harassment, she again framed her job as a matter of women's rights: "I thought, 'Those son of bitches aren't going to do this. They're not going to get by with this. They're not going to get me to quit.' I had just as much right to work there as they did." In spite of her original thought of staying only a year, she remained for almost ten years.

Trudy worked at a variety of jobs throughout the plant in the course of her employment at Oscar, but for the most part she was in kill. The major spatial division in the packinghouse production system is between hot and cold sides of the plant. Kill is done at a temperature of eighty degrees or more. After the kill line has cleaned and eviscerated a carcass, it goes into the cooler, where it is thoroughly chilled before passing onto the cut floor, where work is done at temperatures ranging from freezing to forty-eight degrees. The hot side, the kill floor, which was traditionally male territory, had higher-paying jobs in the past, but this was changing. First, since new-breed packers began taking over the industry by running kill operations, kill wages took the first hard hit. Further, in most plants, including Oscar, cut workers were paid incentive, or piece rate. A worker was required to process at a standard rate and received a bonus for working above standard. The highest-paid workers at Oscar had high-bracket jobs plus additional income from incentive. Although exceptions remained, many Oscar workers with high seniority would gravitate to the better cut jobs. Workers like Trudy with less seniority would often find themselves doing menial work in kill. Having started ten years after the plant opened, Trudy stayed near the bottom of the seniority list throughout her employment at Oscar. Her moving around was not because she was succeeding to better jobs, although she said she was constantly bidding on jobs; it was because she did the jobs they gave her.

Even though the plant operated under formal rules of gender equality, the rules did not have the same impact on men and women, because their lives were not the same. Plant rules permitted sick leave, and men joked about calling in with "brown bottle flu" after drinking. Women, on the other hand, were less likely to have hangovers but more likely to need to stay home to care for sick children, which was not allowed. Trudy took to calling in sick when she had to care for her sick children and nearly lost her job when a plant official made a surprise visit to check on her in the middle of the morning.

The seniority system also functioned differently for men and women, because men and women had different work histories and different experiences on the production floor. Because women like Bonnie and Trudy who came to work in the plant later had lower seniority than the majority of men, they were most likely to be laid off during slack periods. Women clustered in low-bracket jobs. Yet the experience of Alice Anderson, who had worked in the plant since it opened as Iowa Pork, indicates that the seniority system simply did not work the same for women as it did for men.

Men who had worked on plant construction had the highest seniority of initial packing workers, but Alice Anderson had seniority equal to that of the remaining starters. Working on kill, she wanted a quieter and cleaner knife room job that was posted for bidding. Knife room personnel machine-sharpened, sorted, and maintained knives and distributed knives and other equipment to workers at each shift and as needed throughout the day. She bid on it. A male coworker approached her, offering to see that she got the job if she would "go out with him." She turned him down but got the job. Her troubles mounted as knives turned up dull and unusable on the production floor. Another male coworker revealed that the worker she had spurned had told others to dull the knives she gave them. As she related the incident,

> By god, the foreman come to me and told me, he said, "Alice, you're not doing a good job on the knives. You can't have the job." . . .
> I said, "You know why the knives are dull?"
> "No."
> I said, "So and so come and told me that he went up and down the floor, roughing down the steel to make them dull because I wouldn't go out with him. He said he'd get me the job if I would go out with him."
> He said, "Well, I don't know. I never heard nothing about it." . . .
> I never bid on any jobs after that.

Men controlled entry to knife jobs on the production floor since they trained new workers. Because veterans lost incentive pay when new workers came on the line, they had little tolerance for slow or flighty learners (read, women). Although women did take some of the more tedious knife jobs, such as trimming heads, lack of knife skills limited their advancement. There were few exceptions.[76]

A numbing routine of harassment complicated women's work. Trudy told of finding a mouse in her work glove and of having tapeworms thrown at her as she worked. After driving home, she once found the word "whore" written in shaving cream on the back of her car. She received obscene telephone calls at her home, where they might be taken by her husband or children. During a smoke break, a fellow worker turned her over his knee and spanked her with his belt as a group of men, including a union steward, looked on. Alice Anderson also had her share of sexual harassment, especially in the first years of her work. One day while working on the kill line, she felt something warm between her legs and discovered that two men had come up behind her and thrown blood on her. They were laughing, saying that she didn't know what to do when it was "that time of month." She left the line to report the incident to her supervisor, but he did not take her side. She spent the rest of the day in bloody white trousers, although the supervisor gave her a white frock to cover them.

On the kill floor a common form of male entertainment was hosing down women with the high-pressure water hose. Government regulations required that workers wear white clothes, and the heat dictated thin cotton trousers and shirts. The joke was that men would water women down to see what color underwear they were wearing. One day when eying Bonnie, who was working in kill, a man accidentally picked up the hose that had the 180-degree water used to disinfect an area when an abscessed carcass came through. The water scalded Bonnie as it hit her and ran into her boot. She picked up a knife and threw it at her attacker. When he laughed at her she lunged at him. The supervisor led her off the floor and ordered her to tell her attacker that she was sorry. She said she was sorry she didn't kill him and was fired on the spot. Eventually, after threatening to sue, she negotiated a six-week suspension without pay. The man who sprayed her received a three-day suspension.

Trudy, who talked about repeated sexual confrontations during her work, said that she saw no actual violence against women, only grabbing and joking. Then she added, "Some of it was joking, some of it wasn't joking. You didn't think of it as a joke. . . . I was in a ten-year depression. I really was. All I wanted to do when I got home was either go out and get drunk or come home and go to sleep."

The union local did not support the women. Having been friends with the local president before she went to work at Oscar, Bonnie had a great deal of union spirit. Trudy attended meetings with her. The other women, like the majority of the male workers, were too busy or too alienated to put much energy into the union. At some point during the 1970s Bonnie and Trudy learned of a meeting for union women in Omaha. Bonnie's husband, a supermarket butcher and one of the few union members who did not work at Oscar, was on the union's executive board and told them about it. The male officers had already made their plans to attend as union delegates, as they did for all union functions, but Bonnie leaned on her husband to make the case for her and Trudy to go along. With the help of another executive board member, he arranged for the women to go at their own expense. Trudy remembered being captivated by the feminist message: "It was very exciting. It was motivating. It was a stick-to-your-guns type thing. There was a little short black woman who spoke, and I don't remember who she was, but she was a very good speaker, . . . and then Roxanne Conlin spoke. I still admire her to this day. . . . And we went to some seminars that I didn't even understand what we were hearing because it was union oriented and we weren't really allowed . . . we were in the union but we were not really an integral part of it."

Bonnie and Trudy came home inspired but powerless to inject the feminist message into their local. In about 1979 Bonnie decided that she would run for union steward, a male job. Teasing and harassing intensified as the election neared. Her husband felt the pressure acutely. Bonnie recalled an incident when the two of them were at a bar frequented by packing workers: "I was on my way to the bathroom and this guy tripped me, knocked me flat on the floor and said, 'That's how she's going to wind up in this election, too—flat on the floor with egg on her face.' My husband saw it and got up and left. . . . He did not offer me any assistance. He did not back me up and say, 'She's right.' I knew where I stood right then. So I just quit."

Nadine Klaner, a Wilson worker in Cedar Rapids, said of women who tried to work in the union, "You got to carry yourself probably in a little different manner than men to be able to carry on, and I think a lot of women have failed in that way." Union work was not an easy road for women to walk. Ethel Jerred, of Ottumwa, who also failed in her bid for union office, reflected: "I know the same story has come through to me from other women in other places. I've run for office. I've got defeated. You'd be surprised some of the rumors that float around the plant against you. I don't know what they were afraid of unless they were afraid a woman's going to be a little more effective than they were, but I said I never had anything to hide." The significance of whether she had anything to hide hints that the question of "decency" and how she carried herself emerged to sabotage her plans as well.

In the 1982 interview Elsa had told me that when she was young, "decent" women would not work. The question of decency emerged repeatedly in interviews with packinghouse women. Men retained power over women by controlling their reputations. Trudy said that when she had decided to apply for work at Oscar, a friend tried to dissuade her by telling her it was no place for decent women: "I don't remember exact words, but the inference was there that they were whores." A married man who had lived next to Trudy's family for years made a sexual overture to her shortly after she took her Oscar job. Bonnie said that her husband was embarrassed and took a lot of ribbing because of her job: "We [the Oscar women] were looked down upon by the community because we worked there, because if you worked in a packinghouse, you were a slut and that's all there is to it." She and her husband divorced after the incident in the bar, and Bonnie said that it was "80 percent" due to his loss of respect for her. A woman who worked with Bonnie and Trudy committed suicide while employed at Oscar. Trudy's daughter, born the year she started at the plant, talked about her mother having been at Oscar as she grew up: "I looked at it as sort of an embarrassment to have my mother work there, because of the flack I got from people in the community. So I just tried to forget that she worked there. . . . The women who worked there were obviously looked down upon by the community." In the 1980s after a woman IBP worker at Storm Lake had been taking her three sons to a babysitter for a period of time, the sitter complemented the boys' behavior by saying that they didn't act like they came from the household of a single mother or an IBP worker.

Ethel Jerred, who began work in the Morrell plant in Ottumwa in 1942, talked about the problem of "decency" and explained that men resisted women coming into the plants during World War II by saying that it wasn't decent for women to be there. Reviewing her struggle as a woman worker, she said, "In the long run, before it was over, I think the women had proven to the men that we came up there as ladies."[77] The experiences of the next generation of women indicate that this issue was not cleanly resolved. It was a continuing obstacle.

IBP

Trudy and Bonnie quit their jobs in 1983, when wages collapsed; Alice Anderson had quit two years before. But new women were hired into the plant as wages fell. After it repurchased and reopened the facility in 1989, IBP hired a number of these women, having remodeled and expanded the women's locker room to accommodate a workforce that would be 25 to 30 percent female.[78]

"Annie" was among the women that IBP hired. Descended from rural Iowa wage workers and marginal farmers, Annie was born in Perry in 1966 when her father worked on an Oscar Mayer construction crew. She had a short and traumatic childhood involving rape at age four and continuing sexual abuse; at age twelve she became a prostitute and an exotic dancer. A marriage at eighteen left her with a daughter, "Alyce." This marriage and a later brief one both ended in divorce. At age twenty-five, having survived cocaine addiction treatment and numerous batterings from different men, she had missing teeth, a scar across her cheek, and a weight problem that removed her from the first ranks of the sex trade. Through her parents' multiple marriages, Annie had amassed ten half siblings in addition to connections with a large number of foster children raised by her mother. These persons constituted an extensive, if thin, family network.

Annie took her IBP job in the spring of 1991. Alyce was five and looking forward to kindergarten. Annie had a half sister close enough to babysit, but Alyce had frequent throat and respiratory infections that Annie's sister could not handle. Having children of her own and no medical insurance, the sister could not risk the expense of having to take them to a doctor and purchase antibiotics, so she could not care for Alyce regularly. Many IBP workers commuted from Rippey, an unincorporated town ten miles up the road from Perry, and Annie located a sitter and rental house on a dirt road on the outskirts of the town. Her mother and several other siblings lived within a half-hour drive, but for the most part she and Alyce were on their own. At Christmas Alyce's father, "Buck," returned to live with them. He started work at IBP the same week that I did in January 1992.

Annie worked on the upper cut floor as a janitor when I came, but she was determined to get a better job. She learned to drive a forklift (a skill she tried in vain to teach me) and passed the operator's test, but her low seniority generated little hope for a forklift job. These jobs were in high demand, as they took people off the line, saved them from carpal tunnel syndrome, and paid relatively well. Searching for higher-paying jobs in maintenance, which was a man's department, Annie mulled the possibility of learning to weld. I quipped that it could not be too hard because a lot of men did it. She grinned and said I got it right: "I'm a female chauvinist pig," she explained. When I remarked that IBP didn't have many people like her, she said that there weren't many like her anywhere. I had to agree. She pushed through studies on maintenance operations, passed IBP's maintenance test, defied her supervisor by leaving her work to interview, and got a maintenance job. This removed her from my orbit at work. We kept in touch outside the plant, even as our difference in age and background meant that we had different approaches to life. I had much to learn about women meatpackers, and Annie was a teacher.

Considering that employment discrimination had been illegal for nearly thirty years, there was surprisingly open gender segregation in the plant when I was there. A man interviewed me when I applied for the job, a man conducted our orientation, and my supervisor was a man. There was only one other woman, the eighteen-year-old daughter of a longtime Oscar worker and friend of "Clyde," on the belly line with me in the cut floor cellar; "Shirley," an older woman, worked in a cellar corner processing shoulders and was technically under Clyde's supervision, although she had little contact with us. The forklift drivers who scooted around the floor were men, as was everybody who told me what to do. Although some women held management and management support positions, including the safety director and a quality control supervisor along with the secretarial and nursing staff, anyone who had any real authority was male.

"Rosa," the other woman hired with me, and I both started on whizard jobs, electric knives that did not require traditional knife skills. Few IBP workers lasted long on whizard jobs, as these knives destroyed the hands of the average person. I did the job for approximately one week before getting booted down to being a janitor and run-and-fetch specialist. Rosa, whose whizard job was on the upper cut floor, was gone within a few weeks. I never found out what happened to her, but my guess is that she was booted one step lower than I, which was out.

To a large extent, getting along on the floor meant finding my own place. I had my first lesson in this when "Owen," who worked across from me, refused to speak to me and threw untrimmed meat into my tub of belly fat. Even if my hand had survived three months of whizard, Owen's hostility and sabotage made it unlikely that I would qualify in that position. Clyde once directed me to help "Gary," who mixed and boxed meat scraps. This job was more complicated than line jobs, because it involved combining fat and lean meat, blending it in a huge cylindrical machine, testing the fat content, boxing it according to given orders, and stacking it to be carted away. When I went to Gary to offer my help, he refused to speak to me. As there were worse chores than standing there doing nothing, I decided to hang around and watch. After Gary figured out that I wasn't going to disappear, he opened his mouth long enough to tell me to go find someone to teach me how to make boxes. So I got out of his way and started to fold box tops. Clyde never again suggested that I work with Gary. In practice, I did not last where men did not want me.

As a janitor and fetcher, I moved and dumped containers of trash and fifty-gallon barrels of fat and meat. I operated the dry ice machine and pushed barrels of dry ice across the brick floor. Although I tried to cover these barrels with plastic, the possibility remained that a barrel might hit something on the floor and send dry ice up into my face and eyes as I pushed it. I felt the heavy weights that I moved taking their toll on my forty-seven-year-old back. My job required as much physical strength as any in the plant, and I became increasingly uneasy as I observed how many men had back problems. Clyde told me to get a man to help with heavy lifting, but this was extra, hard work above their regular jobs and I could understand their disinclination. If I had no one to help dump a barrel, I had to remove the top third of the contents before I could lift it to dump it myself.

Clyde also suggested that I get a forklift driver to move boxes and barrels for me. But no forklift operator was assigned to help me; they had their own jobs. To ease my work I had to make friends with one of the drivers, all of them male. I had nothing to offer in return for their trouble, and the majority of them simply ignored me. Some were blatantly rude. I had no alternative but to push and shove loads with my own strength.

When I had been hanging onto my job for about two weeks, "Pete," the forklift driver who moved boxes of bellies, called me over and asked me to get up on his forklift beside him. I knew that he was a wise guy and that he knew his way around. With a friendly hand on my shoulder, he told me to ask him when I wanted anything; when he had time he would help me. I could feel my back relaxing as he spoke, but equally significant I was grateful for his friendship. I hoped that this meant I would be accepted, that people would talk to me.

That is exactly what happened. With Pete's sponsorship the other forklift drivers warmed up and often helped, although few men physically lifted and dumped barrels unless Clyde asked them to. When I got too earnest about keeping the cellar in order, Pete admonished me to ease off and let things slide. When I got so cold and tired that my whole body was numb, Pete told me to go to the locker room, rest, and warm up. With Pete's friendship, Clyde stopped yelling at me and only rarely asked what I was doing or where I was going.

Not long after we connected, Pete asked if I wanted to see where they killed pigs. I had no sense of production space beyond the cut floor and the corners of kill and converting that I walked through each day. Trusting that I wouldn't get into trouble moving around the plant with Pete, I walked with him to the area where the pigs came into the building. I saw a worker clamp them into a closed space where another worker stunned them. Then the pigs were hoisted by a leg and moved to the sticker, who jabbed the stickpin into their necks to bleed them be- fore they passed into the scalding tubs. Pete and I then moved from the stickpin into the main area of the kill floor. He explained each operation as the pigs moved down the line and into the cooler. At the end of kill, we walked around the upper cut floor as Pete clarified the various cut operations. At the end of the tour we returned to the belly line in the cellar.

"Just act like we're supposed to be here," Pete calmed me when I stewed about getting into trouble. Although I had had a short production tour during orientation, Pete's teaching was more careful and detailed. I learned more about how the plant operated as I shed my nervousness about encroaching on places where neither of us had any business.

When we returned to the belly line, Pete looked at me with affection and said, "Pete and Ruth, Pete and Ruth." We never took our breaks at the same time, so there was never a question of sitting together in the cafeteria, and Pete showed little interest in getting together after work; but we maintained something of a gendered friendship while I was in the plant. I remained uneasy about the relationship and Pete's constant sexual joking, but I knew that as long as I worked at IBP I would never again place myself in the purgatory of not having a friend and protector in the cellar. Not only did he ease my work, he gave me a social place in the plant. Even though I knew that somewhere I had a life as a feminist, I had never before been so personally dependent on men as I was while working at IBP.

Pete and I talked at length while we worked. I soon told him about my work as an anthropologist and for that matter about almost anything else that came up during my months at IBP. He, in turn, told me that he had murdered his wife and spent seven years in prison. I heard his anguished account of the night he killed her, and I shared his joy the day he completed parole. I listened to his stories of prison, of trying to adjust to the outside world, of his relationship with his son who lived with his parents, of problems with women who used him, and of varied financial difficulties. When his paycheck was garnisheed, I advanced him three hundred dollars to help him out of the hole.

Finding a male protector has been a common coping mechanism for packing women. Trudy Wright talked about a similar relationship that she had had when she was at Oscar, and Ethel Jerred and other women told about it from their work in men's departments during the 1940s.[79] To get jobs, to keep them, to get a man to take the time to show her how to do something, to avoid the worst jobs, and to keep out of trouble a woman had to have the support of a powerful man. This favoritism might come with sexual demands, although it might also be more subtly masked. Women who worked in women's departments seem to have had less need for male protection, and it was undoubtedly a factor in their preference for segregated jobs. Working with women and talking about recipes and children was radically different from what I did at IBP. "Decency" was again an issue.

As least as late as 1974, IBP did not employ women on its kill floors.[80] When I was at IBP, women worked in kill, as they did under Oscar Mayer. Yet invisible gender segregation remained. Even though women worked side by side with men, they clustered in low job brackets. Better-paying jobs belonged to men. "Ardie," who worked on the kill floor at Oscar as well as at IBP, fought to get a job sticking pigs. She explained that the stickpin job was dangerous, as the stunning equipment, which was supposed to incapacitate pigs before they reached the stickpin, was unreliable. At times, as I had observed in my walk with Pete, the stunner did not totally knock the pigs out. A sticker might come face to face with a live, angry, and frightened pig. But even when pigs were properly stunned, the rapid and repetitive motion of thrusting the pin in the pigs' throats was hard on the sticker's arm and shoulder. Telling about getting her job, Ardie said:

> When I first started all women had zero bracket jobs.[81] They wouldn't get a woman a graded job. They couldn't get a sticker to stay there very long. They'd get sick, or they'd get hurt or wouldn't come in. I knew I'd worked there for a day and it was a two bracket job and I wanted it. . . .
>
> I went down there the first time and Jake pulled me out of the stickpin, said there was no way in hell he would have a woman working that end of the kill floor. . . . He said he didn't give a shit how mad anybody got. . . . He said he had a friend once that worked in stickpin and got stuck pretty bad. He wasn't going to have no woman down there getting hurt. I asked him where was the difference in pain between a male and female. You know, just because that man got stuck, does that mean I'd feel more pain than he did? Well, he couldn't answer that. He just said I wasn't going down there and that was final. We argued back and forth from October to March. Then we got mad and I said, "Hey, I want that job down there and if I don't get it I'm going to sue the hell out of you."

Ardie did eventually get the job, although she was disabled after several months of work.

The support of the law was one leg of her argument, but without the assistance of male sponsors in the intermediate levels of the plant hierarchy, it is doubtful that she would have been successful. By union contract, plant management had the sole right to transfer, promote, or demote employees as well as to determine their qualifications and ability, provided it did not do so for the purposes of discrimination.[82] This right, which compromised the seniority system that had governed bidding for jobs in the past, left it to Ardie to prove that gender discrimination rather than judgment of qualifications and ability was

operating. Although Ardie was a union steward, the union was not involved in the conflict.[83]

The IBP plant posted a notice saying that "sexually oriented behavior" had no place at work, and it had a policy prohibiting romances
between supervisory and production workers. Employees frequently
broke these rules. Sexual violations pervaded the IBP plant while I
worked there, just as women who worked at Oscar described. Sexually explicit graffiti appeared on walls and posters; men grabbed their
crotches and made sexual gestures toward women. Men frequently
clutched and fondled women. With this bravado, men controlled the
space on the production floor, in the cafeteria, and in the halls. The
only place where women could relax and converse on their own terms
was the locker room. Ardie's efforts to oppose sexual harassment were
a losing cause. She explained:

> You see, the union steward's job is to protect, go to the office and
> protect whoever is being brought in. . . . You've got to send in a union
> person with the person who's being accused. You've also got to send
> a union person in with the person who's doing the complaint. A lot
> of times it puts us in the situation of being caught in the middle and
> management sits there. Actually it's management's responsibility to
> take care of its problems, but they won't do it. They try to throw it
> back in our laps.
>
> We had a situation where a guy was messing with a girl and I
> turned it in to . . . [the kill floor general supervisor]. I was really
> pissed off—this guy was grabbing this woman on her legs and every-
> thing else. She made the statement if he did it one more time she was
> going to hit him.
>
> He told her, "If you hit somebody on this line I'm going to fire
> you."
>
> It's like, wait a minute, you expect her to stand by and take this
> without hitting him? . . . What they do to us is they take one of the
> union vice presidents into the office on that man's behalf. Then I
> went in on the gal's behalf. They had us right where they wanted us.
> Union personnel cannot argue to get somebody fired, because it's
> our job to make sure they don't.

Through Ardie the union made a motion to protect women against sexual harassment, but it made a greater and opposite motion to protect the perpetrator. "Max," the union president, said that, in his experience, when women claimed sexual harassment against coworkers, it was usually retaliation over a personal dispute. The real offenders, he maintained, were in management; but when women had sexual problems with supervisors, it was usually because they were trying for special breaks, which was not the business of the union.

Annie persisted in being a thorn in the side of Max, complaining about his unwillingness to address safety conditions and complaining about her jobs. When I told her I was working with Max, she looked alarmed and said I should never have talked to him; he would expose me to the company. She was definitely not one of the women he would appoint to be steward. When a harness she was wearing misfunctioned and she fell off a pole, she was out of work with a back injury and repeatedly failed to get her workers' compensation checks. When she and I brought the problem to Max, he shook his head and said nothing could be done about it. Annie also complained of an ammonia leak in the powerhouse and eventually proceeded on her own to make a complaint to OSHA. Max chuckled when he told me he heard this complaint. He countered that when he worked in the powerhouse under Oscar, he smelled ammonia all the time and never complained.[84]

Complaints about health and safety conditions were gendered. One noon while eating lunch with "Don," a coworker in his mid-twenties, I observed that his hands were so badly damaged that he had trouble getting food into his mouth. When I started a discourse on no job being worth his hands, he cut me short, saying that he was a man who earned his pay. Another man supported him, sneering that only women whined about sore hands.

When Jake and I talked about his life as a packinghouse worker, he proudly told me how hard he had worked as a young man. He started in the hide room stacking lime-covered hides and climbing up the piles to shake them out and keep them in order. This job did not exist in the Perry IBP plant, but apparently it was the worst work in the old packinghouses. Jake said that the pollution and stench were overpowering; several times he swallowed his vomit. I have no report of any woman working in a hide room. Indeed, in the plant where Jake started, the requirement that new hires begin in the hide room was given as the reason why no women worked in the plant until the 1970s. Wallace Taylor, who worked in this plant from 1950 through the 1970s, explained, "That separated the men from the boys."[85]

Packinghouse work was hard for men as well as women. Wallace Taylor, who retired at age fifty-five, told an interviewer: "The plant closed in 1981, but I left before then. I took early retirement. My body was not capable of doing anything. I can barely walk. My feet hurt. My back hurts. . . . Gosh sakes, I can't tell you where I didn't hurt. . . . In fifty-five years I was all burned out. I couldn't do nothing."[86] A man who worked for an old-line company reflected that longtime packing workers seldom lived past age sixty-five.[87]

But these were not the words or actions of the exuberant younger working men. Most of them felt challenged to work through the pain that compelled women to pull back. The virtues of strength, endurance, and sacrifice are part of a twentieth-century U.S. construction of manhood, and IBP provided a setting in which to act out these principles.[88] Annie would get no sympathy from Max when she insisted on doing men's jobs.

Toward the end of my stint at IBP I approached Max about the gender and racial discrimination that I saw. Among other things, I believed that I could prove discrimination if I had a list of what jobs had been posted for bidding since IBP opened in 1989, who bid on them and what their seniority was, and who got them. The union could request such a list, and I offered to take it to a colleague in the statistics department at Iowa State University and have her perform statistical tests to demonstrate that IBP discriminated against women and people of color. Max declined to cooperate, reminding me of approaching contract negotiations. Union negotiators would be making major demands on the company at that time; now they didn't want to offend IBP by asking for anything they didn't need. I protested that a finding of discrimination would only enhance the union's position at the bargaining table. He said he would take it up with the executive board and get back to me. I am still waiting to hear what happened when he brought it up.

At that point Max exposed me and my work to Jake, the plant manager, which led to the conversation that opens this chapter.

Trudy Wright concluded our interview with the reflection, "It was a miserable time of my life. I wouldn't want to repeat it." Compare this with "John Kramer's" "What more better work could you ask for?" for a snapshot of gender difference in the experience of a woman and a man working in meatpacking. The difference had to do with pay, division of labor, sexuality, the union, and health and safety. The Civil Rights Act, together with the structural changes in the industry, purported to eliminate gender but in fact reconfigured it. Gender remained a salient means of organizing packinghouse production. The union, in digging in its heels to preserve the old system, conceded gender to the manipulation of packing companies, thereby contributing to the deterioration of conditions for all workers.)

Although a number of events converged to produce a tense and destructive situation in packing plants of the 1990s, these presenting factors were expressions of a deeply ingrained structure of gender inequality. They were not root causes. Changes such as the Civil Rights Act, which might have improved conditions but did not, reveal the complexity of attitudes, actions, and beliefs preserving gender imbalance. Yet change occurs. The more that is known about the roots of injustice, the more likely that change will be liberating.

IBP porkpacking plant west of Perry, Iowa, January 1997. Behind the parking lot stands the guardhouse where workers and hog delivery trucks show identification before entering the inside complex or the plant. (Photo courtesy of Helen Gunderson, Gilbert, Iowa)

The Hausserman Packing Company, Perry, Iowa. Built in 1920, this small meatpacking plant survived numerous bankruptcies and changes of ownership before it was shut down in 1956, when it belonged to the Swift Company. (Photo from Weesner Pharmacy, Dexter, Iowa)

Hog cut at Hormel meatpacking plant, Austin, Minnesota, 1941. The cut floor was a man's work area, although a few women entered this space during World War II. Sharpening steels hung from chains around workers' waists, and they would constantly sharpen their knives as they worked. (U.S. Department of Agriculture Farm Security Administration photo LC-USF 34-63262-D)

Decker Plant, Mason City, cut floor. Conveyer belts moved hog carcasses through a maze of production areas, where workers made their assigned cuts as the carcass was progressively disassembled into smaller pieces. (Photo courtesy of State Historical Society of Iowa, Des Moines)

Wife of a farm owner-operator and wife of a hired hand clean chickens in the farm cellar, Dickens, Iowa, 1936. Farm women earned money through their poultry operations, which occasionally grew to more substantial businesses employing small numbers of women for brief periods. The farmhand's wife contributed her labor to the farm economy without formal acknowledgment of her status as a hired worker; the labor of the farmer's wife was typically informal as well. (U.S. Department of Agriculture Farm Security Administration photo LC-USF 34-10051-D)

Women working at the Tobin packing plant in Fort Dodge. The majority of women hired in meatpacking plants during World War II worked in women's departments, where they wrapped and boxed meat for shipment. (Photo courtesy of State Historical Society of Iowa, Iowa City)

Rath workers, Waterloo, Iowa, ca. 1941. Women did most of the work in the sliced bacon work area, where the final product had to be neat and clean and of uniform weight. Men ran the machinery. (Photo courtesy of State Historical Society of Iowa, Iowa City)

Local Iowa humor, 1913. The Russian revolution evoked fear and hostility in Iowa even before the Bolshevik triumph. These two 1913 cartoons from the *Perry Advertiser* illustrate the pervasive contempt that the established middle class held for women, immigrants, and black persons who seemed to threaten the social order. (*Perry Advertiser*, December 12, 30, 1913)

UPWA Local 46 picnic, Waterloo, Iowa, 1952. The UPWA promoted racial harmony both in the meatpacking plants and in the communities outside of the plants. (Photo courtesy of State Historical Society of Iowa, Iowa City)

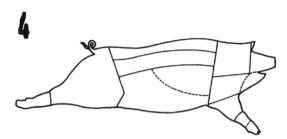

WHO'S FRANCISCO?

RACE/ETHNICITY AND RURAL IOWA WORKERS

"Clyde," my supervisor, called me over as I was working at the Perry IBP plant and told me to take some trash up to the compactor. I said that "Francisco" was doing it.

"Who's Francisco?" Clyde snapped.

Clyde didn't know any Francisco, even though Francisco worked next to us. I had thought that Clyde, having been on the production floor since the plant opened, would at least know everyone I did. Maybe if I had called Francisco "the small Mexican janitor in converting," Clyde would have known whom I meant. Maybe not. I realized that many people—"Francisco," "Pancho," "Chang"—worked in our midst without having real names as far as most of us white workers were concerned. Chang was "that little gook" or "number one son." Latinos, most of whom spoke only Spanish, were little brown people without names. Black workers had names of sorts, but it did them little good.

By my estimate, when I was working at IBP approximately one-third of the workers were Latino; maybe one-tenth were black; one-tenth were Asian American, many of them Laotian; something under half were white. Racial division ran throughout the plant. Except for "Ricardo," who interviewed and hired new workers and sat by himself in the cafeteria, management and supervisors were white. The core of longtime workers who were carried over from Oscar Mayer and knew their way around the plant were white men; they had the best production jobs. The low-bracket, punishing jobs on the line went for the most part to black, Latino, and Asian American workers.

In the cafeteria, workers tacitly staked out segregated tables. When the cut floor took its break, a long line of seats on the wall by the window went to "Pete," "Mike," and the higher-bracket white men. Latino and Asian American workers had different sections and ate their own, different food. Black workers claimed an inside corner of the cafeteria. Early in my IBP employment when I saw "Susan," the black woman whose locker was next to mine, eating there alone, I joined her, only to discover as the table filled up that I had made an awful error. Not only did the black workers make their resentment clear as we ate, my eating with black persons was noted separately by white and Latino coworkers and was later brought up to me by persons not even in the cafeteria at the time. Locker room exchanges with Susan did not mean we were friends in the cafeteria or anywhere else.

By company rule, union contract, and federal law there could be no discrimination in employment on the part of IBP management. What was discrimination? Within weeks of when I started work, "Larry," a young white worker, threw a piece of meat at my surly black teat line partner, "Owen." To be fair to Larry, he probably did not intend a confrontation. Although it was against the rules, white workers frequently horsed around by throwing meat at each other; Larry may have considered his gesture to be one of inclusion. That is not how Owen took it. They were quickly fighting, and Owen's glasses were broken. He was fired; Larry was written up for throwing meat. When Owen returned to the plant to protest his dismissal, Clyde approached me to back him up by saying that Owen had thrown meat at me. I did not see the fight, but apparently the facts did not speak for themselves. I did not speak against Owen, but he did not get his job back. The only other black worker in the cellar at that time was also fired later. Although separately these two black workers would have been hard pressed to prove discrimination before an impartial jury, the overall pattern presented a compelling picture of inequality.

This chapter is about the historical construction of a multiplicity of racial/ethnic "others" in rural Iowa. Although ethnic inequality has powerful historical precedent in Iowa, it has not been monolithic. The content and meaning of ethnic privilege have shifted as has the makeup of the subordinated ethnicities. The shape of Iowa's whiteness is as significant and problematical as is its ideological distancing from the small population with ancestral roots outside of northern Europe. The interests of companies like IBP in promoting division and fragmentation among their workers are obvious, but they do not explain ethnic inequality. Without the tacit or overt consent of many workers and of civic society at large, ethnic inequality would crumble in the plants. In the phrasing of Cornel West, "race matters" in rural Iowa, and "race matters" are an explanatory thread running through the development of the rural Iowa meatpacking workforce.[1]

Unlike the South or the major industrial cities of the United States, the rural Midwest has not emerged as a dramatic focus for this country's ethnic clashes, at least not after European settlement. Robert Dykstra, who examined racism and the "black code" in Iowa's territorial and early state history, concluded that Iowans were only "superficially" racist, because they readily discarded their worst antiblack legislation when eloquent leaders diverted them from their racist behavior. In Dykstra's view, because Iowans had no history of slavery and no economic investment in black inferiority, they did not hold their racist posture forcefully or rigidly. In his words, "[B]lack Iowans could become equal under law without disturbing the prevailing system of labor."[2]

Recent studies of the 1920s emergence of the Ku Klux Klan in the Midwest are consistent with the perspective that would minimize the potency of race and ethnicity in rural midwestern history. As it arose in the Midwest, the Klan was concerned with empowering the average citizen to make an impact on civic life, with protecting Prohibition, with moral reform, with patriotism, and with quality education. According to this research, the midwestern Klan was not greatly concerned with the black population in the 1920s. Although it was anti-Catholic, it was opportunistic in exploiting this homely midwestern credo rather than active in stirring it up. At any rate, the small number of black and foreign-born persons in the rural Midwest meant that the feeble animosity between Catholics and Protestants provided all the juice that the Klan could squeeze out of midwestern ethnic antagonism.[3] If the Klan, which fomented extreme racial terror from the time of Reconstruction in the South, could be transformed into a nonpolarizing agent of moral reform in the Midwest, then surely the well of racial division was virtually dry in this section of the country.

My research suggests otherwise, notwithstanding the apparent mildness and superficiality of racial division in rural Iowa. The logic of the case can be simply inverted: If we begin by assuming that the large measure of ethnic homogeneity in rural Iowa is something to explain rather than to accept as natural, then the absence of overt ethnic confrontation may be read as an indication of the pervasive strength of Yankee whiteness rather than as a sign of its insignificance. The dominance of northern European American ethnicity in rural Iowa may have been so securely and structurally entrenched after the Civil War that extreme measures were not required to maintain it. If the focus is social behavior and economic control rather than legislation or conspicuous violence, then Iowans have been sufficiently racist to maintain the bulk of the state's wealth securely in the hands of the white population. Working-class rural Iowans, as well as the middle class, have sustained structures of ethnic inequality.

Difficulties in arriving at appropriate terminology and analytical categories to discuss ethnic divisions reflect not only divergent theoretical postures but also the shifting and varied nature of the phenomena themselves. Declining to consider apparent ethnic verities as having the solidity and permanence that they present, scholars have deconstructed, unpacked, and historicized them, developing a variety of terms and categories in the process.[4]

The term *race* is used in this study as a folk category, an entity that is not well defined in the real world, although it is frequently used.[5] The ethnic group that I call Latino, for example, has at times been considered a race and at times not. U.S. census terminology currently refers to "Hispanic Origin Persons," who may be of any race; on the other hand, the term *la Raza* (the Race) has been a political rallying point for Latinos outside of Iowa. In the course of my recent interaction with Latino workers, a Latina with dark brown eyes and thick black hair told me that she was white and that it was disrespectful to consider Latinos as being other than white; a similarly colored Latino, on the other hand, said that he was brown, not white. Whiteness could span other biological conventions as well, as could the content of the ethnic group I call black, which in the last fifteen years has been called African American and a number of other terms.[6] In an interview that I conducted with an elderly Scottish railroad worker in Perry in 1993, he defined one of his early Perry coworkers as a white man on the basis of having a white man's job: "We had one fellow that was in engine service. He was black extraction, but he was white; and that was the only colored we had." On the other hand, as David Roediger writes, the fluidity of the category of whiteness might exclude persons of northern European ancestry, as in his examples of Irish falling outside the cultural bounds of whiteness.[7]

Ethnicity (or race) is a historically shaped ideological representation, but it is powerfully ideological rather than "merely" ideological. It is integral to the material reality of social confrontation. Ethnicity has structured alliances and shaped paths of upward mobility, thereby conditioning the class experience of workers. Ethnicity, like gender, is not separate from the construction of class; it is a dimension of it. The inequalities associated with ethnicity are essential to understanding the history of the working class in rural Iowa.[8]

Although the constructed difference between white and nonwhite has defined access to certain social privileges, ethnic diversity has been more complicated than the binary dichotomy suggested by white versus nonwhite or even privileged versus oppressed. For example, within the IBP plant where I worked, a black woman born in Arkansas and a Chinese man born in Vietnam had different languages, different citizenship status, different religions, different political histories, different networks of support, and different access to social resources. Although their position as nonwhite IBP workers gave them some significant commonalities in everyday life, they also had radically divergent life experiences, and IBP supervisors gave them different rights and responsibilities on the production floor. The balance of power in their infrequent interaction would depend on the context, but it was not necessarily equal. As Susan Stanford Friedman asserts, we need "a new geography of identity" that both acknowledges the relevance of the white/nonwhite polarity and goes beyond it.[9] She poses a theory of "relational positionality" in which multiple dimensions of diversity are taken into account, with various of these dimensions carrying weight at any given time. Whiteness becomes one ethnicity rather than the source of identity for all others. This sets a context for the kind of work that David Roediger has done in recentering and problematizing whiteness in a historical context, an analysis that interrogates rather than assumes the significance of whiteness.[10]

So beneficial has ethnic division been to companies such as IBP that a powerful functional argument can be made for the capitalist class as instigators of racial oppression.[11] The history of American slavery establishes a close connection between racism and exploitation of labor, which has continued to the present. Segregation has become a continuing obstacle erected by capitalists and foisted onto their workers. Because of this imposition of division, patterns of ethnicity have channeled how workers have handled conflict. In spite of capitalists' apparent interest in a harmonious workforce, the segmentation and fragmentation that segregation produces within the workforce has bestowed greater advantages than disadvantages on employers. Until 1964, U.S. law, which answered to the interests of industrial owners, allowed separate treatment of workers by ethnicity—or by any criteria that employers found convenient. Although legal changes have erased some of these practices since 1964, many of the old patterns have persisted. As David Griffith has found in his study of low-income rural labor, state policies since then have continued to establish pools of marginal and exploited immigrant workers.[12]

Workers themselves have at times protected their particular ethnic niches. Dominant workers appear to gain the most by discriminatory practices, but subordinated ethnicities may also have incentives to accept what employers offer. Companies have relied on their ability to deliver short-term appeasements through special considerations strategically meted out. A company may be powerfully paternalistic even, or especially, when the favors it dispenses would hardly seem to be worth groveling over. The support of organized labor for ethnic equality has been crucial in some contexts.[13]

ETHNICITY IN RURAL IOWA

The first white Iowans, who moved into the area shortly before the Civil War, were keenly aware and fearful of the possibility of an immigration of freed slaves from Missouri. Although in 1850 only 333 black persons lived in the state, the presence of 115,000 slaves in Missouri, the majority of them in a strip between thirty and fifty miles of Iowa's southern border, provoked a set of severe laws constricting the civil rights of free black Iowans and discouraging black settlement. Favoring the interests of small-scale, white farmers, Iowa legislators disallowed slavery and at different times came close to enacting laws of questionable constitutionality that would have barred free black settlers from the state.[14]

Iowa emerged as one of the whitest states in the United States. Although it has become more diverse in recent years, the movement has been slow and slight. Before 1940 white persons consistently made up over 99 percent of the population; black Iowans and all other "races" together accounted for less than 1 percent. By 1970 the white population constituted 98.6 percent of the total; in 1990 the figure was 96.7 percent. Moreover, nonwhite Iowans' history differs from that of white Iowans in that they were more likely to be wage earners than the self-employed farmers or small business owners who dominated within the white population.[15]

Historically, the small nonwhite population of Iowa was concentrated in urban areas, and the concentration has increased over the years. The population of the state as a whole was predominantly rural until the census of 1960; the black population of the state has been predominantly urban. In Iowa in 1930 there were 17,380 black people, 4,295 of Mexican heritage, and 218 of Asian origin (called Chinese, Japanese, Hindu, and Korean "races" in the federal census report). In 1930 only 2,195 of the black Iowans lived in rural areas, which was less than half the 1910 total of 5,187. By 1990 the number of rural black Iowans had decreased to 1,325, which was 2.8 percent of the total number of black people in the state. By contrast, 40.5 percent of the state's white population was still living in rural areas in 1990. The counting of the Latino population was more irregular, but the small number of Iowans of Mexican descent were also found primarily in cities in the 1930 census. By 1990 there were 30,642 "Hispanic Origin Persons" in Iowa (1.1 percent of the total population), with only 15.0 percent of these persons living in rural areas.[16]

According to 1990 federal census reports, which further broke down residence of the Iowa population by size of city, black and Hispanic per-

Table 8. Birthplace of Perry's Foreign-born
Population by Number of Residents, 1910–1920

Birthplace	1910	1920
Germany	73	70
British Isles	69	73
Ireland	37	36
England	22	24
Scotland	10	11
Wales	0	2
Sweden	46	37
Austria	36	3
Canada	33	25
Italy	33	5
Other	24	43
Total	314	256
% of Perry's population	6.8	4.5

Source: U.S. census manuscripts.

sons were found predominantly in the larger cities. While 14.9 percent
of the white Iowa population lived in small cities (such as Perry) with
populations between 2,500 and 9,999, only 3.3 percent of the black and
10.8 percent of the Hispanic population lived in these cities. In sum, the
rural or small-city environment, which has been home to the majority
of white Iowans since the founding of the state, has provided homes
for only a minority of the tiny minority of people of color living in Iowa.
The black and Mexican American population of pre–World War II rural
Iowa lived in small ethnic pockets rather than being dispersed across
the state.[17]

In Perry the 1910 federal census takers recorded 37 black persons; in
1920 there were 120 black persons, 2 with race recorded as "Chinese,"
and 1 person born in Mexico. Otherwise, the town was white and predominantly native born. In 1910 6.8 percent of the population was foreign born; by 1920 only 4.5 percent was foreign born, the foreign born
coming mainly from northern Europe (see Table 8). The Italian- and
Austrian-born Perry population of 1910 was composed of temporary

Table 9. Number of Perry Residents
with Foreign-born Fathers, 1910–1920

Birthplace	1910	1920
British Isles	416	414
Ireland	244	240
England	108	105
Scotland	55	60
Wales	9	9
Germany	286	283
Sweden	120	119
Canada	60	59
Austria	45	7
Italy	33	5
Other	88	123
Total	1,048	1,010
% of Perry's population	22.6	17.9

Source: U.S. census manuscripts.

railroad crews of single men who lived together in rooming houses; only in exceptional cases did they marry into the majority population and stay. Searching harder for the particulars of ethnicity in the census data, we find that 22.6 percent of Perry residents had foreign-born fathers in 1910 and 17.9 percent in 1920 (see Table 9). Although more immigrant fathers came from Germany than any other nation, English speakers from the British Isles outnumbered them. Nor does more specific European ethnicity dominate among European Americans living outside of Perry. The percentage of foreign born and the countries of origin of the population of the neighboring farm townships of Beaver and Spring Valley were similar to Perry's.[18]

The birthplace of U.S.-born residents of Perry and the surrounding townships shows band migration from Pennsylvania and New York across the middle of the country, a pattern representative of Iowa as a whole (see Table 10). Although the proximity to Missouri accounts for some in-migration from that state, only a small number of persons came from other southern states. A study of the Perry daily news-

Table 10. Birthplace of U.S.-born Perry
Residents and U.S.-born Fathers of Perry
Residents, 1910

Birthplace	No. of Residents	No. of Fathers
Iowa	2,627	1,492
Illinois	455	502
Ohio	233	497
Indiana	175	331
Pennsylvania	139	392
Wisconsin	111	108
New York	94	229
Missouri	90	190
Other states	386	882

Source: U.S. census manuscripts.

paper shows no mention of an Oktoberfest, smorgasbord supper, St. Patrick's Day parade, or non-English language church service. Neither does the town history written by local businessman Eugene N. Hastie in 1962. Perry's entertainment centered around high school sports, movies, club banquets, and downtown business promotions. The name of the town came from a railroad official. Being a railroad division point further identified Perry with the business and cultural life of similar towns across the Midwest. The predominant ethnicity in Perry and the surrounding area might be termed midwestern Yankee. If there was anything atypical about Perry as an Iowa town, it was its lack of self-conscious ethnic identity. Sufficiently representative of textbook Midwest, it could pass as not having an ethnicity.[19]

Growing numbers of Mexican Americans entered Iowa early in the twentieth century. Recruiting at the border and illegally in the interior of Mexico, railroads hired individuals displaced by the prolonged chaos of the Mexican Revolution. Mexican immigrants then dispersed northward along major railroad routes, although some of them sought other jobs such as mining and farm labor when they were available. Mexican immigrants eased the serious labor shortage caused by World War I.[20]

A small cluster of Mexican-born farm workers settled in the sugar beet growing area around Mason City in northern Iowa, but the majority of the Mexican immigrants in rural Iowa worked in railroad gangs. Paid less than white workers, they lived in housing provided by railroads and were further dependent on their employers for medical care and transportation. Mexican settlements for Iowa railroad workers were established by the Rock Island Railroad outside of Des Moines and by the Atchison, Topeka and Santa Fe Railroad outside Fort Madison in the southeastern tip of the state. In the Fort Madison settlement the first homes consisted of boxcars in the railroad yard. When the Mississippi flooded the area in 1926, the Santa Fe built a set of brick barracks on higher ground. Many of the Mexican workers and their families lived in the barracks; others built their own small homes between the city limits of Fort Madison and the railroad yard, an area that became known as "the Village." It bordered another neighborhood just outside the town that was home to a small black population.[21]

The great northern migration of rural black southerners in the early twentieth century brought small numbers of black workers into coal camps in rural Iowa. Research on the Buxton camp in southern Iowa documented this movement and the cohesive social base that grew out of the shared economic circumstances of black coal miners. Black miners and their families lived in company housing in coal camps and were subject to being uprooted and moved from place to place as existing coal mines gave out and new ones opened. At least some workers who left the Buxton camp when the mines began to taper off around 1914 migrated north to the Perry area.[22]

The Milwaukee Railroad, for which Perry was a division point, recruited a crew of black workers in 1912 when it needed more labor for the expansion of its Perry yards. Perry's black railroad workers were not originally housed in Perry, being assigned instead to a "Camp Lincoln" outside of town. But from there they moved into boxcars on railroad property in town and later to two housing areas on the western and northeastern outskirts of town. When their temporary railroad employment ended, these workers and other incoming black persons took jobs in the Moran and Zook Spur coal mines east of Perry. The black miners and their families lived either in company-built coal camps or in the Perry enclaves, with daily and weekly commutes provided by an interurban trolley.[23]

Iowa town society was tightly segregated. The 1920 federal census manuscripts from Perry show that white households and black households were totally disjoint except for one white woman who was married to a black man and lived in a black neighborhood. Similar to the companies' treatment of the black population of Perry, the Santa Fe Railroad originally housed the Fort Madison Mexicans two miles outside of town. When these Mexicans eventually tried to buy land to build their own houses in Fort Madison, they were not allowed to do so. Mexicans were excluded from restaurants and were required to sit in segregated areas in movie theaters. They sat in a special section in the back of the Catholic church. When a Mexican couple married, the wedding was held in the basement of the Catholic school rather than in the church.[24]

In 1913 when Perry police arrested a group of black men for playing craps, the Perry Advertiser noted the protest of one of the men:

One of the colored men arrested, John Duncan, declared that the colored men had no place to go in Perry. They are barred from the restaurants and the pool halls, and shunted into a corner at the movies. It is impossible for them to gather at the home of a friend for the evening without having police called in. It [playing craps] takes the place of their club life and they protest that the game was not a stiff one, which was probably true as the Milwaukee pay checks for other than enginemen did not come until yesterday, so it was hold over change which went into the game when the arrest was made.[25]

Nevertheless, the city took over fifty dollars in fines from the black workers. When someone in Camp Lincoln broke a small pox quarantine, black persons were barred from all public places in Perry. Excluded from the existing churches, Perry's black churchgoers built three Protestant churches of their own.[26]

The Mexican and black communities of Fort Madison and Perry came into existence because of the needs of the railroads for workers, but the railroads depended on the rural domestic and informal economy for the daily reproduction of the workforce. In Fort Madison, the Santa Fe allowed the Mexican households free use of small plots of land adjacent to the railroad tracks where they could grow potatoes, corn, squash, and tomatoes, both for sale and for household consumption. Some women raised poultry and made a little money through egg sales; some households kept goats. Butchering of hogs, which were purchased from local farmers, was a family enterprise that produced a small income, as fresh meat would be sold within the settlement when it was available. Men also fished in Mississippi River inlets close to the railroad yards.[27]

Calling her childhood home a "shed," "Agnes Brown," a black woman who grew up in Perry in the 1920s, described the house where she lived with her parents and eight siblings:

> Well, my father fixed it (the house). It set on two lots. He planted cherry trees, apple trees, raspberries and a grape arbor and hedges. But when we first bought it, it was just—you know—nothing. It had an old porch with great big white posts . . . and it had one big bedroom for my mother and father and another big room where we all slept. All of us slept in that one big shed—five or six beds. Then there was a kitchen. . . . We had a great big back yard and a barn. . . .
>
> We had chickens, but my mother would never have [pigs]. We didn't have the room in the first place. But almost everybody else did. "Mrs. Jolly" had pigs right behind our back yard.

One of the black Perry families rented thirty-five acres of land from the Milwaukee Railroad for $110 a year. This family raised corn and fruit trees and kept hogs, geese, turkeys, and a cow. Like other black residents of Dallas County, members of this family fished in the Raccoon River, which ran along the west side of Perry. For income, they sold about ten hogs a year to a market buyer and sold buttermilk and turkeys in the mining camps. Although the Milwaukee Railroad employed some black women laborers during World War I, including seven who were still working at the time of the 1920 census, this was an exception. The railroad companies did not ordinarily employ women as line or yard workers.[28] Women, on the other hand, did much of the subsistence production that allowed for the tenuous survival of families. Men, married and single, did both wage labor and subsistence production.

Employing black and Latino workers that could generally not get comparable alternative jobs, railroads and mines further secured their dependence by providing housing and services that could not be purchased in the general rural economy. Iowa's black and Latino railroad workers received lower wages than did white workers, and none of them were union members until the CIO organizing of the 1930s.

By the 1930s the Zook Spur and Moran mines had completely shut down, as had the entire coal mining industry in Iowa, removing the economic base of the black community of Perry.[29] Agnes Brown recalled, "The depression was the most devastating thing that had ever happened, because the mines shut down and there was nothing, absolutely nothing." People were hungry and desperate. With no steady jobs for black men, the black community relied more heavily than before on the income of women and girls, who earned money washing dishes and cooking at a restaurant in addition to doing housework for white families in Perry. The generosity of some of the white women employers was helpful. With the intervention of one of these women, a black man got a job as a janitor in the local hospital. Black men found scattered work washing cars for a car dealer or emptying boxcars but nothing that provided enough money for people to live. Agnes Brown continued, "There was never a feeling that you could go downtown and get a job as a clerk or a job as a secretary. We just knew you couldn't. So we gravitated to Des Moines when we got out of high school. . . . Never, never, never could the average person get anything other than a maid job."

Nor was there any point in black persons trying to get jobs at the Perry packing plant; those jobs were also reserved for white workers. Black porters who rode the trains would stay overnight in homes of black residents of Perry, leaving some of their money in the community. In the absence of jobs, a number of black persons ran bootlegging and gambling operations, which filtered some money in from the white community. The frequent arrests of black persons displayed in daily newspapers may not reflect the actual racial composition of gambling and liquor violators, but it does document that a number of black men and women were accused. On occasion black persons entering the court system were given stiff fines and sentences that were forgiven if they left town.[30]

The black and Mexican communities of Perry and Fort Madison were founded on short-lived economic bases. In Perry, jobs on the railroad and in the mines ran their separate courses in approximately fifteen years. After World War I, when the labor shortage eased, Fort Madison Mexicans' jobs with the Santa Fe were irregular. Seasonal agricultural jobs were an inferior alternative to Mexican railroad labor; most other employment was closed to them. In the 1930s, with little railroad work for the Mexican community and little income, some availed themselves of railroad passes to return to their families in Mexico. Most of these workers were gradually able to return to the United States. Some within the minority communities of Fort Madison and Perry simply sank roots and persisted; there was nowhere else to go.

In addition to increasing economic marginalization in the 1920s and 1930s, the experience of minorities within the dominant midwestern Yankee culture was shaped by the xenophobia and ethnocentrism engendered in World War I. As if in answer to the wider employment openings of the wartime economy, the Iowa Yankee population claimed its superior status more intensely in overt and belligerent intolerance after the Great War. During the war the state of Iowa had forbidden the speaking of any language other than English in public places, a measure heartily supported by the editor of the *Perry Daily Chief*, who stated, "There can be no true patriotism except in the American language."[31] Crews of eastern and southern European railroad workers were transferred out of the Dallas County area. A loyalty committee was formed for the railroad workers, whose allegiances were carefully monitored. A black railroad worker in Perry was forced to kiss the U.S. flag. The slightest indication of opposition to the war was punished by vandalism or personal violence.[32]

Harassment of ethnic minorities intensified in the 1920s. The Ku Klux Klan, which flourished in Iowa in the 1920s, found a large following in Perry. The Perry press reported enthusiastic crowds turning out to hear eloquent Klan speeches urging Americans to squash communism and to bar immigration. A 1924 Klan rally drew 15,000 persons, the largest crowd in Perry's history. With fireworks, music, food, and speakers, it was a community event. The Klan represented itself as the only refuge for true patriots. Consistent with the research of Robert J. Neymeyer on the Iowa Klan, there were no reports of vigilantism or violence in the newspaper, and certainly no evidence of murder or massive property destruction, such as occurred in the South.[33]

Yet research on the Ku Klux Klan is complicated by a pattern of secrecy and local autonomy. Furthermore, the retrospective embarrassment and reticence of Klan members and witnesses make interviewing

difficult. But there is unmistakable evidence that behind the respectable facade the Perry Ku Klux Klan fomented antagonism and fear. Klan
members burned a cross on the lawn of Agnes Brown's family shortly
after the family moved to Perry. They also burned crosses on the prop-
erties of Catholics in and around Perry. One Catholic, born in the mid-
1920s, remembers the fear he felt seeing his parents' helplessness and
terror when the Klan burned a cross close to their farm home when he
was four. The Perry Ku Klux Klan had fewer people to intimidate than
did the Klan in southern towns, but the smaller number of targeted
persons may have increased their vulnerability.

Consistent with Neymeyer's analysis, however, Perry's black and
Catholic survivors of the 1920s chuckle over their memories of the
Klan. "Jacob Harvey," part of a large Catholic family, told of two relatives laughing about scaring the wits out of a Klan member by pulling
the sheet off him. "After it was over there was no hard feelings. . . .
Most of them were good people, really," he said. "Ed Jefferson," a black
man born in Perry in 1913, said that when a group of white-sheeted persons approached his grandmother's home, she let loose a mouthful of
profanity that sent them running. For him, the Klan was silly; he knew
some of the members personally and could not take them seriously.

The last *Perry Daily Chief* reference to the Klan in the 1930s concerned
plans to host the state Klan convention in Perry in 1933, but not a great
deal of interest arose. By then the Klan had accomplished its purpose
and run its course. World War I had opened new opportunities for black
Americans and other marginalized persons, and the Ku Klux Klan of
the 1920s reacted; by the 1930s there was no upward economic mobility
for the Klan to squash. In 1941 a Catholic family bought the Perry Klan
property, which became a vintage family joke.[34]

Interviews with black persons who lived in rural Iowa before World
War II stress that survival depended on the black social nexus. In Agnes
Brown's words,

> The main thing that you should be concerned about . . . is that in
> spite of the economic hardships we carved a life out for ourselves and
> generally speaking it wasn't based on crime. There was an element
> there, . . . but most of them were church-going people, God-fearing
> people, and hard-working people. And we were close. The commu-

nity was close-knit. We cared about each other. When somebody had a problem everybody had a problem. That is the main thrust of this story. There may have been segregation. There *was* segregation. There was discrimination. But we were so busy carving out our own life we didn't become bitter.

Black churches in Perry were social centers. Residents opened their homes to each other, shared food, and offered assistance at crucial times. The black community had baseball teams, picnics, and musical events. Surviving residents have warm memories of community solidarity and security within the segregated setting.[35]

The separate Latino and black communities in themselves seem to have been sources of comfort and hospitality, just as the midwestern Yankee ethnicity was for its members. Yet it would be misleading to romanticize these situations. They were based on unfair exclusion and economic exploitation. Even as the subjugated communities formed bases for economic and psychological survival, internally they too often displayed violence and coercion toward their most vulnerable members, particularly women.[36] For all minorities there was a clear and powerful awareness of crushing discrimination. Sebastian Alvarez of Fort Madison said, "We were *really* discriminated."[37] Economic discrimination was destructive. Both the Latino and black persons who migrated to cities and those who remained in rural areas have expressed regret that their economic base fell short of what was needed for many young people to maintain homes in rural Iowa.

ETHNICITY AND MEATPACKING, 1940–1960

Before World War II meatpacking companies, like other employers, hired workers according to their ethnicity and separated them within the plants. In Iowa, white, U.S.-born workers predominated in meatpacking, as they did in the population of the state as a whole, but packing plants recruited crews of eastern European immigrant and black workers. Meatcutting and curing technology drew on European culture, and these immigrants brought much-sought skills to the production floor. Russian and Polish immigrants worked in the packing companies of Sioux City. The Sinclair Company recruited Bohemians in Czechoslovakia for their Cedar Rapids plant. The Mason City Decker plant imported German workers. Black workers came to the packinghouses of Sioux City in the early 1900s, and they formed a significant minority of the workforce in the Waterloo Rath plant in the 1930s. The Tobin Company recruited six skilled butchers, including four black men, from Chicago to train local workers when it opened its Fort Dodge plant. A small number of workers of Mexican descent were in both Decker and Rath. Notwithstanding valuable skills that ethnic minority workers brought to their employers, the majority of them did dirty jobs for less pay than did their Yankee counterparts.[38]

The practice of recruiting workers through families and other social networks reinforced segregation patterns. Thus, workers within a given gang tended to speak the same language and cooperate in training and problem solving. A Sioux City packing employee from the 1930s stated, "Now, I know a lot of people quarrel with this, but the facts are that the whole mechanical department almost without exception was Catholics. You could get into other departments, and you'd find that they were pretty much all Lutheran. You couldn't work in the branch house, for instance, at one time unless you could show your penny, you know, was a member of the Masons."[39] Plant superintendents often assigned black and immigrant men to the kill floor or the hide room; they gave black women jobs as janitors or assigned them to clean out intestines. Yankee workers held the inside track on respectable, "skilled" jobs.[40]

Some of the more rural-based plants, including Morrell in Ottumwa, Swift/Arnold Brothers in Perry, Tobin in Estherville, and Kingan in Storm Lake, hired almost entirely white, native-born labor. The Tobin plant of Fort Dodge would not hire local black workers in the 1930s, notwithstanding the four skilled black butchers from Chicago. According to one Fort Dodge black man, it was townspeople, rather than the company, who would not permit local black persons in the Tobin plant.[41]

The AFL's Amalgamated initially accepted racial and ethnic division within the workforce and concentrated organizing among skilled workers. The strong card of the CIO in the 1930s and 1940s was its appeal to workers at the bottom of the packing hierarchy, including people of color and immigrants. With the labor shortage of World War II, many plants were more willing to hire previously excluded workers, and this further contributed to the success of the CIO's Packinghouse Workers Organizing Committee (PWOC) and United Packinghouse Workers of America (UPWA), which prided itself on its civil rights record, organizing "men, women, Negro, Spanish-speaking, Catholics, Protestants, Jews."[42] The kill floors, with their large contingents of black and immigrant men, became strong bases of CIO organizing.[43]

The UPWA did not drop the issue of race and ethnicity when it captured its membership. Before the emergence of the civil rights movement in the national media in the 1950s and 1960s, the UPWA was working for ethnic equality within the union, on the production floor, and in packing communities. In 1945 Local P-46, which represented Rath workers in Waterloo, placed one of its members on trial for making racial slurs. Going beyond statements of nondiscrimination, P-46 worked for structural changes such as revamping the seniority system to enable workers to transfer out of segregated departments. This local also monitored the rate at which black persons applied for and got hired at Rath and kept statistics on racial composition in the industry as a whole.[44]

Because packinghouses were often the major employers in Iowa communities, the racial equality movement within the plants effected change in the towns outside the plants. A union member tells a triumphant story about an action in Fort Dodge when fifteen to twenty UPWA members went into a restaurant and the restaurant refused service to a black man who was in the group. All the union members walked out of the restaurant and began a campaign that opened up Fort Dodge restaurants and bars to black people.[45]

The UPWA Oral History Project interview with Anna Mae Weems demonstrates the political power that came from the local level on the civil rights issue. Weems, a black woman born in Waterloo in 1926, began to fight local employment discrimination when, unlike her white classmates, she was unable to secure a decent job after high school graduation. In 1954, with the encouragement of P-46, she applied to Rath for a job. Although black men had worked in kill, women's departments remained white. Plant policy was that a black woman had to work a year as a janitor before moving into another job. When the union intervened and succeeded in placing Weems in sliced bacon, she met resistance and hostility from the white women. P-46 backed her up, telling the existing workers that they would have to leave if they could not work with Weems. Although she had trouble working her way into the production line, eventually she became highly adept. Because the women worked on an incentive system that paid bonuses for speed, Weems's speed and the quality of her work made her popular. She was elected union steward and served as chair of the union's human rights committee. Outside the plant, Weems used the leverage of her union support to prod the local NAACP and black clergy, both oriented toward middle-class issues at that time, to address concerns of black workers. The union and NAACP together pressured the *Waterloo Courier* to stop racial stereotyping, they sat in and desegregated lunch counters, they opened job opportunities to Waterloo black persons, and they successfully pressured the city to establish a human rights commission. The district and international UPWA supported these efforts and in turn drew on the Waterloo experience and Weems's leadership in promoting their civil rights agenda.[46]

However, the UPWA did not erase ethnic division either in the plants or in the communities. Although the white women with whom Weems worked came to value her skills on the job, she could not involve them in her civil rights activities. She also recalled that some of the white board members opposed the union's civil rights work. Moreover, the number of black workers in the Rath plant dwindled during the 1950s in spite of UPWA efforts, and few black persons had management or supervisory roles.[47]

Although ethnic groups were powerful building blocks, it was not only, or even primarily, ethnic minorities that organized packinghouses in Iowa. Some plants remained almost completely white, in spite of being organized by UPWA. Local P-1, the first UPWA local, was organized in Ottumwa's Morrell plant; its membership was based on a close-knit, native-born, white, Protestant ethnicity. The Tobin plant of Fort Dodge hired its first local blacks during World War II. Marshall Wells, a Fort Dodge black man who got a packing job in 1942, said that the local UPWA Ladies Auxiliary asked him and his wife to speak on community relations but then told them not to come to the meeting. He also remembered that when a black union organizer from outside the community was called into a local meeting, the white union men walked out.[48]

The question of how hard to push the civil rights issue split the UPWA itself. The locals of Chicago, the site of the international office, were largely black in the 1950s. Plans for a major black power movement emerged from a group of black Chicago unionists, but this plan could not be implemented at the local level outside of Chicago. The large, predominantly white locals in Nebraska and Iowa were major obstacles. Even where substantial local black membership existed, such as in Omaha, these blacks tended to be attuned to the need for diplomacy and compromise in their home communities and hence unreceptive to the confrontive agenda of the Chicago office. P-1, the predominantly white local of Ottumwa, declined to participate in the antidiscrimination program that came down from Chicago and thereby lost the backing of the international for some of its local efforts.[49]

The Storm Lake Kingan plant, among the smaller number of Iowa plants organized by the AFL Amalgamated, tended to be white and to avoid the race issue. The Perry Swift/Arnold Brothers plant, some of whose workers belonged to the UPWA, hired only white workers during World War II, as did the local poultry processing plant, which had a few Amalgamated members.[50]

In spite of lingering segregation, rural Latino and black Iowans believe that substantial social and economic progress occurred in the years from 1940 to 1960. Sebastian Alvarez said that, because he and so many other Mexican Americans fought in World War II, discrimination against the Mexican community in general eased after the war. Before the war he had tried to apply for a post office job and was never called; afterward he took a civil service exam and with veterans' preference he scored over 100 percent. He became a custodian in the post office, a job he kept until his retirement. Juan Vasquez, born in the Village in 1939, stated, "In that area, in west Fort Madison, that was the late forties and fifties, we kind of like broke the barrier of everything."[51]

In retrospect, Ed Jefferson managed a philosophical chuckle when he recalled that when his wife went to apply for a job at the Perry poultry processing plant during World War II, the manager told her he would never hire a black person. The manager did not realize that he was talking to the woman who worked as a maid in his house. But even in Perry, the war effected some forward progress in race relations. In 1943, with many white workers gone, Jefferson got his first job on the railroad, working as a hostler's helper. He worked there for thirteen months, although he was never allowed to join the union. By the end of the conflict three black employees remained in the Perry yards. Jefferson got another wartime job working for a construction company, but after the war a brick mason said that he would call his workers off the job if Jefferson stayed. Jefferson was fired. The city later hired him for street maintenance, a job he kept until retirement. The city engineer and other city officials were good people and had a conscience, he explained.

Perry as a whole remained quietly segregated socially, although a few low-income whites mixed in the black neighborhoods as the black population diminished. "Betty Tice," a white woman born in Perry in 1941, grew up with no black classmates in the 1940s and 1950s, although her grandmother lived next to a black woman on the west side. She recalled that her grandmother talked to this neighbor over the fence but had no other contact with her. She herself grew up avoiding blacks: "People didn't treat them like they should, you know. They usually ended up calling them 'nigger.' . . . I just never spoke to them. They would walk around town, and Mother would say, . . . 'Just don't say anything. If a black goes by you, don't say anything to them.' " A railroad worker recalled, "The colored fellows . . . here in [Perry], they wasn't much of a problem. They stayed pretty much to themselves."

Although plenty of evidence of discrimination remained, after World War II doors were not as tightly sealed to black and Latino individuals as they had been in the 1930s. Older white people could talk to black acquaintances outside, even though it was not something to teach children. In rural areas, public employment seems to have been more accessible to black and Latino workers than private employment such as meatpacking, although UPWA made significant strides on behalf of its members and other black persons in the larger packing communities.

RESTRUCTURING DIVERSITY

With the meatpacking industry restructuring that occurred after the founding of IBP in 1960, the politics of race and ethnicity reverted to echoes of early twentieth-century patterns. New-breed meatpacking companies in rural Iowa benefited from ethnic discrimination that isolated and disempowered groups of their workers, a pattern that continued the employee relations of railroads and mining companies in the early twentieth century. Company practices built on social ostracism that the population of northern European descent imposed on all others, but most uncompromisingly on black and Latino persons. One by one the old-line urban packing plants closed. The Swift, Cudahy, and Armour plants of Sioux City shut down, as did the Rath plant of Waterloo and all of Omaha's major packing companies. The plants opened by the new-breed leaders—IBP, ConAgra (Monfort), and Cargill (Excel)—tended to be in rural and small-town locations rather than in cities. For example, Armour closed in Sioux City in 1963, but in 1964 IBP established its flagship plant and corporate headquarters in Dakota City, Nebraska, a small town just across the Missouri River from Sioux City. In 1968 the UPWA, which had vigorously promoted a civil rights agenda, merged with the Amalgamated, which by this time was larger and more powerful than the confrontive UPWA. The plants that had the largest numbers of blacks and the most radical union agenda closed, and the more rural locations gave new-breed packers a whiter, less militant workforce.[52]

New-breed companies' conquest of the industry is evidenced most dramatically in the fact that in 1970, at age ten, IBP slaughtered more beef than any other company in the world. However, IBP used up workers fast, and the move to more sparsely populated areas made it impossible for the firm to hire enough local workers to keep running. Frequent labor clashes intensified the problems. In 1969, with workers striking in Dakota City and Fort Dodge, IBP began bringing in Mexican workers from the Texas border area. The number of Mexican workers increased in the following decade. In 1982, in response to another strike at the Dakota City plant, IBP began to recruit Asian Americans from California. Asian American workers moved into other IBP plants; the Storm Lake plant that opened in 1982 became a center for Lao workers. The worker recruitment practices of new-breed packers spilled back over into the old-line companies that were frantically scrambling to compete. During a 1987 Morrell strike in Sioux City, that company recruited Indians from South Dakota reservations and black workers from New Orleans, as well as Latinos from the Texas border; IBP recruited black workers from Chicago for rural Iowa in the 1980s. Although Amalgamated/UPWA unionized IBP in Dakota City and Fort Dodge, and the Denison IBP plant had a company-sponsored union, most of IBP's new plants were nonunion. When IBP brought its cheap imported labor into towns such as Storm Lake and Columbus Junction that had formerly had unionized plants with mostly white workers, further racial polarization was virtually inevitable.[53]

Packing companies' recruitment brought an explosion of ethnic diversity in rural Iowa in the 1990s. White-nonwhite remained an axis of tension, but the greater numbers of nonwhites, their greater diversity, the instability of their employment and residence, and the more homogeneous social context of rural communities all worked together to produce a new dynamic. Like the earlier rural employers, new-breed companies took advantage of recent arrivals, who were more expendable and had less social capital with which to mount effective protests than did native-born white workers. Rather than melting into the life of a packing town, new arrivals forged separate social networks to confront parallel problems of discrimination within the plants and ostracism in the community outside. As was true in the study of packing workers in Garden City, Kansas, the separate ethnic groups tended not to forge links. They coexisted, but they did not interact. Outside of the network of professional social workers and clergy, few rural whites even attempted to crack ethnic boundaries.[54]

Primarily in response to the recruiting practices of packing companies, the Iowa legislature enacted the Non–English Speaking Employees Law in 1990. Aimed at increasing the cost of recruiting workers from outside of Iowa, the law states that if more than 10 percent of the employees at a given worksite do not speak English and speak the same non-English language, the employer is required to provide an interpreter for each shift and a person whose primary responsibility is to refer workers to community services. If a company recruits workers from a distance of over five hundred miles, they have to provide written statements specifying (1) the minimum number of hours the new hires can expect to work, (2) wages, (3) a job description, and (4) the health risks associated with the employment. In addition, if a worker quits or is fired within four weeks of being hired, the company has to provide return transportation to the point of recruitment.[55]

The Oscar Mayer plant in Perry operated in its own sphere in the seventies and eighties. Just as with the hiring of women, it moved enough on the hiring of black workers to keep out of trouble. By the mid-1980s three black men worked among approximately six hundred white workers at the plant, which may have been something like a representative number of working-age persons among the small elderly black population of Perry. It was hard to get a job at Oscar, which did not need to recruit.[56]

When Oscar announced that it would close in February 1989, IBP materialized as a miracle. The largest meatpacker in the world was coming to Perry to replace the crumbling Oscar Mayer Company. Yet even before IBP began production, it occurred to some of the citizens of Perry that IBP could mean some unwelcome newcomers. Gene Leman, the executive in charge of IBP's pork division, soothed the nerves of the townspeople by assuring them that IBP did not import minorities; the only minorities that it would hire were the ones already in the community. In July 1989 IBP began hiring in Perry; in August the plant went into production.[57]

In August 1990 IBP brought in the first group of Latinos, recruited in East Los Angeles. By the time I went to work at the plant in January 1992, it had imported Asian Americans as well as a number of black workers either hired in Des Moines or recruited from rural Arkansas or Louisiana. This was not turning out as the town fathers had planned, but IBP was able to call up and use a history of 150 years of racial polarization to its advantage. Racial discrimination occurred among both managers and workers in the plant. If anything, this discrimination was less intense among supervisors than among production workers. Formal rules compelled supervisors to behave differently from workers. The shape of discrimination experienced on the production floor and outside the plant differed for each of the major groups: Asian American, black, Latino, and white workers.

CHANG

Once a month, after the line stopped, the cut floor at IBP would crowd into the cafeteria for a general meeting on a safety or procedural topic. At one of these meetings, on March 19, 1992, a crew of us from the cellar sat around a table. This time we had forms to fill out about vacation leave preferences. When a supervisor brought around the pencils and papers for us, "Chang" picked up a form and a pencil and started to write his name. Larry jerked the pencil out of his hand and injected a preemptory "Shut up!" in case Chang decided to say something, which he did not.

This was a small incident. Rudeness was not unusual at IBP. I learned that the proper response to such a gesture was a string of obscenities and a reverse grab. But for Chang, the proper response was submission. I had seen a cellar worker violently push Chang down onto the wet floor. Chang was known by a variety of stupid names; I never heard another worker call him Chang. No one else in the cellar was held in such general and unmitigated contempt. Except for brief periods when the upper cut floor sent a worker down, there were no other Asian workers in the cellar.

Chang worked the whizard on the belly line, and usually he was there all day. He stood up remarkably well under pressure, a characteristic believed to be an advantage of Asian workers. Chang had come to Perry from the San Francisco area in November 1991, just two months before I started work. He called himself Chinese, although he was born in Vietnam. He spoke Chinese and Vietnamese, but his English was not good enough for me to get a clear picture of how he got to San Francisco or how he came to work for IBP in Perry. He seemed to have no family. Most of the other Asian Americans were from Laos and did not particularly like Chang, who looked different, spoke different languages, and had more gregarious mannerisms. Chang got to know the family that ran a Chinese restaurant in Perry and took a job working in the kitchen after he got off at the plant.

Like most of those working on whizards, Chang had hand trouble. Although bellies were not supposed to have bones, occasionally a rib bone lodged in a piece of belly. Chang hit a bone with his whizard, which sent the bone through his glove and into his finger. When the wound did not heal, a doctor put him on light duty. With this, he moved off the line and was set to folding boxes.

One afternoon as he was folding, I went over to ask how his finger was. Not good. He pulled off his glove and showed me a bright red swollen bulb. He had just been to a specialist, who told him that he needed surgery; there seemed to be something inside the finger. But the surgery would cost two thousand dollars. Chang didn't have the money, and IBP wasn't going to pay. I told him to go to the union. He said that he wasn't a member, but I urged him to go anyway. Just then Clyde walked up and started explaining to me that Chang came into the plant with a bad finger and that his previous employer was liable for medical expenses for seven years after he quit that job.

Why was he telling me this? Wasn't this what he should tell Chang, who was right there?

"He can't understand this, see?" Clyde said to me.

I couldn't understand it, either. I noticed something that needed doing somewhere else.

"Lowell," a main floor cut worker, and I later found Chang and told him again that he needed to get to the union office. "Don't fuck around with the company," said Lowell, "just go to the union."

Chang was skeptical, but Lowell insisted. The doctor was also willing to support Chang. The very next day Chang gave me the news that IBP was going to pay. The surgery was scheduled and he would be on light duty until then.

One evening in the Loft, the bar next to the plant, I talked to "Lee," a forty-six-year-old IBP worker. Lee had been in Vietnam from 1963 to 1967. Most people didn't like Vietnam, he stated, but he went back a second time because he liked it. He said Clyde had been a sharpshooter in Vietnam. Clyde could pick off a "gook" from one thousand feet and he killed seventy-six of them, but he never liked it. Lee, on the other hand, was a knife man and he liked it. He would kill a "gook" by slashing the throat from right to left. If he did it left to right they died right away, but right to left it took four minutes for them to die and that was a kick. He killed twenty-six. He wore a baseball cap saying "Vietnam Veteran and Proud of It."

According to Lee, he had worked under Clyde making combos in the cellar before I was there. One day a "gook" came into his area, and Lee stalked over to Clyde and demanded that he keep the "gook" away from him or something bad would happen. Clyde told Lee to take care of it himself. So Lee warned the "gook," "I got paid fifty-five dollars a month to kill gooks in Vietnam; and I killed a lot of them. But you're free the next time you come into my room." Lee savored this punch line, rolling it over several times before moving on.

After Chang's surgery he got placed on light duty in the knife room, but before the surgery he stayed in the cellar. Unlike some of us who had free-ranging light duty for long periods, Chang had a small notebook and was set to counting boxes as they went by on a conveyor coming down from the upper cut floor. It was an exquisitely boring job, especially designed for Chang, and without logic, as boxes were counted more efficiently once stacked in storage. At quitting time Chang left his post and hurried toward the door, doubtless looking forward to the warmth and friendliness of the restaurant kitchen. Clyde caught him by the shoulder: "Where you goin'?" Chang looked at him in surprise. "You ain't goin' nowhere," leveled Clyde. Chang was going to be sticking around until Clyde said he could leave, and that would be sometime later. No sense having them think they could just clock in, sit around all day, and then clock out. They were always trying to get away with something.

Chang was the only Asian American I talked to in the plant, and he was not typical. He was the only one with a room in Perry; the others commuted every day from Des Moines. I never heard any of the others speak English, and they seemed to move through their jobs without seeing the rest of us. Although a few Lao women came to work, it was only for short periods, and they stayed close to the men. Some people just aren't friendly.[58]

SUSAN AND FRED

By 1990 the Perry IBP was hiring black workers from outside the area. In the midst of a general resurgence of Ku Klux Klan activity in eastern Iowa that year, a cross was burned on the lawn of a houseful of young black men who worked in the plant and lived together in Perry. Again, it got written off as something done by someone with less than a full load. It was some yahoos, not the real Klan. But Ed Jefferson didn't think it was funny this time around. The black men left town, although one of them subsequently returned. By 1992 most of the black IBP workers carpooled or rode the IBP bus from Des Moines.

Ed Jefferson's grandson worked in maintenance at IBP, but the majority of the black persons in the plant did not have roots in Perry. Some black workers came north from rural Louisiana; others were from rural Arkansas. Many were from Des Moines and applied for their jobs through the Des Moines Job Service. Like most IBP hires, the majority had only short stints of work in the plant. I knew of four black women who worked there continuously while I did. One of them was married to another black worker and lived in Perry. There were, maybe, fifty black men on an average day.

Susan, who worked in converting and whose locker was next to mine, was one of those commuting from Des Moines. Aged thirty-three, she was a single mother with a fourteen-year-old daughter and a six-year-old son. Living with her children in an apartment in a black area of Des Moines, she frequently ran low on money by the end of the weekly pay period. Sometimes her lunch was a few pieces of bread that she dressed up by adding onions, mustard, and pickles from the condiment station in the cafeteria. She once asked me for five dollars for food and paid it back as soon as she got her next paycheck, the only time any of my co-workers got around to repaying one of my loans.

Susan was dead tired most of the time. A heavy woman, she had trouble with her feet. Once she stayed out two days with swollen feet, but usually she tried to make it through. One afternoon when she seemed particularly tired, I suggested that she report in sick. I would have. She said that the only way to get off work was to have a temperature, and she didn't know how to do that. I thought it might be effective to say that she was going to throw up on the meat, but she said that didn't work either.

As we talked, Susan tried to convey the weight of innumerable small insults that go with being a working-class black woman. One Thursday night after she had received her weekly paycheck, she rode the IBP bus back to Des Moines and then took the city bus to a grocery store so she could buy food. The store had a check-cashing service, which she had used before, but this time the service was out of money. Susan had enough money for a loaf of bread and return bus fare to her apartment, but as she left the store she noticed a white man cashing a payroll check. She had spent an evening on her feet after a full day on her feet and still had almost no food for her children and herself.

Susan observed that black workers had a harder time than white workers in qualifying for jobs at IBP. They got written up more than white workers did. She herself had been written up for attitude, which sounded incredible considering other attitudes that I had observed. Most of all, Susan said, she couldn't handle it when one of the supervisors shoved her around on the floor. She didn't want any of the supervisors to ever touch her.

Shortly before I left the plant, Susan bid on a maintenance job, and she had the highest seniority of the bidders. She did not get the job, it being stipulated in the union contract that IBP had the exclusive right to determine the qualifications and ability of employees.[59]

Fred, an easygoing and friendly black man in his twenties, was among the four black hires who started in my orientation group on January 14. He was the only new black hire still around after two weeks, but he was assigned to loin boning in converting, so I didn't see him very often after the first days. On March 19, as I was getting ready to go home after the line meeting, I saw him making a telephone call at the pay phone in the hall. I hurried over to say hello and ask how things were going.

He was in a bad way. He showed me his thumb, which was sticking out at a strange angle and said the pain was driving him crazy. I reached over to it when he held it out, but he whisked it back and warned me not to touch it. He had just been through a terrific scene in the dispensary. He had gone to see the nurses about five times in the past weeks, and they told him to stop faking a sore thumb and get back to work. This day, while waiting to talk to a nurse, he stepped out into the hall for a smoke. The nurse stormed out and accused him of coming to the dispensary to catch a smoke. She ordered him back to work. Fred said she treated him like a kid, and he lost his temper, yelled, and quit his job.

Now as we talked, he was cooling off and regretting having given up his job. We knew from orientation that anyone who quit was irrevocably out. Still, Fred had been treated badly and there should be some redress. On the other hand, because we were probationary employees, the company could fire us at will with no grievance allowed. We talked to a union steward, who suggested that we find the union president, "Max," in the local office downtown. Fred and I then rode downtown in my car to see what could be done.

Fred had not joined the union; for Max, this was a chance to reach out to black workers. He told Fred that he should have come to him right away; it was hard because the rules were against him. "Jake," the plant manager, was out of town, but he would try to reach him and talk to him. Chances were Jake could get Fred back on light duty. As it happened, he did, and Fred was soon back in the plant.

Five days later I talked to Fred again and learned that the nurses were still jerking him around. We decided that Fred should never go into the dispensary alone; he needed a union steward each time he talked with someone about his hand. We consulted a steward, who informed us that IBP could stall a long time on medical conditions. "You need to sign a union card," he told Fred. Fred assured him that he was going to, and I reminded them both that the union represented all workers whether or not they joined. But Max was pleading his case and Fred did get to see a doctor, who backed him up, affirming that there were verifiable signs of damage and that he was in the early stages of carpal tunnel syndrome. He had been on his job for only about two months.

Fred, a towering, muscular man, must have looked like a good candidate for one of the more arduous jobs. But what do you do with a black man who is used up before the end of probation?

The company fired Fred on the last day of the ninety-day probation, having suddenly discovered that he had attendance violations in the first weeks of work. In addition, he got written up twice on his last day of probation—once for poor work performance and once for looking around the room.

I did some rattling around, calling Fred, talking to Max. Max went over Fred's disciplinary record with me. By February 28 he had three unexcused absences and had come back three minutes late from break. That was a violation of probationary attendance rules, whatever they really were. But why didn't they fire him in February if that was the reason?

Would the same thing have happened to a white man? My guess is that race mattered in terms of his brutal job assignment, his treatment by the nurses, and his negative performance evaluation, but also in the time and effort Max expended to show both Fred and me that he had something to offer black workers. He was willing to call in whatever chips Jake owed to secure his intervention. For Fred's part, he had been convinced that nothing much was going to come of our efforts. After being fired he tired of my crusade. I imagine that his hand healed once he got out of the plant.

A monotonous list of small indignities marked the experience of black workers at IBP. Petty harassment occurred daily, and I never saw a supervisor defend the rights of a black worker. One black man was promoted to trainer before I left, but basically black workers were out of the promotion loop. Equal employment laws and some popular education on race issues doubtless stemmed some overt discrimination. Any one of the small irritations would not in itself necessarily indicate prejudice. Everyone gets a few bad calls from time to time, but for black workers the grinding predictability of the bad calls shot the odds.

ROBERTO

Clyde was having a tantrum on the belly line. Pork bellies, rectangular slabs about three inches thick, were weighed and sorted for bacon or rejected and sent through the skinner and from there down a whizard line where the lean meat was robbed, the fat cut off, and any remaining skin conveyed to a combo. Unlike my teat line job, the belly whizards had to keep up with the meat as it moved by them. The whizard was a terrible job, but a row of anonymous Latino men worked away at it. It was not a job for long-term workers. When quality control found skin in the fat tub, it was unpleasant for everyone, not least Clyde, but the line speed was set upstairs. Clyde could put more whizards on the line, but what was the matter with these guys? He was up on the scaffolding carrying on while the workers were trying to work through the bellies as they came by. Most of what he said must have been unintelligible, but they could doubtless grasp the drift. Finally, Clyde threw up his hands. "I'm tired of hearing, 'I can't.' Get up to the cafeteria," he said to "Pedro," whose English was minimal.

Between breaks, the cafeteria was the woodshed. Pedro was going to be disciplined and possibly fired.

Next to native-born, white Iowans, the most numerous ethnic group in the plant was Latinos, and many of them worked in the cellar or the adjoining area of converting. Because my job allowed me to range around the cellar and even into a corner of converting, I spent quite a bit of time getting to know these recent arrivals to Iowa. Although most of them had similar coloring, small builds, and spoke little English, actually a great deal of diversity existed among them. The majority came most recently from East Los Angeles, but they included Mexicans, Salvadorans, and Nicaraguans. Some arrived in family units and hoped to make Iowa their home. Others were just passing through and sending much of their pay back to families south of the border. The few women usually lived in some form of family setting; many of the men shared living quarters with several other male workers.

Although the conditions these immigrants faced as Iowa workers were oppressive by midwestern Yankee standards, Latino workers did not necessarily assess them in the same way. Recent scholarship on Latino immigrants in the United States has moved away from a victimization model toward a discussion of agency. A survey of the service needs of Mexican immigrant women in Marshalltown, Iowa, another packing town that has seen a rapid increase in immigrant workers in the 1990s, found that the women did not define themselves as disadvantaged. They saw themselves as having taken a decisive step toward a better life. Similarly, a study of a Latino immigrant organizing project in California discovered that recent immigrants believed that they had found their economic niche in the United States by doing jobs that Yankee workers would not do for the same wages. For them, perhaps, it was not a question of whether they would be under Yankee domination; it was a question of whether they would experience this domination in Latin America or in the United States. Latino immigrants might simultaneously improve their condition and experience exploitation; they focused on the improvement rather than the exploitation. Conditions that seemed appalling to me, as a middle-class Yankee, might not have seemed as appalling to those who had had no prior expectation of niceness.[60]

"Roberto Salinas" was born into a rural family in 1950 in Mexicali, just south of the Mexican border in Baja California. By the age of six he was milking and herding his family's cows, but his golden memories of growing up in Mexico are of ranging out on the arid plains, of fishing and swimming in a stream that went by his house, and of hunting and roasting rabbits for meals. He had a cohort of about thirty male cousins and brothers, and they were welcome in each others' households as well as in their grandmother's home.

In 1963, when Roberto was thirteen, his mother died, leaving his father with ten children. Roberto was the oldest. His father, unable to continue his marginal farming operation, took Roberto and the next oldest son, "Reynaldo," north to California to try to make a living. The plan was to send for the rest of the children when the father and two oldest sons were established.

Roberto and Reynaldo had attended a crowded, one-room Mexican school sporadically. Although they enrolled in a California high school for a short time in 1964, not knowing the language or the culture and never having been in a graded school system, they did not catch hold. The boys lived with their father in a room without furniture and caught and roasted squirrels outdoors in order to eat. Soon they were following the crops up and down the coast. Later they connected with Cesar Chavez's United Farm Workers. Roberto helped organize tomato harvesters, and the family earnings rose. More of his siblings were able to join the household. The father remarried and settled in Los Angeles, adding a stepmother and later three half sisters to Roberto's family circle.

In Los Angeles, Roberto shifted from farm labor to making his living in the informal economy. For a time he had a waged job as a groundskeeper at an Air Force base, but in general he was on the street. He dealt in drugs and transported different kinds of goods back and forth across the border; he brokered various services. Over the years he acknowledged and contributed to the support of four sons born to three women, but his closest family ties were in the households of his father and siblings in California and in those of a sister and his grandmother, who remained in Mexico. He became bilingual and acquired rudimentary English reading and writing skills.

In 1989, hard pressed from different directions, he entered a Comprehensive Employment Training program that held out the hope of a general equivalency diploma (GED) as well as training in computers, typing, welding, and forklift operation. The program also offered help in finding a job. The main attraction of the training was the hope of a GED and a job, neither of which actually materialized.

In July 1990 he and some of his classmates saw an advertisement in a Los Angeles newspaper for IBP production workers in Perry, Iowa. The IBP officials who had set up a recruiting station in Los Angeles had a Spanish language video that pictured peaceful, rural Iowa with woods, rivers, and affordable housing. It said IBP had good-paying jobs with fine opportunities for advancement. The company would hire people on the spot and would pay for bus tickets to Iowa plus two weeks of lodging at a Perry motel. Roberto applied for a job, passed a physical examination in California, and became an IBP employee. A group of Latino hires traveled by bus to Des Moines, where "Archie," the orientation leader, met them and transported them to Perry. Roberto recalled that when he arrived in August and saw the Raccoon River running west of the plant, it was a flashback to his happy days in Mexico. He wanted to sink his roots in Iowa.

He was soon rooming with "Damiana," a Salvadoran woman who was in the job training program and rode the same bus to Iowa. She had three daughters with her and she also worked in the plant. Roberto, being older and more experienced than most of the other Latino workers, served informally as translator and helped others adjust to their jobs and to the new territory.

The number of Latino workers in the Perry plant grew rapidly. Most of them worked on the line; some were part of the overnight cleaning crew. Roberto started on the line but was promoted to forklift driver in converting. Except for Ricardo, who worked in management, Roberto had the best IBP job of any of the Latinos at the time I started at IBP. His job involved carting combos of whole hams to keep the ham boning line supplied and hauling away boneless ham from the end of the line to the scale and then to storage.

The majority of the new arrivals found housing in Des Moines and rode the IBP bus each morning and evening.[61] Roberto and Damiana, among the few who found housing in Perry, lived together off and on for about a year. In January 1992, depressed by some of Roberto's habits, Damiana broke her ties with him, loading up her children and as much else as she could in his car, which she took back to California. Roberto was living in a Perry apartment with Francisco, my fellow janitor in converting, when I got to know them both through the proximity of our work. Within a few weeks Roberto and Francisco had a falling out, as another Salvadoran woman moved into the apartment with Roberto.

Roberto kept his contacts with his California and Mexican relatives by frequent telephone calls and by making trips back to see them every few months. Returning to Iowa, he brought Mexican food, clothing, cassette tapes, and art objects, which he traded within the local Latino community. He also sent money and gifts, including a guitar and a computer, to his sons in California. Reynaldo, his California brother, advanced him money when he was low, and Roberto in return brought back Reynaldo's son and helped him find jobs and enroll in an Iowa college.

The company was flexible in accommodating the habits of some Latinos. Roberto's side trips nurtured an ongoing network of exchange involving both information and goods between Perry and southern California and Mexico. Other Latinos took time off for family affairs or took advantage of time off through injuries to return to their homes. In this respect, some of them counted on being exceptions to IBP's draconian attendance policies, which allowed no time off in the first year of work. But this varied. Roberto would take ten days to two weeks off when he needed some downtime, but Francisco was fired for missing only a few days of work. Unlike some others, Damiana was unable to reclaim her job at IBP when she returned from California the following year. (When I checked IBP's rehire policy, I learned that it varied from day to day; it just depended.)

Roberto helped to recruit other Latinos to work at IBP, and this may have given him some leeway in bending the attendance rules for himself. My guess is that Roberto's attendance privileges were related to at least two additional factors. First, IBP perceived him to be a leader among the Latinos and therefore cultivated his good graces. Second, he had caught onto how to unobtrusively juggle the ham supply and weighing system so that it appeared that the ham boning line was producing a great quantity of boneless ham in relation to the weight of the whole hams fed into the line. This boosted the performance statistics of the general supervisor in converting, who observed that the ham line always seemed to work more efficiently when Roberto was present. That the inflated boning ratios simultaneously played havoc with cut floor numbers was someone else's problem.

With exceptions such as Roberto, the low-paid, silent Latino workers seemed interchangeable in the plant. Their names baffled the supervisors. One of the Latino men regularly slipped out of the plant at the time of the daily changeover from sows to butchers. He returned to clock out with the other workers, and apparently his supervisor did not miss him or assumed that he was assigned to another work area at that time.

The firings and injury layoffs functioned to expand Latino social and economic networks. Roberto's trips to California and Mexico also circulated information and goods. After being fired, Francisco was able to locate a job as a waiter in North Carolina through an informal Latino network. After he left, he telephoned back, giving news of the kinds of jobs and living conditions available there. When Damiana was unable to get back on at IBP, she found a job at the Monfort meatpacking plant in Des Moines and from there moved into another factory job, providing a model and contacts for other Perry Latinos to move away from IBP. The company itself took advantage of these networks when it skirted Iowa's recruiting law by ceasing to do direct recruiting of workers in Los Angeles, instead paying existing Latino workers $150 for each worker successfully recruited.[62]

Increasing numbers of Latinos are appearing in Perry schools, a solid indication that more families are coming. Damiana's family is one piece of the widening breadth of Latino kinship networks in Iowa. Her extended Iowa family now includes her sister and brother and their spouses and children, two of her own four children, and four grandchildren, together with another male partner whom she brought with her when she returned. Her family celebrations now take place in Perry.

Roberto also has members of his California family in and out of his household as they look for jobs and educational opportunities in Iowa. In addition, he now has three Iowa-born sons.

Some Perry churches have reached out to the Latino population, including one that sponsors a Hispanic ministry. The Catholic Church has begun a Spanish language service. Yet Latinos have been slow to warm to the overtures. They have not gravitated to the churches, nor do they trust the union. According to my reports, Latino union membership has actually declined since the first months of their arrival.

The Latino population itself has been rent with ethnic and personal factions. Low IBP incomes compound community problems of drugs, alcohol, and domestic abuse. Moreover, Perry Latinos do not mix well with other Latino immigrants in Iowa. Because many other newcomers come from the predominantly interior rural areas around the Texas border, a marked cultural gap divides them and the ex-Californians with urban experiences.

Leaving the warmth and familiarity of their homes to work in a cold and strange setting lay a thick and heavy blanket of sadness on Latino immigrants. But the sadness—profound and powerful as it was—did not necessarily define them. Although I have tended to focus on the injustice experienced by Latinos at IBP in Perry, most of them have resisted any representation of themselves as victims. Many believed they were doing well. I should have paid more attention when the first Mexican worker I met in the waiting room at IBP asserted that IBP meant good money and that he preferred going to work to staying home. Latinos who came to Iowa understood discrimination. They knew that their attraction to IBP was their willingness to do jobs under conditions that Yankees would not accept. The Latino persons I met through my IBP connection accepted the money I occasionally advanced; they continued to solicit my help in a myriad of ways in regard to housing, children, jobs, medical services, and legal problems. Yet, at least until the latter months of 1996, they have resisted an overtly confrontive approach to righting the wrongs against them. They have been making their lives in Iowa their way.

LOWELL AND TOM

Like the other ethnic groups in the IBP plant, the Yankee workers were a diverse lot. They included those with years of work in the Oscar Mayer plant, young persons just out of area high schools, and a range of singletons like me who came to the plant through various idiosyncratic routes. Only a minority lived in Perry; the majority of us were scattered across the countryside in old farmhouses or in tiny towns such as Rippey, where "Annie" lived. The Loft, the bar next to the plant, was as much a social center for white IBP workers as existed anywhere, but some never entered it.

Most white workers were aware of the low status generally accorded to meatpacking workers, and few intersected with middle-class churches or organizations in the community outside the plant. Yet within the body of IBP workers, we were privileged, and we knew it. When "Tom," one of my white coworkers, was musing over his work and his life prospects after leaving IBP, he said, "I want a white man's job." This meant a job with decent pay and decent hours of work, a job that would not destroy his health but would leave him with enough time, energy, and money to pursue a life outside of his work. Not all IBP jobs were "white man's jobs," but his had been.

The union was not limited to white workers, and not all white workers were members, but its local leadership and the majority of its members were white. It was attempting to include Latino and black workers. Never did I stand in higher esteem with Max, the local president, than when I brought persons of color into the union office. Yet the union was ambivalent with respect to the prospect of giving up white privilege in exchange for a broader and more united collective voice. It was only in the 1990s that significant numbers of Latino, black, and Asian American workers came into the Perry plant. Although the old United Packinghouse Workers of America had intervened forcefully to break down racial barriers in packing plants and communities in the 1950s and 1960s, this had not impinged as directly on the rural, predominantly white workforce of Perry in the 1960s as did the sudden racial transformation of the 1990s. Many white workers were cynical and negative toward union leaders who had overseen the sharp drop in wages in the 1980s, but they were not ready to withdraw from the union completely.

Lowell, who helped Chang get his finger cared for, maintained a burning hope that workers would rise together against IBP. Yet he was a loner. An intense leftist who rode the bus from Des Moines, Lowell had few, if any, friends in the plant; Pete teased me when he heard that I ate lunch with him. Lowell was on the job only a short time before I came. Like me, he tried to work for better conditions through the union. Although he was one of the few workers interested in the union and was later appointed a steward, Max considered him a pain. He left the plant not long after I did, and no one seems to have kept in touch with him.

Tom, on the other hand, had been a longtime Oscar worker as well as an IBP employee. A union officer, he was highly respected by almost everyone. He believed that a broadly representative union would benefit all IBP workers, and he encouraged Latino participation in particular. As Tom mulled the prospect of running for union president against Max, he was abruptly fired, in spite of having a long-term, excellent work record. Although Max filed a grievance on his behalf, the union's support for Tom stopped with a formal minimum. Tom had been in maintenance and I had known him only by reputation when I worked in the plant, but he called me after he was fired and we got to know each other then. He and I pursued legal options after his grievance was dismissed, but Max turned against him and enlisted the support of the international union hierarchy. When the union and IBP stood together on something, it was hard to contest, and Tom and I were nearly past the statutory time limit when we started to press the issue.

Notwithstanding the individual efforts of workers such as Lowell and Tom, I found no organized movement among white workers to end discrimination in the plant. Max tried to get Roberto to work for him, taking him to Des Moines to meet with union officials in a plush downtown hotel and promising him the use of a car and a cash payment for each worker that he would sign up. But Max conceived the issue in terms of full plant representation rather than racial or ethnic justice. In fact, contrary to Max's assumption, Roberto had no power to deliver Latino workers to the union, and he knew that other Latinos would not buy what Max was selling. Roberto himself lost status with other Latino workers when they perceived that he was conspiring with Max.

Most Iowa-born meatpacking workers nursed an underlying resentment of the newcomers who appeared with the structural changes in the industry. "John Kramer," a union president before Max was appointed, articulated the dominant viewpoint:

> They (IBP) say they can't get workers. . . . That's bullshit. All they got to do is pay them decent money and treat them right. They can get all they want, but they want these people that can't read and write that they can take advantage of, that they can monopolize. They can do anything they want with them. . . .
>
> I think it's pretty pathetic when we got a border down there. When you go to Switzerland to go to work you got to get out in six months or a year and you can't come back in for like thirty days or sixty days or something. You never get any citizenship or nothing. You got to protect your own economy. You got to protect your own people. I mean, I got feelings for these people down there, too; but, you understand, can we take them all to raise? Can we take the whole world to raise? We got a problem.

Midwestern Yankees are diverse in their perspectives. Although opposing opinions surfaced, John Kramer's attitude was the rule. Without accepting his suggestion of turning back the newcomers, I can nevertheless concur that "we [read native-born white Iowans] got a problem."

The power of the 1990 law protecting non–English-speaking workers is compromised by the fact that having an interpreter in a large plant does not mean that the interpreter is available when needed. Although many Latinos worked in the cellar, I never saw the interpreter there helping workers understand their jobs or communicate with their supervisor. Nor do the majority of non-English speakers fully understand IBP's obligations to them.

After I left the plant a worker brought me news of an accident. "Dolores," a Salvadoran woman who spoke no English, had been transferred to the cut floor and put to work. Unable to fully comprehend the finer details and dangers of the new job, she caught her right hand in a machine after working there only about ten minutes. Her supervisor was not there at the time, and no one in the area could understand Spanish. They did not realize what was happening or that they needed to turn off the machine. It was drawing her into it before she was able to extricate her hand, ripping off her third and fourth fingers and part of her little finger and bruising the side of her body where she fought with the machine. Clutching her hand, Dolores walked to the dispensary, where the nurses took charge and transported her to a hospital in Des Moines. Heavily sedated, she was back on the job, minus part of her right hand, in four and a half days. Max advised her to wait and see what IBP planned to do before she took any action.

Yankee whiteness has carried privilege since the early period of white settlement, although it has not been monolithic. Whereas southern and eastern European immigrants once stood with a very few Latino and black individuals outside the bounds of the chosen whites in rural Iowa, European immigrants no longer fill out the ranks of the lowest-paid wage workers. Asian American, Latino, and black workers, together with a minority of whites, have become the core of the modern low-wage rural meatpacking workforce. The specificity of each group's condition with respect to citizenship, language, education, and cultural capital assigns them to different niches, making a fragmented and often internally conflicted rural working class.

Any effective mobilization of workers will have to confront the ethnic inequality that is deeply ingrained in rural Iowa. Research done in California indicates that the longer Latino immigrants live in the United States, the more extensive their social networks and the less likely they are to accept the economic crumbs.[63] Other newcomers may also become more assertive as time seasons them. This offers hope that is currently hard to find in the actions of the UFCW as a union. Labor organizing spanning ethnic boundaries will occur only if those who are involved look race and ethnicity squarely in the face. Consideration of the history of whiteness within Iowa's working class will be integral to the effort, but it will be only a part of the whole.

5

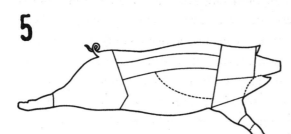

HEY! YOU GUYS ARE NOT ENTITLED

THE WORKINGS OF CLASS

At the 1991 U.S. Senate Hearing on Concentration in the Meatpacking Industry, a representative of the Western Organization of Resource Councils warned that powerful meatpacking companies with oligopolistic control of livestock markets threatened to overwhelm independent livestock producers: "I do believe that there is a miracle in American agriculture and its free enterprise system, and its miracle is its independent producers. . . . *They are turning these people from farmers into workers*, and if you don't have management and motivation on a farm, people don't produce" (emphasis added).[1]

Wage labor was the consummate humiliation for farmers; no one at the hearing disputed the point. Its truth was grounded in the powerful agrarian writings of Thomas Jefferson, which have framed discourse on rural society since the founding of the country. Jefferson's frequently quoted paean to farmers, "Those who labor on the earth are the chosen people of God, if ever He has a chosen people," continues, "Dependence begets subservience and venality, suffocates the germ of virtue, . . . generally speaking, the proportion which the aggregate of the other classes of citizens bears in any State to that of its husbandmen, is the proportion of its unsound to its healthy parts, and is a good enough barometer whereby to measure its degree of corruption."[2] Jefferson believed that whereas independent craftsmen retained the virtues of the self-employed, those who sold their labor rather than their products weakened the social fiber. He later modified his abhorrence of hired workers to advocate a balanced economy, thereby avoiding dependence on European manufactures, but he continued to believe that farmers were inherently superior to all other people. Modern agrarians seldom even note his later acknowledgment of manufacturing labor as a necessary evil, nor do they ponder the irony in Jefferson's failure to confront squarely the reality of nonowner labor in agriculture.[3]

The agrarian vision of a society of small landowners denied class division, an ideal that persists to shape the modern image of rural life.[4] Most accounts of the rural Midwest have been about self-employed farmers; some have been about small-town business owners. Numerous studies exist on farm laborers in other regions of the United States, but ethnographic analyses of rural midwestern labor have appeared only recently. Theoretical discussions of class in the rural context rest on differences among farmers, especially the amount of land held and whether or not the farm employs nonfamily workers. The defining character of rural economic enterprises, that which sets them apart from urban industrial bureaucracies, is self-employment. Honest dirt under the fingernails of the owner distinguishes rural from urban businessmen. The dissonant presence of rural wage workers serves only to confuse the picture.[5]

Yet wage workers are solidly embedded in the fabric of rural midwestern life. Riverboatmen, railroad crews, miners, farm laborers, domestics, and construction workers of all kinds laid the groundwork for rural life.[6] They appear in the crannies of almost every account of the Midwest. Catherine McNicol Stock, writing about the old middle class in South Dakota in the 1930s, said that work was the defining characteristic of the rural middle class; not included in this account was an amorphous group of " 'common laborers,' tenant farmers, drunks, drifters, prostitutes, peddlers, troublemakers and other 'riff-raff' " — together with Indians.[7] These persons were present, but their presence was not as historically interesting as that of the individuals belonging to the middle class, who were the critical rural actors. In rural Iowa the nonowner working class encompassed the majority of the small black and Latino population as well.

As in Stock's book, wage workers appear most frequently in midwestern histories as incidental others rather than as the subjects of narratives on rural life. Curtis Harnack's memories of growing up in rural Iowa in the 1930s include a frank appraisal of the benign contempt in which his farm family held Barney, their hired hand: "We took his second-class status in our household as matter-of-factly as Southerners might regard Negro servants."[8] Barney did muscle work rather than brain work, smelled bad, chewed tobacco, used the outhouse rather than the toilet, never took a tub bath, and went to town to drink and court loose women on Saturday nights—all traits that fell outside the standards of Harnack's farm family. But Barney's labor was central to the maintenance of the family's middle-class patterns of life.

Harnack describes Barney with unusual detail and empathy, yet his retrospective sensitivity in itself requires him to respect the social and cultural distance between Barney and the family. This chapter is about the shape and control of this intervening distance as it existed in the 1930s between the Harnacks and Barney and as it was progressively reconfigured with the arrival of the corporations that dwarfed both Barney and the Harnack family. It is about class relations as formed and manifested in a continuing stream of events throughout each person's life. The ramifications of class are both deeply personal and overtly political.[9]

The virtue of family farming, the solid core of the rural middle class in agrarian ideology, has historically dominated the collective meaning of rural life. Accordingly, Osha Gray Davidson grounds his analysis of the disintegration of the fabric of rural Iowa in what has been called the "farm crisis" of the 1980s.[10] At this time many farmers were forced off their farms. But the trend toward larger farms through the forced departure of smaller operators has been continuous since the 1930s; it has occurred in times of high farm incomes and in time of low returns. The fixation on the farm situation intrudes on and denies the specificity of what rural wage workers have experienced both in the past and since the adjustments of the 1980s and 1990s. The positional integrity of rural labor has tended to disappear or be subsumed under that of farmers. Yet wage workers have maintained a perversely independent reality.

Defining ideology as "the collective production of shared moral meanings for the conduct of social life, critique, and change," Marc W. Steinberg describes the ways that dominant groups maintain power by controlling this construction of meaning and value.[11] Yet this control is rarely, if ever, complete. Differentiating their experience from that of the middle class, the working class of rural Iowa has developed distinct systems of knowledge about what a person could legitimately expect from the world and what guiding principles would be practical and appropriate to carry one through life. Countering the agrarian reality, workers' struggles have generated different claims over cultural definitions of meaning and value. These claims have arisen in the context of a history of social action that has continually crafted new lessons, that has continually revised workers' sense of agency. Ideology, as Steinberg theorizes it, cannot be reduced to discourse; it develops as a product of both discourse and action. The contours of class struggle emerge in the interface between the dominant framework and that developed by the working class. The conflict and contradiction between the divergent constructs carve out a field of struggle on the boundaries, a space where competing claims to legitimacy are matched against each other. In rural Iowa, the dominant agrarian worldview and the distinct patterns of logic of the working class have formed a counterpoint, sometimes harmonious and sometimes dissonant, that reflects the accommodations and the tensions creating a historical narrative.[12]

Corporations like IBP have introduced a new dimension to class relations in rural Iowa. June Nash, in her study of the electrical industry in Pittsfield, Massachusetts, describes a process by which corporations have weakened the social contract between themselves and the communities in which they are located. Rural communities have been even less prepared than cities to require that large corporations pay their own way and contribute to the general well-being of the community. In fact, as David Griffith has demonstrated, the well-being of a rural community may be inversely related to the success of its major corporate employer. Increasingly since 1980, values and meanings that would oppose those of dominant corporations have been fragmented and silenced. Large corporations and their profits have become synonymous with progress and inevitability. Opposing voices have been forced into ridiculous positions, while the giants have controlled the fertile rhetorical ground.[13]

The rural working class has historically been more ethnically diverse than has the farming class, and neither the self-employed middle class nor the class of corporate capitalists has undergone anything like the recent explosion of ethnic diversity that has occurred among rural Iowa wage workers. Even though the rural working class has not produced a coherent ideology, even though the ideological shape of the emerging working class remains diffuse and diverse, it is time to begin to delineate these voices and to counterpose their evolving worldviews with those of the elite. Because of their different histories, rural wage laborers have negotiated every historical development in a different spirit from that of farmers and businessmen.

CLASS DIVISION IN PERRY BEFORE IBP

The Perry Daily Chief expressed a strikingly consistent view of class relations from World War I through the 1960s.[14] Like most small town Iowa newspapers, it supported the Republican Party and the free market. A booster of local economic development, the voice of the Perry press sought smooth, amicable relations between capital and labor. It encouraged local businessmen to act with benevolence and generosity toward their workers. With a strong preference toward locals over outsiders, the Chief even supported railroad workers over the distant Milwaukee management during the strike of 1922. The worst villains, however, were outside labor agitators, foreigners to the local scene who lurked in the wings waiting for their chance to disturb the good order of the town. In different eras these agitators materialized as immigrants, eastern Europeans, Bolsheviks, the International Workers of the World (IWW), socialists, New Dealers, the CIO, communists, or the United Packinghouse Workers of America (UPWA).[15]

Overseeing the smooth running of the town, the Chief assumed a fatherly tone, calling forth local workers' loyalty and good behavior. Each Labor Day the paper affirmed its high regard for workers in a front-page statement and picture, praising them for their steadfastness in fulfilling their appointed roles. In 1927 the statement supported laborers while attacking labor organizers: "American laboring men are not greatly concerned with the old-world shibboleths. Such phrases as 'class consciousness' have little meaning here. . . . This gives our European friends much pain. To them, American labor is 'fifty years behind the times.' . . . But there is another way of looking at it. Isn't is possible that American labor, instead of being fifty years behind the times, is fifty years ahead? . . . And so it is that the very calm way in which American labor greets Labor Day is, after all, the most significant thing about the whole occasion." [16]

The *Chief* excoriated socialist Eugene V. Debs at his death in 1926, charging that he brought violence rather than peace to workers.[17] In the same year the newspaper could favorably observe the rise of Benito Mussolini in Italy, an event that brought forward "the dream of the perfect Fascist state, with capital and labor working in cooperation for the common welfare." With Mussolini, "the constructive role of organizing the masses of Italy for smoother and intensified productivity has begun." [18]

The opposition of the *Chief* to organized labor intensified with the New Deal and the 1935 Wagner Act, which protected the right of workers to organize. The Labor Day message of 1935 pleaded for sanity and tolerance: Everyone should consider the needs of the community as a whole. Capital and labor were "Siamese twins" that had no choice but to work through their differences in a spirit of cooperation. Supporting the 1936 presidential candidacy of Alf Landon, the *Chief* claimed that he stood up for labor by opposing unions. Labor would have a strong voice, but only if it operated in the framework of existing political institutions. A Labor Party or a Farm-Labor Party would be a catastrophe.[19]

Meanwhile, the *Chief* carried regular stories of violence and disruption attributed to the labor movement and the communists declared to have taken it over. With the reality of 1930s eruptions of labor agitation, the paper championed the cause of the AFL in opposition to the radical CIO. The CIO's Packinghouse Worker Organizing Committee (PWOC), which organized meatpackers and called strikes against Morrell in Ottumwa and Armour in Sioux City, appeared repeatedly as a force that would pull people out of their jobs and destroy the threads of security and independence that workers and employers together were weaving. Moreover, the expense of putting down strike violence drained public coffers, diverting money that was needed for economic recovery during the depression.[20]

Although the press could praise the smooth and harmonious industrial life of the Perry community, the experience was anything but smooth and harmonious for the workers. "Abe Mohr," who lived in and around Perry during the interwar years, observed labor relations from the perspective of a worker. No one in Perry purchased a daily newspaper to read his words, and he did not speak in the abstract and authoritative style of the newspaper editor. Nor did he necessarily disagree with it. Interviewed in 1993, he drew on a different reality that spoke to different material questions and different concerns about relations between workers and employers.

Born in rural Iowa in 1913, Abe moved to Perry as the young son of a Scottish railroad worker. His life with his parents was short: at age seven he left them to live in the Perry home of his widowed grandmother. Of his parents, Abe said, "I couldn't get along with them. My folks had no use for me whatsoever. . . . I left there and never went back." He finished eight years of school before quitting: "I just didn't care to go to school. I don't know. There was nothing there for me as far as the foreseeable future." As a young teenager in the late 1920s he worked for a grocer, making from ten to twelve dollars a week.

Although the wages of a 1920s grocery boy were low by the standards of the 1920s, they were generous within the economic context of the 1930s. When Abe was seventeen he married a young domestic worker who was one of eleven children reared on a small, poorly run farm. He, his young wife, and a baby moved to a farm after securing employment as hired laborers in 1930:

Working on the farm, my wife and I, I got twenty-five dollars a month.

(DF [Deborah Fink]: You still remember after all these years!)

Gracious yes, when you work as hard as I did! . . . You was up in the morning at about five o'clock. You went to the barn, did the chores— fed the hogs and milked the cows, harnessed the horse, got ready to go to the field. Then you'd come back in, eat breakfast. You was in the field by eight in the morning. You disked, harrowed or plowed for corn or whatever it was. Those days when there wasn't anything to do you hauled manure out.

This work lasted from the early morning until late at night. His wife, in addition to the care of their baby, did housework and chores for the farm owners.

Work in town was preferable. It was easier and generally better paying than farm work, although there were food and housing expenses in town that they didn't have while living on the farm. Town work also had the advantage of freedom from the continuing direct control of the employers. Abe recalled applying for a job at the Perry packinghouse: "Out to the old packinghouse, when the word got out that they was going to hire, there must have been six- seven hundred men out there waiting for a job. . . . I wanted a job so bad I was the first one up there and I was the first one that they hired. . . . I think there was ten or twelve hired that day."

Eighteen years old, Abe processed offal from the kill floor. He made eighteen dollars a week, working from 7:00 A.M. to 5:00 P.M. from Monday through Saturday. Recalling their household economy during the packinghouse years, Abe described meager living arrangements and the birth of their third child:

> I had to give three dollars a month for a house that had no toilet, had the outside privy, no water in the house, no heat, no lights, no nothing. . . . You got by. . . .
>
> I walked from West Fifth Street clear out to the packinghouse (about two miles), couldn't even afford a car. [Here is why:] The third child was born then. I couldn't pay the doctor bill. It was twenty-five dollars. I told Dr. Connally, "the only thing I could do is to give you my car." So I gave him my car and then I walked to the packinghouse.

After several years of packinghouse work, he quit or was laid off: "I got to the place where I just couldn't hack it. . . . Fact is, when I quit out there it took three guys to run the operation and they never did have a good batch of tankage. . . . Man, you worked! They didn't have a union."

In 1936, at age twenty-three, Abe made his first "student run" with the railroad, but this was an irregular source of income. He talked about the multiple jobs he took after leaving the packinghouse:

I went down to the fairgrounds and picked up lumber and built a leanto. . . . I went out to the old railroad yards there and they had two by sixes out of flatcars that they was tearing up and I got them and with them I built the garage over there. Then I put an ad in the paper that I'd solder radiators. . . . I worked. I worked long and hard. There for a period of time—I forget just when it was, but . . . prior to World War II, I dug basements. I dug all but one basement around town for all the houses. . . . I did everything. . . . I went out and did wiring. When I didn't have a regular job I would wire houses. Or whatever there was to do. Paint or roof or anything. All that stuff.

Abe also did hauling in a truck that he bought for ten dollars down. His wife, with three young children, was apparently not earning wages at this time. They raised their own vegetables in a garden. He recalled that wages were so bad during the 1930s that it was not uncommon for workers to steal in order to survive.

Seeking and keeping work in itself was time-consuming and exacting. It was a continuous necessity:

At that time you didn't get no unemployment compensation. You didn't get nothing. You'd just have to work at anything you could get. . . . It was just tough. You had to hold onto the job you had. You had to give it a lot when there was somebody waiting, maybe as many as a half dozen people [waiting] for the job. . . .

There wasn't enough wages, but you didn't stop and think about that. You just had to work and work and work. . . .

It didn't come to you. You had to go after it. I was fortunate in getting a good name—that I would work. I would come when they called me. I would show up. That was very important. . . . Today, people don't go to work if they're sick. They call in for sick leave or something like that. Then, you just didn't do it. You either went to work or you looked for another job.

When Abe was able to get steady work on the Milwaukee Railroad, the pay was better, but he had sixteen-hour workdays. He eased into steady railroad employment as World War II loosened the job market, but not too long after his regular railroad job began an accident broke both of his legs, leaving him in excruciating pain. Unable to return to his job after being sidelined for a lengthy convalescence, he received a retirement sum. Although he did not recall the amount, he said that the railroad took in a lot of money; it was reasonable to expect it to pay out when someone was hurt.

At some point Abe's wife divorced him. He was seldom home, he explained, and she would "badmouth" him: "You'd just lose them. That's all. You'd lose your family. . . . There was a lot of it. I saw a lot of families break up. I loved them very dearly and wanted to spend as much time as I could [with them]. Working on the railroad, you didn't have no time. . . . I would come home, I heard my wife screaming at the children, 'You wait 'til your dad gets home and you'll get a beating!' Well, what kid wants to see their dad come home?"

The need to earn money drove Abe's young life, and he apparently became the pliant and cooperative worker that the editor of the *Chief* would have applauded, except that he would not have known Abe personally. They had disjoint social circles. After World War II, with his settlement from the railroad, Abe was able to outfit himself to make a more comfortable living doing a variety of indispensable mechanical jobs around town.

THE RURAL FACTOR

As indicated in Abe's narrative, Iowa farmers both complemented the packinghouse hiring schedule and competed with the packing industry. In the nineteenth century, meatpacking provided off-season work for farm laborers. Pigs were usually killed and processed in cold weather after the corn harvest was completed, and porkpacking tapered off in the spring as the weather grew warm, leaving workers free for planting. Seasonality in porkpacking persists to some degree in the present, but it was more pronounced in the 1930s, and workers were more likely to spend part of the year on farms and part of the year in packinghouses.[21] Yet farm labor, as Abe Mohr knew, was notoriously low paying and intense. Jarvis Hiles, who did farm labor in the 1930s and later became a railroad and meatpacking worker, stated, "After working on the farm for a dollar a day for sixteen hours a day, you can believe it wasn't hard to make a union man out of me." [22] Abe and his wife together actually made less than a dollar a day on the farm.

Rising wages for packing work would put pressure on farm wages, and farmers as a group did not support union efforts. Neither Abe Mohr nor the *Chief* provides evidence of meatpacking union activity in Perry in the 1930s. Organizing in the small and isolated plant may have been too costly for the limited available resources, or there may have been an unsuccessful effort that I have not discovered. Even with formal legal protection for union organizing, justifiable fear of employers' political and economic power remained, and organizing was a financially strapped, uphill struggle. But PWOC was aggressively organizing in the larger Iowa packing plants. There workers heard a rebuttal to the conservative rural text, a rebuttal grounded in the reality of their daily experience. Those won over by the union movement spoke with clarity about their perceptions of working conditions and about the political economy of rural Iowa.

Unionists with family farm backgrounds had to overcome a primal distaste for labor organization. Willys Stearns, a packer and the son of an Iowa homesteader, identified this antipathy as he told of signing on as a union member while working at the Tobin plant in Estherville: "I joined the union June 6, 1939. I was kind of leery of the CIO. Being a farmer, I didn't know much about labor organizations, and they was kind of radical." [23] Nadine Klaner, born into an Iowa farm family in 1932, articulated a similar association of farmers and union opposition: "Of course, my father being a farmer, he was a nonunion man. In fact, I think he was a Republican. I was always taught in prior years that we didn't need unions, and all they did was strike [for] higher wages. That's all I ever knew about unions when I was growing up." [24] Conversely, Velma Otterman, who went to work at the Waterloo Rath plant in 1927, traced her union politics to her father's stance as a Democrat and a unionist. [25]

Animosity between farm people and union members arose when farmers and farm laborers scabbed during strikes. Wilson Warren's comprehensive study of labor organizing in the Morrell plant in Ottumwa draws a clear picture of the division between plant workers who were solidly behind the union and farm people who later edged into plant work and weakened the union. Many Morrell workers came from the farms and mines of southeastern Iowa, and Warren believed it was the union experience of the miners that originally won over the anti-unionism of those from farms. Jeanette Haymond, who worked in the Wilson plant in Cedar Rapids in the 1930s, also identified rural people and farmers as scabs. Unfortunately, the descriptions of farm persons as scabs seldom specify whether they were farm laborers or self-employed farmers. If they were self-employed farmers, they were probably economically precarious or they would not have resorted to wage labor, but during the 1930s this would have included most Iowa farmers. However, those who had realistic expectations of independent farm operations in the future would logically have been less likely to make the short-term sacrifice for future improvement in packinghouse jobs and more likely to settle for whatever they could get to tide them over the short run.[26]

Rural Iowans' general antipathy toward unions hit me in the face when I was doing fieldwork in northwestern Iowa in 1982. I escaped one afternoon to spend a few hours shooting the breeze with UFCW officials and Wilson meatpacking workers in a restaurant in Cherokee.[27] That evening, flush with union spirit, I joined a group of women for dinner at a friend's home in a nearby town. While there, a hospital worker took advantage of dinner, drinks, and friends to vent the miseries of her job. After a lengthy rendition she flicked my switch by ending with, "We need a union!" I then joined in too readily with a proposal to put her in touch with union organizers who would help her. She backed off at once. Rather than let the subject die, I pressed on until she finally shook her head and set her jaw in a clinch that I recognized as "stop."

The next morning I walked into a group of persons at a small business open house and met ice cold silence. Remaining only a short time, I managed to latch onto the friend in whose home I had eaten the evening before. We left together. Through her, I discovered that in less than twenty-four hours my indiscreet union talk had spread through the town. I was branded a "troublemaker" who had come to unionize the hospital workers. The word came back to me repeatedly during the year. I could not imagine a more visceral reaction if I had arrived to sell cocaine. A farmer who now and then talked over life, death, and books with me while I was in the field reflected that among farmers, including himself, being in favor of unions or being a Democrat was seen as "not quite decent."

Although not all modern farmers have subscribed to the traditional antipathy toward labor unions, it remains a continuing factor in rural politics. Gaylen Klinker, employed at the Cherokee Wilson plant, explained his conversion from farm boy to union activist: "Due to my bringing up, born and raised on a farm and everything, my own personal feeling was that I didn't think unions was necessary, you know. I couldn't figure out why a person would have to have a job and pay union dues and things like that. But after I got in the packinghouse I could see where somebody had to have a voice in there for you, because there was just no way you was going to make it without."[28] Union workers interviewed for the Iowa Labor History Oral Project repeatedly articulated this lack of fit between the anti-union mindset of the farm population and the union experiences of workers. Although the AFL-CIO helped with the organization of the National Farmers Organization (NFO) at the time of the steep drop in hog prices in 1956, close cooperation between the two organizations was brief. Farm-labor committees organized within the packing unions had scattered success when a dominant person bridged the divide, but overall farm and labor politics in Iowa have been separate. Describing farm-labor coalitions in the Midwest, Daniel Nelson wrote, "Local farmer-laborer parties were in reality disguised labor parties. They were short-lived and inconsequential."[29]

In 1982 flippant remarks about unions elicited passive aggression that can never be taken lightly in the context of a rural community. A genuine movement to mass and direct the power of rural workers has historically evoked stronger measures. In Estherville, where PWOC was organizing the Kingan plant in 1938, workers saw class conflict in the hostility of townspeople who used shotguns and pitchforks to run union organizers out of town.[30]

Why were the Estherville townspeople, like so many across the state of Iowa, violently opposed to the union? According to Barney Hassel, a packing worker, "They was scared to death of it. They was afraid it was going to get in here and just run the town. The union was going to run the town. That's what it was. Scared to death of it. . . . The guy that run the paper, . . . he had my picture in the paper. He smeared it all over the paper. I was a radical and all this and that."[31]

Town fathers were no friends of organized labor by any measure. Yet rural town settings provided more fertile ground for labor than did dispersed farm settlement. Even small neighborhoods of workers nurtured solidarity. Wilson Warren's study of Morrell organizing in Ottumwa brought out the significance of the clustering of almost two-thirds of packinghouse workers' housing in the shadow of the Morrell plant. Here, working-class families could see their own condition reflected in that of their neighbors, thereby giving them a deeper understanding of the social as well as the personal contingencies shaping their lives as workers. In addition, the town was small enough so that they could observe the living standards of plant managers and reflect on the grounds for this difference. The large size of the Morrell plant in the relatively small city presented dilemmas for organizers, but also for plant managers needing to hire workers.[32]

Unions represented a destabilizing force in the small-town economy. Workers, if they accepted the union message, saw the possibility of improvement; farmers and other businessmen saw the possibility of losing the predictable labor supply to which they were entitled. If they saw a need for change they—and not the union outsiders—would make the change. If they did not see any need for change, then workers ought to be satisfied as well.

CLASS FORMATION IN SCHOOL

Notwithstanding the occasional dramatically pitched confrontation, class generally manifested itself in subtle ways in rural Iowa. As persons matured and learned the accepted cultural patterns, class differences would blend with the social landscape, becoming simply the shape of neighborhood life. Children and youths, more than adults, were inclined to articulate class divisions, as they were in the process of discovering and internalizing the rules of social stratification. In 1923 Ethel Minor, a Perry high school student, won five dollars from the Rotary Club for her essay titled "Why Continue My Education." In this winning essay she expressed class division with charmingly simple candor:

The other night as I was going home from school I saw an old man, bent by age and toil returning home from work. He was dirty and greasy and an expression of weariness and dis-content was on his face. It looked pitiful for one so old, who should be enjoying a little comfort now for the few remaining years of his life to have to work so hard. Then a large car drove by, a doctor at the wheel. Age adds dignity to him and we respect him because of his gray hair, for we know that he increases his knowledge as the years go by. Education enables him to have, not only every comfort of life, but it gives him the privilege of helping thousands of people. The difference between these two men is education.[33]

Her belief that class division rested on education rather than wealth reflects a Yankee emphasis on individual effort, an emphasis that dismissed the reality of unequal access to public education.

Public schools culled students by social class, a fact that working-class youths could not escape and middle-class youths could not confront. Even those working-class students who showed aptitude for learning in their early years frequently faded away from school as they realized how different their lives were from those of students whose classroom experiences progressively mirrored and confirmed the lives of their parents and families. From the Fort Madison Mexican Village, for example, all of the families were working class, and students of all stripes and bents evoked an increasingly uniform response from their teachers as they matured into their accepted social roles as workers. Those who remained in school typically received vocational diplomas rather than regular high school graduation diplomas.[34]

Fidel Alvarez, born in Fort Madison in 1938, quit school in his early teens, although he later completed high school and went to college as an adult after becoming involved in government farmworker programs of the 1960s. In spite of an aptitude for learning, he had found no opening for an academic track when he was in primary school. He talked about his early decision to leave school:

I dropped out of the eighth grade. I didn't see any real future. When I entered high school one of the guidance counselors said to me, "No use in even talking to you because I know what you're gonna be doing. You're gonna be working for the railroad."

And I told him at that time, I said, "Me? I'm not gonna work in no railroad. I know what it's like working in the railroad." I said, "That's not for me."

And he says, "Na, all you people will end up working for the rail-road."

And I just walked out of there rather frustrated. So I dropped out of school because I didn't see any real future in there because everybody seemed to want to put you in a classification that I didn't agree with.[35]

Steering any young people toward work in the railroad industry when it was folding down all around them was pointless, and the Mexican heritage of Alvarez undoubtedly contributed to his perfunctory dismissal. But "Henry Wilson," an Anglo son of a Fort Madison railroad worker, lived close to the Mexican Village, went to the same school, and also experienced discrimination:

"Miss Long" used a paddle on me pretty regular when I was in third grade. Somehow or another she had me picked out. . . . Usually "Walter Comstock," the black guy, would be across the aisle some-place. And she would always say, "Walter! Henry! Into the cloak-room!" She'd whack you twice and send you back in there. . . . When you get twenty-five or thirty kids in there there's always a couple that the teacher really likes that can do no wrong and there's some that can do no right. . . .

(DF: Do you think working-class kids got hit more?)

Oh yes, that made a difference!

In Perry, "Betty Tice," the daughter of a divorced woman who supported her children with work in a poultry plant and with social welfare in the 1950s, recalled, "The teachers were very much for certain kids. . . . In fact, I had a teacher tell me I would never graduate . . . because I was from the other side of the tracks."

Yet Betty persevered and graduated, as did increasing numbers of working-class students like her. Higher wages, welfare checks, and the more frequent incidence of mothers rather than children earning wages enabled more households to support young people through their high school years. In addition, working-class persons' memories of public schools are laced with stories of a gentle teacher who gave a child a gift of a special book, a school counselor who provided the understanding and encouragement needed to keep an awkward and isolated adolescent in school, or a coach who stood up for the rights of his players. These individual gestures were critical in a number of cases.

Nevertheless, many teachers continued to maintain low expectations for working-class students. After World War II, college or university training was becoming a more salient class indicator than was high school, and working-class youths seldom even considered this step. Those working-class persons who did attend college are often moved to explain how they happened to deviate from the expected pattern rather than how their childhood prepared them for higher education. A woman whose mother worked in the Decker plant in Mason City described the reaction of high school teachers when she became a National Merit semifinalist in 1959: "[It] astounded all the high school teachers, mostly because of my family background. . . . Everybody else was the son or daughter of someone from the professional classes. How did this upstart, the daughter of a Decker worker, [score so high]? . . . I had this attitude about myself that I was an outsider. . . . Maybe they were putting me into this category, that I'd not be college bound, because of my working class background."

Some students refused to be sorted; others acceded temporarily or permanently to assigned slots. The GI Bill of 1944 helped to turn some working-class ex-soldiers toward the possibility of college. Henry Wilson returned home to Fort Madison without a job or a plan after a very short hitch in the army at the close of World War II. Recalling his decision to become a civil engineer, he said that a veterans' administration counselor encouraged him to consider not only college but also a major institution and an engineering program: "If it hadn't been for him, I don't think I'd even given [college] a thought."

This academic sorting was part of a complex, multifaceted social system that apparently seemed logical and natural to the majority of both working-class and middle-class persons. Yet working and middle class did not experience it in the same way; they did not view it from the same angle or at the same level of consciousness, nor did they have the same commitment to maintaining it. The nationwide meatpacking strikes of 1946 and 1948 occurred with high drama in some locations in Iowa (but not in Perry). Meatpacking was the largest sector of organized labor in Iowa, and a number of writers have discussed the importance of these actions in clarifying boundaries and defining the terms under which packing workers and companies would operate. But labor's movement was not uniform or comprehensive.[36]

PERRY WORKERS EMERGE

Class division, which had discreetly structured Perry society throughout the century, thrust itself into the open in the 1960s, when the UPWA moved into town to organize the workers of the Iowa Pork Company, a subsidiary of Iowa Beef Packers. The Iowa Pork Company, built in 1962, was the child of Perry Industries, a group of local businessmen operating in conjunction with the Iowa Development Commission. The Perry Daily Chief supported this development and articulated a vigorous protest when the UPWA appeared. The actions of the UPWA, in turn, shaped a counterpoint.[37]

As before, the Chief stressed themes of harmony and benevolence within the town and the dangers lurking as outside troublemakers tried to weasel into the simple minds of workers:

> About a year ago a group of Perry and Perry Community people got together with some experienced meat plant operations, and through a lot of hard effort and sacrifice they raised a million dollars to build the local Iowa Pork Company plant. These people wanted to create a place to give employment to local men and women. . . .
>
> Now there is another picture to present—the union organizers came to Perry. . . . They live well and seem to prosper well, and they have been telling many tales to the employees of the Perry pork plant. They have been reciting, I am informed many horrible stories and painting some other rosy pictures. . . .
>
> It seems to be just a simple question for the employee, and the stock holder. Do you want your job, and or do you want your stock to be safe and profitable or do you want big union control. The closed plants are proving that there can't be both the job and the big union.[38]

One of the workers, "John Kramer," had belonged to the UPWA as an Armour worker in Omaha in the 1950s. With a frank embrace of working-class status and an easy way with words, he helped to bring

UPWA organizers into the workers' fold. Unlike the old Swift plant, the Iowa Pork Company was expanding, allowing new union supporters to enter and creating a shortage of workers in the Perry area. The growing number of workers, the ready availability of jobs, and the vulnerability of the company as it constantly sought new hires all strengthened the union cause—but not sufficiently.

The union representation vote held in March 1963 resulted in the landslide election of the Dallas County Industrial Labor Union, a company-supported organization. The Chief editor was jubilant over the triumph of home rule and rejection of the "imported delegates" of the UPWA. [39]

However, once the UPWA came to town, union supporters among the workers had powerful allies in pressing their claims against the company and the local business community. In addition to the power of the UPWA, the National Labor Relations Board (NLRB), under the Democratic administration of President John F. Kennedy, provided critical support for the union cause in Perry. The UPWA immediately filed a protest with the NLRB over the March election, alleging that the company had held a mandatory employee meeting in which management stated that it would close the plant if the UPWA won, a threat also minuted at a stockholders' meeting. The NLRB upheld UPWA charges, finding that threats of closure had occurred and that management had posted anti-union editorials from the Chief on a bulletin board in the plant. For its part, the Chief ran anti-union news stories almost daily throughout the representation campaign period. [40]

Just one month after the NLRB ruling, in September 1963, plant workers again voted and again elected the company union over the UPWA. Again the Chief lauded the victory of unity and prosperity over the insubordinate outsiders. Again the UPWA appealed the election results, citing forced anti-union meetings and threats to close the plant. And again the NLRB upheld UPWA charges and invalidated the election. [41]

In December 1964, only eighteen months after the first election, workers voted overwhelmingly to be represented by UPWA. Negotiations between UPWA and Iowa Pork, which began in January 1965, deadlocked immediately. A short walkout occurred that month; a full strike began on March 10. [42]

The Perry business community and the workers faced off. Union members found a chilly reception when they solicited local businesses for strike support. Merchants complained that UPWA members obliquely threatened them when they refused to cooperate with strikers. The president of the Chamber of Commerce informed the union that any solicitations required its approval, which it had not given. In response, the UPWA stocked the commissary it opened for strikers with goods purchased in Des Moines rather than from local businesses.[43]

The strike, which included a parallel stoppage at the IBP plant in Fort Dodge, was bitter; its outcome was decisive in reshaping power relations in the community. Iowa Beef brought in strikebreakers. Cars were bombed, tires slashed, people assaulted. In Fort Dodge, Iowa Beef had men with rifles behind the plant fence, and armed strikers with high-powered rifles blocked roads leading to the plant. A fire in the Perry plant was put out before causing extensive damage. The dispute eventually involved Iowa's Governor Harold Hughes, federal mediators, and UPWA officials from the international office in Chicago as well as rank and file from other midwestern locals. As Hughes recalled in his autobiography, "There was a scent of blood in the air."[44] The result was largely a victory for the workers.[45]

After agreeing to most of the union demands, IBP sold the Perry plant to the more union-friendly Oscar Mayer Company. This result was a win for Perry businessmen in that it established a prosperous and stable core of workers to support the local economy; it was a defeat for Perry businessmen in that it established a prosperous and stable core of workers to challenge the local political structure. An electorate that had faithfully delivered its votes to the usual leaders and to the Republican Party switched over to join the majority in the national Democratic landslide of 1964 and has remained in the Democratic column in every election since that time.

The rise of packing unions during and after World War II generated a liberal political voice across Iowa. Although opposition to unions remained, it more frequently evoked a response rather than silent acceptance. As in other towns with a major unionized factory workforce, Perry's Oscar Mayer workers wielded new economic and social power. John Kramer explained, "We were financially amongst the elite, you may

say, the higher paid of the blue collars. It was good for the community."
Overt opposition to unions disappeared in the Perry press, although
subtle opposition can be inferred in the absence of coverage of union
activities. The annual Labor Day tribute to workers disappeared. In
1969 when the *Perry Chief* published an enlarged centennial edition,
the packinghouse local (which was the Amalgamated after the 1968
merger of the Amalgamated and the UPWA) did not appear among the
business, church, and organizational histories solicited by the newspaper staff. It did, however, purchase a full-page advertisement presenting the history of unions and unionism in Perry. Juxtaposing the
six-year Amalgamated history with the celebrated histories of brother-
hoods of railroad workers, the Amalgamated statement grafted itself
into centennial nostalgia to stake a similar claim for acceptance and respect. But nothing ever happens twice the same way, and even railroad
workers may be more honored in memory than they were in the flesh.[46]

Even with successful union organizing, Iowa meatpacking workers
collectively withstood disparaging treatment, as the rural establishment regarded them as unjustly wealthy upstarts. Roy Clabaugh, a
packing worker from Estherville, talked about being a unionist in that
town: "Some of the people didn't go along with what our beliefs were,
and we'd argue with the community—townspeople, businesspeople,
many times. We just never paid any attention to it. We just kept on the
way we was going."[47]

John Kramer, president of the Perry local at different times in the
Oscar Mayer period, recalled,

If we would go on strike, . . . that whole town would swarm
together, the city daddies, and that was terrible. . . .

I went to the Chamber of Commerce, I said, "Wait a minute, you
guys. You know, it bothers me. The more money we make, the more
money you make." I said, "You siding with the company all this time,
it isn't really necessary." I said, "You don't have to jump on your
bandwagon and fly banners, 'yea, yea union.' But," I said, "You just
kind of remain neutral." . . . I said, "We're not going to get any more
money than what industry pays." I said, "Why do you fight us? Why
do you want to make everybody hate one another?"

(DF: Were they jealous of all the money you got?)

Yeah. They said, "We can't hire people to work in our stores. They won't work there because you guys make that big money."

And I said, "Well, you know, get your kids or something. Do what you got to do. But," I said, "I just do not see why you do not want us to make a decent wage. Or more than a decent wage. A proud wage." ...

They used to be terrible. They would get out there and tell us to get back to work, and what's wrong with you. The minute we got too many pickets or something they'd call out the damn highway patrol and they'd come running.

(DF: You must have been about the best off people in Perry.)

We were.

As Merlyn Wee of Estherville summed up the attitude of town businessmen toward the packing workers, it was, "Hey! You guys are not entitled to do that well." [48]

Iowa packing unions and auxiliaries sponsored baseball and softball teams, bowling leagues, and parade entries. They gave college scholarships and donated infant car seats to a public health program. Union members were elected and appointed to boards and committees. With union support a meatpacking worker became mayor in Fort Dodge. But even after reviewing the solid community participation of union members, Dean Hanson of Estherville came back to, "We was the outcasts, you know. They liked our money, and we had a good living. I mean we made a good living, but we was still in the background." [49]

Without the security of strong labor legislation at the state level, without the attendant advantage of social legitimacy, union power was fragile. Violence shored up the structure of labor organization in meatpacking, bringing a semblance of strength overlaying a tenuous foundation. Strike violence associated with packing unions, the most dramatic and openly confrontational aspect of labor organization, has been frequently reported. A nonstriker shot and killed a striking worker in Waterloo during the 1948 strike; an IBP informer was wounded and her sixteen-year-old sister was killed in the 1969 Dakota City strike; fifty-six bombings, twenty shootings, numerous tire slashings, and death threats were further associated with this 1969 strike, in which an IBP vice president's home was destroyed by fire.[50]

As John Kramer described his feelings about the violence that occurred in connection with the Perry meatpacking local,

> Gandhi's theory is wonderful, you know, if someone pays attention to him. . . . They say [violence] is wrong, but I'm telling you, if you're standing on that picket line and you're protecting your job and that and somebody comes along and says, "I'm going to take your job; I'm going to take your money; I'm going to take your food; I'm going to take your livelihood; I'm going to take your future," you have to be kind of not right to not protest it. You know what I'm saying. They say you can't do that; violence gets you nowhere. It gets you in trouble, but it gets attention, also [laughs]. And it's too bad that any of it has to be.[51]

Everyday violence has been even more pervasive than the publicly staged dramas. Iowa being a right-to-work state, union membership can never be formally required as a condition for employment, but membership was expected and informally enforced in packing plants. Those who did not join the union were quietly pushed down steps or beaten up, or they would have their tires slashed or car windows broken. Dick Sturgeon, whose parents worked at the Armour plant in Sioux City, said of the UPWA, "They were very militant folks. If you didn't join the union after thirty days you found yourself hanging upside down inside of a hide chute or in some predicament."[52]

Disputes within the unions could also lead to violence and vandalism. In Ottumwa, Ethel Jerred's six-year-old daughter was threatened and her new home was vandalized over a union dispute. Workers would refuse to speak to scabs for decades. Such experiences inevitably produced resentment behind the facade of conformity to the union program. Jerred herself pulled back from union participation because she believed that the union was fighting against women rather than taking up their cause.[53] Women constituted the most apparent and consistent pocket of resentment within the packing unions in the 1960s and 1970s, but union men have also given accounts of incidents in which dissenting voices were silenced through heavy-handed practices of union leaders. John Kramer, for example, gave an account of a union officer who threatened a would-be candidate into withdrawing; Kramer himself was physically threatened by two union enforcers when he did not go along with a union policy as determined by the international office.[54]

Packinghouse union leaders enforced labor unity against the common enemy—the major meatpacking companies. In the meantime, another dialogue was occurring, a dialogue that would shape workers' future, a dialogue that went far beyond the labor issues that were apparent in the immediate post–World War II years, and a dialogue that largely excluded workers.

CAPITAL AND LABOR IN IOWA ECONOMIC DEVELOPMENT

Since World War II, local development agencies such as Perry Industries have continued to promote industrial growth at the community level. But local development efforts, which operated largely on an independent basis in the early twentieth century, have increasingly come to be advised and coordinated by statewide economic development networks. Discussions about economic development in Iowa have occurred almost exclusively within business and government circles; seldom have workers or their representatives been present in the planning rooms. The words and actions of development experts appropriated the field of political discourse relating to jobs and economic development in Iowa.

In 1993 I interviewed a prominent liberal businessman and politician of the 1980s on the subject of rural development.[55] Lower taxes, he observed, were overrated as a drawing card for business development. His program for rural Iowa stressed the construction of rural recreational facilities and improvement in postsecondary education. Disturbed that the evolving rural workforce was increasingly nonwhite, he stated that with improved education the high quality of Iowa's workforce would draw higher-quality industries. He blamed unions for resisting companies such as IBP, which were the wave of the future. When asked about the role of the worker in economic development planning, he stopped talking. Becoming more cautious and tentative, he reflected that he did not know what to do with that question. Then he continued, "I don't know whether American business has humanitarian aspects or not. I simply don't know." Although he expressed a need for a higher minimum wage, he cautioned that this would lead to higher food prices and hence an inflationary spiral.

Although a push toward the development of manufacturing industry in rural Iowa occurred in the early twentieth century, government demands for food during World War I and World War II and the interim economic stagnation of 1920 to 1940 had quieted rural industrialists. But even before World War II was over, the Iowa Postwar Rehabilitation Commission of 1945 set a tone for succeeding development efforts. Although farming would continue to be the number one industry in Iowa, farming could not be counted on for new jobs. Modern farms would be larger and more mechanized; farm labor would decrease. In contrast to the existing economy, which lately had been heavily supported and regulated by government-sponsored New Deal programs and by government management of World War II, the 1945 report projected an economic future in which the economy would be turned over to the private sector. The report recommended a reversal of the rapid urbanization that had occurred with World War II; but rather than supporting a denser farm population, the goal was to shore up rural communities by locating nonfarm jobs in them. In 1945 the Iowa legislature created the Iowa Development Commission out of the Postwar Rehabilitation Committee. Its charge was to promote the growth of private industry.[56]

The dominant agrarian ethos has meant that there was little inclination to construct labor legislation at the state level, and benign neglect buttressed the propertied power bases. Iowa's becoming a right-to-work state in 1947 was used as incentive for industrial relocation. Iowa could sell itself to industrialists in that, unlike the corrupt Chicago-based politics on its eastern border, Iowa was pristine territory ready to receive the benefits of industrial development. "There are no Big City political bosses or machines in Iowa!" crowed a 1950 publication of the Iowa Development Commission, which went on to advertise that Iowa was 99.3 percent white and 94.7 percent native born.[57] An intelligent, yet well-behaved workforce would boost production without introducing extraneous matters like workers' rights.

Lacking significant sources of energy or metals, Iowa developers wrote their industrial recruitment text around a cheap and dependable supply of rural labor. As with existing images of the rural Midwest, a 1950 Iowa Development Commission report neglected to mention non-farm labor and sold the Iowa labor force as coming from the farm and having all the hardy qualities that this entailed. Manufacturers could escape the labor problems of the cities by locating in Iowa, which had "a steady source of the finest youth of this country, waiting to be utilized in the further development of Iowa as an industrial state. Iowa possesses no finer national resources, awaiting industrial development, than this endless supply of young men and women."[58] An Iowa Federation of Labor spokesman added, "These Iowa ex-farm boys are just plain God-fearing Sons of Toil. They know how to work. They aren't radicals. Farm boys don't believe in radicals."[59]

Rural efforts to attract the manufacturing industry accelerated as farm labor declined. Nationally, rural industrialization was part of the 1967 Rural Poverty Program of President Lyndon B. Johnson. Rural Iowa-based industries such as Maytag and Amana expanded, and new ones, such as Winnebago of Forrest City, grew rapidly through the 1970s. The 1980s rural economic collapse severely strained not just the farm economy but all of the industries in rural Iowa, spawning renewed efforts to shore up nonfarm industry. In 1986 the Iowa Development Commission was reorganized to become the Department of Economic Development, whose mission was to coordinate broad-based economic recovery and development undertakings.

In the late 1980s IBP's six Iowa plants harvested over $14 million in various public subsidies through economic development programs.[60] But even this support paled in comparison to the development grants of the 1990s. In 1993 the Lennox Company of Marshalltown received an incentive package worth $18 million to expand a heating plant. In 1994 $73 million lured Ipsco, Inc., a Canadian steel manufacturer, to build a plant in rural Muscatine County. These awards, made in the context of tight budgets and broad public spending cuts, generated concern that development money might give unfair advantage to chosen businesses as they competed with other Iowa enterprises.[61]

Contrasting experiences of economic development bring class struggle into relief. Developers framed their dialogue around themes of economic growth and increasing numbers of jobs rather than around the needs of workers. The stark realities facing low-income workers of the 1990s have emerged as a countercrescendo. Studies have revealed that this divergence is predictable rather than accidental. The rural United States, which has approximately one-fourth of the country's population, now has about one-half of its low-skilled, low-wage manufacturing jobs. Advances in telecommunication technology, widely touted as a lifeline for rural businesses, actually contribute to economic polarization rather than integrated development. Although management consultation and critical decision making continue to depend on the intimacy of face-to-face contact, goods production can be relegated to cheap labor points that do not participate in central management functions. Cheap labor secured within the United States, while presently more costly than that of many developing countries, may be preferable for a variety of political reasons as well as for the substantial infrastructure and other incentives provided at public expense in the United States. The rhetoric of the market as the natural economic regulator survives, masks the substantial public assistance afforded businesses, and justifies the continuing neglect of workers' reality. Although workers have been able to vote for particular legislative or executive department leaders at the state level, their absence at the development discussion table is generally unnoted.[62]

Discussions of economic development seldom reach beyond the interests of capital. Pressed for how economic development will benefit workers, development specialists get vague and philosophical. In 1996 the Iowa Senate Economic Development Committee chair answered a *Des Moines Register* question about quality jobs with allusions to biotechnological research and a more highly educated workforce laid over an agrarian foundation:

> I think we need to return to our roots. We have the ability to create wealth and recreate wealth every year in our fields. . . .
>
> Genetic engineering will enable us eventually over time to engineer our corn and our soybeans so that they can be uniquely different from field to field to field, so that when industry A needs a certain oil content in their corn farmer B over here will be able to do that. Whereas over here the livestock industry wants a feed that's not going to create as much cholesterol.

There's an unlimited need for that kind of activity in my view in this country. And all of those high value-added jobs have a single thread that runs throughout and that is they need a highly trained and skilled work force.[63]

The devilish detail to be worked out is what this development offers to a thirty-year-old IBP worker whose hands have been destroyed by carpal tunnel syndrome. His situation is on the far margins of development discourse.

At the close of my interview with the development-oriented politician, after I had asked him to consider how workers fit into economic development plans, he succinctly confirmed my growing sense of the disconnection between his world and that of workers. Slipping into a text on the nobility, energy, and resilience of workers, he scoffed as he described the practice of an unspecified packing company that awarded each worker a birthday ham and a day off. With a mischievous grin, he digressed to say that he would guess that every worker's birthday would fall on a Friday. Continuing the thread of the hard-working and thrifty Iowa worker, he declared that in fact workers did not want a day off; they would be happier with two cents more in their paychecks.

This meatpacking company may have been IBP, which was the largest industrial employer in the politician's county. The company does give workers a birthday holiday, although I know nothing about hams. But his image of the worker's experience was eerily skewed. If he had actually known a worker, he could never have thrown off this remark. First, IBP or any other industrial employer invariably knew each worker's birthday. No one could change this holiday without negotiation. Most workers were subject to close surveillance and control; they did not talk their way through anything and especially not into taking a long weekend. Second, if a worker did seek a long weekend, it would have involved taking extra time off on a Monday, Tuesday, or Saturday. Friday was not the end of the workweek for packing workers. Third, the hunger for a little bit of free time was infinitely more palpable than the hunger for two cents more in their paychecks. Workers were constantly putting their jobs on the line by pushing attendance rules to the limit and past, even though they were not paid for these absences and often lost their jobs. Even with poverty level paychecks they craved unstructured time, making attendance one of the centrally contested issues in packing employment. Fourth, ham was a genuine luxury for an IBP worker. In short, IBP's understanding of workers and time control far outstripped that of the liberal politician.

CLASS CONTROL

Economic development colonized and defined ever increasing chunks of workers' experience in the 1990s. But just as Abe Mohr's reality was distinct from that which the editor of the *Chief* projected onto him as a worker, the reality of a rural meatpacking worker of the 1990s was distinct from that which the developers constructed for her. Being an IBP worker in rural Iowa in the 1990s means having a low income, but beyond this lies a range of afflictions that are connected with low income but reach beyond it. I saw these most clearly as I recovered from my IBP job while making a heroic effort to maintain connections with the workers I knew in the plant. Seeing them wrestle with their problems brought the chasm separating me from them into focus.

Several weeks after I quit work, "Annie," my twenty-five-year-old plant friend, inhaled toxic welding fumes while working in her new maintenance job. Although not initially overcome, she suffered chills, vomiting, and diarrhea during the night, and a Perry doctor sent her to a Des Moines hospital in an ambulance. After a brief recovery she returned, shaken and noisily indignant, to her job, her only work restriction being to avoid toxic fumes.

A few days later she was even more severely injured, possibly as a result of lingering vertigo from the first accident. Again working in maintenance, she fell from a pole she was climbing. Although she wore a safety harness and connecting lanyard, the lanyard proved to be too long to protect her. Rushed to the emergency room, she emerged with no broken bones but with a severely traumatized back, which largely immobilized her. Strong painkillers took the edge off her agony but clouded her mind.

As the heat of an Iowa July descended in full force, Annie faced her predicament from her four-room rented house on a dirt road on the outskirts of Rippey, the unincorporated town where she lived. Her daughter "Alyce," six years old and looking forward to first grade, was her best friend and first concern as Annie tried to figure out how to proceed. Alyce's father, an IBP worker who had lived with them briefly a few months before, was gone. "Ben," another IBP worker, had then moved in with her. Suffering from severe carpal tunnel syndrome, he constantly dropped dishes when he tried his hand in the kitchen. Without a driver's license, he depended on Annie for his transportation, but Annie was also barred from driving while taking her pain medication. Because public transportation does not exist in rural Iowa, Annie, Alyce, and Ben had to count on catching rides with neighboring IBP commuters whenever they needed to leave Rippey. Although Annie was optimistic that Ben would be a father to Alyce, she conceded that it was unrealistic to count on him. She had tried to get him to bring home toilet paper shortly after her fall but accepted his failure to follow through with a characteristic combination of blunt words and loving indulgence: "He's okay for being a male, but men ain't worth shit. My mom says men are okay to have around but don't expect them to support you. You gotta take care of yourself."

Although extended family members offered some succor, their distance and their limited resources circumscribed what they could do for Annie. Annie's mother lived within a thirty-minute drive, but Annie could not expect much from her. She worked in a nursing home and somewhat supported herself, but she had little excess time or money to offer. Nor were Annie's half-siblings able to give much immediate help.

Even though Annie had family and friends, she alone shouldered the care of herself and Alyce. Unable to work at IBP, she stationed herself by the telephone on the couch in her living room and tried to take hold of her responsibilities. Alyce and Ben provided some food, and occasionally Annie would move painfully to the kitchen or the bathroom to take care of the most urgent necessities. Each day was a challenge.

Two days after her fall she was scheduled to begin physical therapy in Des Moines. Without being able to drive, what could she do? Alyce went to the neighbor who babysat for her and Annie caught a ride to Perry with one of the IBP workers, reaching IBP in time for the 7:00 A.M. shift. She walked through the security check, up the stairs to the plant dispensary, and waited there until a nurse was ready to transport her and two others to their physical therapy appointments in Des Moines.

Riding in the back seat of the car was a torment for Annie. When they returned to Perry from Des Moines, rather than walking to the dispensary, she waited in the July heat in the IBP parking lot the rest of the day until she caught her ride back to Rippey with the returning workers.

Workers' compensation checks would take two weeks to come, which further complicated Annie's predicament. She had no money. Ben would get paid, but could she count on his checks?

She called me to take her to her doctor appointment in Des Moines three days later. It was her twenty-sixth birthday. After driving forty miles to Rippey, I greeted Annie, Alyce, and Annie's mother, who was there for a short time before going to work. Alyce, who had been set to picking up toys and clothes scattered around the house, seemed relieved to jump on her bicycle and pedal to her babysitter before we left.

Annie was a specter. Her back was rigid and straight, and she did not turn her neck. She took small, careful steps to reach my car, where we cushioned the bottom and back of the seat with pillows to partially protect her from the inevitable jolting of the drive. Never before had I had seen her subdued. Although she took pain pills, she could not sleep; her anxiety for Alyce and herself pierced the drug-induced fog. How could she care for Alyce? She feared that she would never regain flexibility in her back. In addition to the toxic fumes inhaled in the previous week, she had read up on the dangers of ammonia fumes that she had smelled in the plant and was afraid that the pregnancy she was anticipating would be endangered. She was terrified that she might never have another child. The IBP doctor whom she consulted for the fall was trying to get her to go back to work by equipping her with an electronic pain block. That had been somewhat effective on her upper back, she said, but her lower back still tormented her. The doctor seemed to be working more for IBP than for her, and she believed that the IBP nurses had forewarned him that she was obnoxious. She dreaded their encounter and vowed that once recovered from this injury she would leave IBP behind her for good.

Driving to Des Moines, we assessed her options. The union would do little for her, she stated, a fact that I had already confirmed independently. It functioned largely in terms of personal favors dispensed by the president, "Max," and she and Max were not friends. Nor were Max and I on the best of terms at this point. If only she could find a decent doctor. But without money, she was limited to the medical services provided by IBP. Both of us felt sure that an independent doctor would confirm that her injuries were more severe than had been acknowledged. I could not imagine her returning to work in her condition. We decided that she needed a copy of her medical records. I assured her that she had a legal right to them.

Arriving at the doctor's office, we went through the slow process of getting Annie out of the car and propped up on pillows in the waiting room. I parked the car, joined her in the waiting room, and read magazines while she was with the doctor.

Annie emerged after a short time, and I heard her asking the receptionist for a copy of her medical records. The receptionist perfunctorily informed her that the doctor's office could communicate only with IBP about her case. They could not release her records to her. Annie turned away, too weak to press the matter.

I stepped up to the receptionist's desk. The Labor Center people were right: my hair, my glasses, my teeth, my clothes, and my speech all told that I was middle class. I said that Annie wanted her records. The receptionist tried telling me that only IBP could have her records. I replied that the records were Annie's. The receptionist in turn contended that if Annie wanted her medical records, she would have to get them from IBP. My procedure at such an impasse is to stand firm and continue to state my position; refusing to go away sometimes resolves such standoffs. As the exchange continued the doctor emerged, gracious and eager to satisfy my request. Of course Annie could have her records. They were hers. There was no problem with that whatsoever. A doctor had fifteen days to produce the records, which would have to be photocopied. We concluded by arranging for the records to be sent to Annie's home address. At least one step was taken.

Annie and I picked up her pillows and started to leave the waiting room. As I put my hand on the door, it suddenly occurred to me that Annie had not signed any form. Almost always there was a form to sign. I returned to the receptionist's desk and asked if Annie would have to sign a formal request before her medical records would be released. Now that I mentioned it, there *was* a form that had to be completed for the release of medical records. Annie returned to the desk and filled out the form, writing her Rippey address and putting her signature on the end. Finally we asked if anything more was needed, and we were assured that Annie would have her records within fifteen days.

We had a birthday lunch in Des Moines before returning to Rippey, and I caught up on more bizarre details. As soon as she fell, she had been ordered to take a drug test—in spite of having followed all safety procedures. The company had clearly been at fault in providing her with a lanyard that was useless in breaking her fall, but they were trying to say it was her fault. What difference, I asked, did that make? The question floated. Now this doctor was a turkey. He was an occupational health specialist, but not the back specialist that Annie needed. Annie knew he was against her. He told her not to even think of suing IBP, because IBP was more powerful than she was. How was she going to survive the two weeks until she could get her workers' compensation checks? She was taking her pain pills with alcohol. Alyce was the anchor that brought her down to earth and set her planning how she would make it through the ordeal and taking stock of who might help her. I took her back to Rippey and drove home.

Annie's recovery continued as a nightmare. Her doctor did refer her to a back specialist. By the end of July, four weeks after her fall, she was released to return to do restricted work for four hours a day. For unknown reasons, some of her workers' compensation checks did not come through; others arrived late. A month after we assertively requested Annie's medical records, the doctor sent them to IBP rather than to her. When she tried to get them from IBP, the company informed her that they would be released to her lawyer, not to her. Surprisingly—and against my pleading—she used the lawyer Max recommended to workers. This lawyer agreed to work for her on contingency.

A year after her fall, several months after Annie had quit work at IBP and left the state, her lawyer got around to requesting her medical records from IBP and charged Annie thirty-five dollars for the photocopying and letter writing involved. Annie complained about him, saying that he was working for IBP, not for her. In late 1993 she was still sorting through her medical and legal affairs, saying that she would sue the back specialist for malpractice.

Repeatedly as I interacted with IBP workers I found myself vainly trying to transport them into the world I understood. Most frustrating was that nothing I ever tried to do to give a hand up to my packing plant

coworkers was ever helpful as other than a minor and temporary ame-
lioration. Nothing I could say or do on a personal level was useful to
them. Moreover, they perceived this with frightening clarity. They knew
that the logic of my life was not their logic. They accepted the "loans"
that I occasionally made, but almost never did they accept my advice.
Neither were they grateful.

To my surprise, I have learned that it is standard operating procedure
that doctors engaged by employers for their injured workers communicate with the employers who pay them rather than with the patients.
For workers, the wage relationship with employers supersedes their
rights as medical consumers. Doctors' attention to those who pay the
bills displaces their legal and ethical responsibility to their patients in
much the same way that a doctor might be responsible to communicate
with a parent rather than a child patient. Consulting the Iowa workers'
compensation law on this point, I find that it stipulates that full medical information be provided to all parties in a workers' compensation
case, but it does not specify the route by which this information is to be
provided.

In short, my assumption that patients have a right to their medical
records is true for me as a middle-class consumer of medical services,
but it is not in practice uniformly true for working-class persons. A
middle-class person may assume the right to knowledge of one's medical condition; the right to act on this knowledge is taken as fundamental. Working-class reality and working-class rights are different in
the 1990s. Working-class and middle-class rural Iowans had met and
contested each other at the ideological boundaries in the 1960s and
1970s; by the 1990s workers such as Annie had ceded much of their
personal space.

Nothing I experienced with working-class persons ever suggested to
me that as a group they were born losers or that their verbal or problem-
solving skills were deficient. I have observed a similar distribution of
insight and stupidity in every community in which I have been involved.
Rather than separate orders of intelligence or talent, I perceived distinct
systems of logic, reflecting distinct ways of making sense of what was
possible, acceptable, and inevitable. Middle-class assumptions allow

for some flukes and bad breaks, but the belief remains that, overall, people have a reasonable range of control over their lives. Systematic study and preparation often pay off for the middle class in a way that they have not for the working class. Belief in merit allows middle-class persons to deny privilege even while nourishing and protecting it.[64]

The middle class and working class have different histories in rural Iowa. From the perspective of town businessmen and from the perspective of the family farmer, the rural past opens onto a glorious agrarian era of hardy individualism, family values, and community vitality. On the other hand, a worker such as Abe Mohr lacks the golden memories of being in control of his own time, of being his own boss, of enjoying rural leisure activities. He had too much hard work. While the farm families were tenaciously holding onto their farms during the hard times, Abe desperately grasped for the job that would take him away from the farm. Abe Mohr and Annie both had chaotic personal lives.

The closest thing to nostalgia that most Perry meatpacking workers experienced was the memory of the fighting days of UPWA and Oscar Mayer, and this pertained largely to white male workers. Coming off substantial government regulation and having the support of national legislation, these working-class lives approached those of the middle class during the post–World War II period when unions were strongest. This necessarily engendered a struggle over what should constitute a social claim on wealth. John Kramer argued forcefully for the dignity of workers. Under the domination of companies like IBP, a dominance that has permeated the state development discourse of the 1990s, the world of the working class has become increasingly disconnected from the meanings and values that structure middle-class life. Annie expresses herself with clarity comparable to John Kramer, but workers no longer have the economic, political, legal, or social capital with which to press their points. As a woman, Annie was further disregarded. An analysis that reduces rural disintegration to a farm crisis erases a significant element of Iowa history.

Capital is more powerful in the 1990s than it was in 1970, and the colonization of rural areas by such companies as IBP is a fact of late-twentieth-century America. The workers of the Perry IBP plant do not represent all members of the U.S. working class, but the contradictions that they have experienced have reverberated through the rest of American society. Not only has the rise of the kind of rural manufacturing represented by IBP circumscribed and impoverished the bodies and souls of rural workers, it has also drained social resources from a broader segment of the U.S. population.

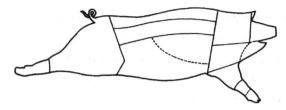

EPILOGUE

In the summer of 1992 "Pete's" attendance demerits added up to his dismissal from IBP. Although IBP sometimes followed a policy of re-hiring such workers after thirty days, this was erratic and arbitrary. Pete was not rehired, even when he returned to the plant twice to plead for his job. Later in 1992 he was sentenced to a total of thirty months in prison for violating a no-contact order by running down and nearly killing his girlfriend.

"Annie" continued to recover from her injuries and cope with her financial problems in August 1992. Driving her aged car, which was in need of a front-end alignment that she could not afford, she spun it out of control and into a gravel pit. "Ben" and "Alyce" were riding with her. She and Ben escaped without serious injury, but Alyce drowned. After the funeral she married Ben. In October, having missed paying rent, they were evicted from the house in Rippey and moved into a camper for the Iowa winter. Her life has continued to unravel.

In October 1993 "Susan" stabbed her boyfriend in the heart dur-ing an argument. Although critically injured, he survived. Susan was charged with assault. I do not know where she is now.

"Roberto" has thrived in the years since I worked with him at IBP. I helped him secure an initial job outside the plant, but he has done better moving from job to job on his own. He reports that he has turned down offers to work for the union and for IBP as a translator or re-cruiter. Although he has had a series of minor brushes with the law in Iowa, he has managed to negotiate fines, suspended sentences, and probation.

In 1995 IBP recruited twenty Sudanese refugees as workers in the Perry plant. East African workers had been in various other meatpacking plants in rural Iowa for over a year. Perry churches opened their arms to the newcomers to try to do what they could to ameliorate the conditions they would face in the plant.[1]

Neither Pete, Annie, Susan, nor Roberto now works at IBP. "Jake," the plant manager, has also left, as has my supervisor, "Clyde." It is probably no accident that among my closest plant friends, the person who emerged from IBP in fighting form came to Iowa from a baptism in the streets of East Los Angeles. The distress of the majority of packing workers emerges repeatedly in newspaper items on crime or personal tragedies.[2] Often, as when Pete's attack on his girlfriend got headlined because of his prior conviction of murdering his wife, the packinghouse connection was not reported. So familiar was the state penitentiary at Anamosa that plant workers spoke of their prison terms as "visiting Annie." Those packinghouse workers who have not experienced major problems related to the stress of their jobs in the 1990s are the exceptions rather than the rule. Most of the stable workers are holdovers from the era when union strength secured a cushion of security and personal freedom. New workers without resources twist in the wind. In one way or another, society picks up the tab for the disintegration.

Although conditions in the Perry IBP plant were far from bucolic, they rose logically out of the economic and social history of rural Iowa. Industrial development and agriculture grew together from the early days of European settlement in the Midwest. Hog processing was a natural adjunct to Iowa's farm economy in that it complemented the labor cycle of farms, enhanced the value of farm produce, and provided diversity in investment. The hired hand, domestic helper, and packinghouse worker fit into the farm picture as consistently and seamlessly as red barns and dairy cows. Wage workers also built and operated railroads and other businesses that advanced the profitability of farm commodities.

Like farms, the U.S. meatpacking industry grew through various government subsidies and contracts, particularly those connected to wars. Meatpacking and farming drew on and in turn supported each other. A small number of large packing companies have dominated the industry since the nineteenth century. The early packing industry centered in major midwestern cities. Notorious for the destruction of workers, packinghouses improved the conditions on their production floors and raised wages in response to government regulation, union power, and evolving ethics of fair play.

When Iowa Beef Packers appeared in the 1960s, local developers embraced it as a rebuttal to the urban agricultural industries that thrived on farm production at their expense. Put together with baling wire and duct tape, Iowa Beef entered the industry through the back door and nestled into the faultlines of rural society. What it lacked in grace it made up in brutal pragmatism. When the power of the government tilted away from labor and toward business, IBP, together with ConAgra and Cargill, overthrew the existing industry leaders and became the core of the new-breed packers.

For workers, the triumph of the new-breed packers meant the dissolution of gains made through union organization that had taken hold during World War II. The power of the packing unions was crushed. Workers could do little more than watch their incomes wither and the control they had achieved on the production floor disintegrate. Most urban packing workers lost their jobs or relocated to rural areas to work in new-breed plants; rural packing workers, such as those in Perry, sometimes kept shreds of jobs at reduced pay and with greater stress. Some maintained personal stability as a result of escaping the worst packinghouse jobs, in addition to having purchased homes and raised their children in better times. New workers endured agonies outside the plants that paralleled those experienced inside.

Gender contradictions with solid roots in rural Iowa weakened the position of packinghouse workers. Although rural Iowa women historically did a wide range of hard and dirty work in support of their families, they received less pay than men and much of their work was informal. The ideal of the male breadwinner effaced the significance of women's work. Meatpackers took advantage of women's low status by hiring women as cheap labor to replace men.

When packinghouse unions organized the majority of the midwestern plants during World War II, they included women in their ranks but not as men's equals. The fact that women's jobs everywhere were low paying concealed the problems that this created in the union structure. Women's position in post–World War II packinghouses continued to erode until the situation came to a head with the passage of the Civil Rights Act of 1964. Women challenged both the meatpacking companies and the unions in the courts, bringing underlying tensions to the surface. The formal equality that women achieved with the Civil Rights Act laid bare informal mechanisms with which men maintained power in the plants. These included sexual harassment, control of orientation and training, control of management and supervisory positions, and gender-skewed work rules. Working-class feminism emerged most powerfully for meatpacking workers in the 1960s. Distinct from middle-class feminism as articulated by Betty Friedan in *The Feminine Mystique*, it nevertheless borrowed from it, just as middle-class feminism eventually borrowed from other traditions.

Even when overt discrimination against women was illegal, patterns of gender inequality persisted. The prevailing disdain for women's rights permitted meatpackers to carry out their agenda. Contempt for women facilitated their use of women's labor to bypass powerful packinghouse unions, deskill jobs, and lower wages.

Ethnic discrimination was also a venerable rural Iowa institution. The agrarian ideal pertained primarily to the white population; few Latino or black Iowans settled in rural homes. Those who did tended to be wage laborers rather than entrepreneurs. They lived in segregated enclaves where they made lower wages than did workers of the majority population. Only by combining subsistence production with their wages could they hope to survive. Economics continually drove them to cities.

From the beginning, meatpacking companies exploited ethnic diversity. Many of the early immigrant packing workers were from eastern Europe. Black and Latino workers had entered midwestern packing by World War II, and their numbers increased in the urban packing centers in the postwar years. Although the UPWA made bold strides toward erasing ethnic division in the plants and in packing communities, their successes were modest when measured against deeply rooted and pervasive discrimination. UPWA antidiscrimination efforts had less effect in rural communities than in urban centers.

Rural relocation of new-breed companies overturned some of the social advances made in old-line packing plants. Importing Latino, black, and Asian American workers into packing plants in rural Iowa, the companies were able to reinstitute ethnic divisions in their workforces. Although civil rights legislation reconfigured the terms under which companies could employ workers, its application left deep chasms in place. These chasms persisted, in part, because some workers found short-term, but vital, advantages in them. Workers who suffered most immediately from ethnic divisions had the least power to confront them.

Gender and ethnic inequalities have been elements of a rural class division that violates the agrarian vision of a classless community of small property owners. Unpropertied laborers were not supposed to be there, notwithstanding their indispensability to the rural economy. Historically, the fact of not being afforded official credence or acknowledgment muffled the collective voice of the rural working class. Yet class division can be read in the continuing business boosterism of the middle class, in the persistent hostility of business to organized labor, and in the contrasting life experiences of the working class. Economic developers spoke a language of capital, technology, and profits that, while beneficial to some workers, bypassed the reality of many. The formal educational system solidified and legitimated class privilege.

The rural milieu shaped the packing industry, and the packing industry shaped the rural milieu from the first intermeshing in the nineteenth century. The recent rural recentering of the packing industry is based in distinctive advantages of the countryside over the city. Not only is livestock more readily at hand, the sparse population and the historical antipathy of rural communities to labor organizing shaped the new labor force. Rural workers of the 1980s and 1990s were more dispersed and more isolated than urban workers, making the packing plants their major point of contact with each other. The community of the early 1990s IBP workers was thin, and the high turnover of workers maintained an unsettled and unrooted sense of confusion. My tenure of four months as an IBP worker was longer than that of the majority of IBP hires. Establishing friendships and learning who can be trusted takes time. As IBP workers we were trying to find our balance on rough and unpredictable terrain. False starts and betrayed trust led to cynicism. The result of industry changes is a widening gap between the middle and working classes. Income is but one aspect of this gap. Unequal legal rights, unequal health care, and unequal personal freedom widen the separation.

In the twenty-five years after World War II the meatpacking labor movement had generated a substantive challenge to the existing order. By raising the reality of class and by frank articulation of the interests of workers, packinghouse unions increased wages, improved working conditions, and inserted the voice of labor in the political arena. Yet the political power of the labor movement was unsustained at the local, state, or national levels. In the 1980s and 1990s internal weaknesses of unions converged with the growing power of capital to annihilate or neutralize earlier gains.

The disintegration of the packinghouse unions left labor with scant ideological or theoretical foundation with which to confront the tactics of new-breed packers. The ability of IBP to exploit gender and ethnic division demonstrates the need for basic reconception of workers' struggle. The UFCW bureaucracy, which has shown little stomach for the gritty and costly process of addressing both internal and external contradictions, has added little to the cause of the workers. On the contrary, its power contributes to the continuing oppression of workers by stifling progressive stirrings that arise among packing workers. Although individual workers have achieved some clarity in their understanding of the labor politics of the 1990s, union structure as a whole has constituted a barrier to them rather than an avenue through which they have been able to effect positive changes.

Although IBP projects an image of triumph and inevitability, its power is not monolithic. Even without organized union opposition in the 1990s, it has backtracked, relented, and modified its course. The speed with which "Chang" was able to press his claim for IBP to pay for his surgery is but one small indication that the company can be moved.

In addition to its advantages, the rural milieu has drawbacks for new-breed packers. Because a rural area is by definition sparsely populated, an industry that employs large numbers of workers, turns them over rapidly, and excels in occupational injuries and illnesses faces a chronic worker deficit. As a result, IBP has never been able to take for granted that it will have a full contingent of workers on any given day. This is why my IBP orientation stressed attendance as one of the first principles of IBP discipline; it is also why the company did not uniformly enforce attendance rules. Jake once remarked to me that the biggest change in meatpacking from the time he started in the 1960s to the 1990s was that in the 1990s no one really wanted to work. The numerous Latinos brought in to relieve IBP's labor shortage were notorious for not coming to work when they got fed up, and IBP had no choice but to accept and adapt to this fact. Seventeen kill workers called in sick one day to protest an obnoxious supervisor, and their protest was effective. Coaxing and threatening as well as recruiting workers consumed resources without relieving managers of the worry of having a rotting pile of dead animals or a backup of thousands of live hogs with no place to go.

Individual workers have the power to disrupt production and resist rules even without the support of their union, and this resistance is costly for IBP. At the Perry plant a cut floor worker got disgusted enough to urinate in a large combo of meat. The line speed encouraged workers to sabotage quality control measures by throwing meat back on the line after it fell on the floor, dripping mucous on the meat rather than blowing their noses, or not following prescribed procedures for washing meat or equipment. Slapstick horseplay and meat thrown around the production floor were workers' answers to stress and boredom, as were the ever-present drugs and the constant "bathroom breaks" that took workers off the line. Workers further sabotaged management plans by haranguing and driving away those not wanted in their midst. Whereas there were fifty to seventy-five workers per supervisor in old-line packing plants, an IBP supervisor might be in charge of twenty-five workers. Supervisors as well as workers violated rules as they answered to other supervisors in a hierarchy of power that could leave them trapped between the reality of workers' limits and the output demands handed down from above.

Yet erratic resistance and insubordination lack form; they do not necessarily give workers more collective control. By supplying IBP with grounds to fire workers without paying unemployment compensation, spontaneous resistance may actually contribute to the flexibility and power of the company: Without the support of a principled union — or with the treachery of an unprincipled union — any potentially effective resistance by IBP workers can be easily squashed. Informal resistance sets an outside limit on management actions, but this limit may nearly coincide with the outside limits of human capability. Many workers have been willing to sacrifice their health to maintain IBP employment.

Much of the existing union structure reinforces rather than challenges the isolation and weakness that workers experience. Effective organizing of workers would address the gender and ethnic divisions that fragment the meatpacking workforce; it would build a program of study, education, and outreach designed to overcome the practices that marginalize and silence the majority of workers. Such a movement would rigorously root out corruption within the ranks of labor leaders. It would work to create solidarity that would link the production floor to the home and community. It would address a range of working-class issues in addition to those having to do directly with the job. These would include health, education, housing, recreation, and transportation.

As important and central as is the struggle of the workers, it will be futile without the active engagement of the wider community. The close alignment of IBP and other new-breed packers with the philosophy of the free market obscures the significant social resources they marshal as well as their dependence on social consensus. Not only have they absorbed untold millions of dollars in direct subsidies from taxpayers, they have also received considerable indirect subsidies. The Iowa Job Service does initial processing of employment applications, and IBP's high turnover requires many hours of Job Service workers' time each week in offering information, distributing employment forms, and conducting screening interviews before sending applicants to IBP. The Perry IBP's 1994 threat to close the plant provoked a full community response as well as negotiations involving the governor of Iowa and other development officials. Perry clergy and social workers joined the business community in reaching out to the company and the workers to make every accommodation. The low pay and high stress that IBP workers experience lead to subsidized medical care and use of furniture banks and public mental health services. Widespread substance abuse problems, along with other criminal activities, clog the district court docket and the state prison system as well as placing the health and well-being of the rest of the community in jeopardy. Workers educated at public expense who are consumed by their jobs rather than set free to participate in civic life represent a net loss to the society as a whole and a corresponding gift to the corporation that destroys them.

Companies such as IBP have effectively externalized many of their social and environmental costs. The process of determining the costs and returning them to the companies would be exacting and extended. The companies would resist and throw roadblocks at every juncture. But awareness of the costs might lead to the realization that toleration of such companies is a social decision that can be rescinded.

Local and regional policy development, however necessary, does not substitute for a national policy that guides and shapes development. The absence of an articulated national industrial policy and accompanying legislation encourages states and localities to bid against each other to give the most away to industries. Setting the development of rural Iowa in a national and global context would provide a more comprehensive and realistic basis for determining goals and investing resources.

Corporate flight, whether between states or countries, is a continuing threat that can be most effectively addressed at the federal government level. Some of the international displacement of industry occurs because of trade and immigration legislation permitting industries to span national borders while keeping pools of low-paid workers in place. Although this legislation has some impact on new-breed packers, they are not among the most mobile industries. Unlike the garment and electronics industries, new-breed meatpacking cannot be easily dislodged from the political geography of the United States. Although beef is currently being imported from Central and South American countries, this rests on the politics of cheap land and land appropriations rather than on profits extracted in processing. New-breed pork processing has remained within the United States and Canada, notwithstanding the passage of NAFTA (North American Free Trade Agreement) legislation opening the way for the development of Mexican plants. The United States offers the companies an infrastructure that affords a massive clean water supply and an extensive and intricate transportation network that cannot be provided in Mexico at this time. In addition, new-breed porkpacking draws on an agricultural system that produces feed grains and uniform livestock on a scale large enough to keep the plants operating. All of these conditions might eventually be available in Mexico and other Latin American countries but not in the immediate future. At present new-breed meatpackers, especially porkpackers, have no choice but to engage the industrial policies of the United States and Canada.

One proposed remedy for abuses by such companies as the new-breed meatpackers is to return to the situation as it was before the structural changes occurred. Some economic developers and workers have looked longingly to days when men supported their wives and children, and rural Iowa was filled with descendants of northern European immigrants. This, as we have seen, is an airbrushed picture of gender history. Notwithstanding the whiteness that Iowans have historically cherished and protected, black persons can no longer be denied their rightful place as U.S. citizens. The challenge of late-twentieth-century immigration is more complicated.

As outlined by Robert Hackenberg, "The stream of immigrant labor entering the United States is not exclusively Hispanic, nor does it derive entirely from Mexico. But . . . an unlimited supply of unskilled labor will continue to drive wages down. . . . It becomes necessary to block or greatly reduce the volume of immigrants."[3] He goes on to propose the monitoring of the Mexican border to keep undocumented immigrants out of the United States, thereby allowing existing immigrants to be more satisfactorily absorbed into the social and economic mainstream.

Sealing the Mexican border promises to limit the number of immigrant workers, but its promise is questionable. Latino workers enter the United States because of intolerable political and economic conditions in their countries. Intensified border patrols diminish the number of crossings at a given site, but no evidence demonstrates that anything short of a militarized wall would actually stem the flow. The image of the United States building a fortress around itself to protect its economic privilege is one that few persons would countenance. In the meantime, the presence of undocumented immigrants gives employers a state-enforced pool of underground, exploitable workers. A counterproposal would be for the United States to cease its support of corrupt Latin American politicians and to promote the kind of broad-based economic development that would take the pressure off the Mexican-U.S. border. Such a policy would offer more hope for long-term stability than would efforts at exclusion.

A democratic future entails planning by a widely diverse citizenry. For my part, I weigh in opposed to changes that would reject the industrial revolution and return the economy to small enterprises, sometimes called "appropriate technology." In Upton Sinclair's 1906 novel, *The Jungle*, the immigrant Jokubas stands in amazement as he observes a turn-of-the-century Chicago packing plant: "It was pork-making by machinery, pork-making by applied mathematics. . . . It was like a wonderful poem to him, and he took it all in guilelessly." [4] I have a similar awe of the technological process that turns out meat through a fantastic array of interlocking human and machine operations. The industrial division of labor unites workers in a way that I had never experienced before IBP. In spite of the stupidity, obscenity, and horror of the work, leaving the plant has been wrenching. The industrial revolution holds the promise of health and leisure for workers, and that promise can be fulfilled if technology is oriented to the needs of workers and placed at the service of society at large rather than the production of enormous corporate profits. The machine runs according to the way it is built and programmed, not according to laws of destiny.

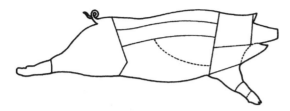

NOTES

PREFACE

1. Deborah Fink, "Women's Work and Change in a Danish Community" (Ph.D. dissertation, University of Minnesota, Minneapolis, 1979).

2. María Patricia Fernandez-Kelly, *For We Are Sold, I and My People: Women and Industry in Mexico's Frontier* (Albany: State University of New York Press, 1983); Louise Lamphere, "Bringing the Family to Work: Women's Culture on the Shop Floor," *Feminist Studies* 11 (1985): 519–40.

3. "Draft AAA Code of Ethics," *Anthropology Newsletter*, April 1996, 15.

4. Judith Stacey, "Can There Be a Feminist Ethnography?," in *Women's Words: The Feminist Practice of Oral History*, edited by Sherna Berger Gluck and Daphne Patai (New York: Routledge, 1991), 111–20; Daphne Patai, "U.S. Academics and Third World Women: Is Ethical Research Possible?," in *Women's Words*, 137–54.

5. Patai, "U.S. Academics," 139.

6. Ibid., 145.

7. From this seminar comes Shelton Stromquist and Marvin Bergman, eds., *Unionizing the Jungles: Labor and Community in the Twentieth-Century Meatpacking Industry* (Iowa City: University of Iowa Press, 1997).

INTRODUCTION

1. In this study "rural" is taken to include areas outside of population aggregates of 10,000 or more, a definition that is slightly broader than the official census threshold of 2,500. For studies of the 1980s, see Osha Davidson, *Broken Heartland: The Rise of America's Rural Ghetto* (New York: Doubleday, 1990); Rachael Kamel, *The Global Factory: Analysis and Action for a New Economic Era* (Philadelphia: American Friends Service Committee, 1990); and Donald D. Stull, Michael J. Broadway, and David Griffith, eds., *Any Way You Cut It: Meat Processing and Small-Town America* (Lawrence: University Press of Kansas, 1995). Data on occupational injuries and illnesses are found in U.S. Department of Labor, Bureau of Labor Statistics Bulletin 2455 (Washington, D.C.: GPO, 1995), 5–7.

2. For an exposé of IBP porkpacking in Storm Lake, Iowa, see Stephen J. Hedges

and Dana Hawkins with Penny Loeb, "The New Jungle," *U.S. News and World Report*, September 23, 1996, 34–45.

3. The canons of Iowa political history include Leland Sage, *A History of Iowa* (Ames: Iowa State University Press, 1974), and Joseph F. Wall, *Iowa: A Bicentennial History* (New York: W. W. Norton, 1978). Social history sources are Dorothy Schwieder, *Iowa: The Middle Land* (Ames: Iowa State University Press, 1996), and Thomas J. Morain, *Prairie Grass Roots: An Iowa Small Town in the Early Twentieth Century* (Ames: Iowa State University Press, 1988). For Iowa labor history, see Shelton Stromquist, *Solidarity and Survival: An Oral History of Iowa Labor in the Twentieth Century* (Iowa City: University of Iowa Press, 1993), and Dorothy Schwieder, *Black Diamonds: Life and Work in Iowa's Coal Mining Communities, 1895–1925* (Ames: Iowa State University Press, 1983).

4. Books on black people and women in Iowa include Robert R. Dykstra, *Bright Radical Star: Black Freedom and White Supremacy on the Hawkeye Frontier* (Cambridge: Harvard University Press, 1993); Dorothy Schwieder, Joseph Hraba, and Elmer Schwieder, *Buxton: Work and Racial Equality in a Coal Mining Community* (Ames: Iowa State University Press, 1987); Glenda Riley, *Frontierswomen: The Iowa Experience* (Ames: Iowa State University Press, 1981); and Deborah Fink, *Open Country, Iowa: Rural Women, Tradition and Change* (Albany: State University of New York Press, 1986).

CHAPTER ONE

1. "Teat line" refers to the row of teats running the length of each side of a sow belly.

2. Whizard is a brand name for these circular electric knives. Like Kleenex, it is also used as a generic name.

3. Clyde knew that he had more workers than he usually needed, and he did not want the general supervisor coming down and seeing us doing nothing.

CHAPTER TWO

1. For a discussion of the evolving rural Iowa economy and the farm crisis of the 1980s, see Osha Davidson, *Broken Heartland: The Rise of America's Rural Ghetto* (New York: Doubleday, 1990), 13–46.

2. U.S. Bureau of the Census, 1920 Schedule, Dallas County, Iowa. Assessing the relative inputs of owner and nonowner labor in agricultural enterprises is complicated by the fact that family members have been irregularly recorded as workers in state and federal censuses, but we can safely assume that the number of non-owner laborers was at least what is shown in census reports.

3. U.S. Bureau of the Census, *1990 Census of the Population: General Population Characteristics: Iowa*, 1990 CP-1-17 (Washington, D.C., 1992), 59; Dale Kasler, "Iowa Manufacturing Sees a Rural Rebirth," *Des Moines Register*, February 18, 1996.

4. Brian Page and Richard Walker, "From Settlement to Fordism: The Agro-industrial Revolution in the American Midwest," *Economic Geography* 67 (1991): 281–315. See also Daniel Nelson, *Farm and Factory: Workers in the Midwest, 1880–1990* (Bloomington: Indiana University Press, 1995).

5. Iowa Census, *Census for the Year 1915* (Des Moines, 1916), 100–101.

6. U.S. Bureau of the Census, 1910 Schedule, Dallas County, Iowa; Eugene N. Hastie, *History of Perry, Iowa* (Fort Dodge, Iowa: Walterick Printing Co., 1962), 46.

7. U.S. Bureau of the Census, 1910 and 1920 Schedules, Dallas County, Iowa; Hastie, *History of Perry*, 187–97. For discussion of rural midwestern wage labor in the early twentieth century, see Nelson, *Farm and Factory*, 13–14, 28–32.

8. U.S. Bureau of the Census, 1910 Schedule, Dallas County, Iowa; "Garden Time; Pen Up the Hens," *Perry Advertiser*, April 9, 1915; "Chickens Must Be Kept Penned Up," *Advertiser*, October 20, 1922.

9. Dorothy Schwieder, "Rural Iowa in the 1920s: Conflict and Continuity," *Annals of Iowa* 47 (1983): 107–8.

10. "We Are All Farmers," *Perry Daily Chief*, April 29, 1940.

11. Willard W. Cochrane, *The Development of American Agriculture: A Historical Analysis* (Minneapolis: University of Minnesota Press, 1979), 100–101.

12. "Bureau of Commerce," *Chief*, January 30, 1922.

13. Donald Lay, assistant professor of Animal Science at Iowa State University, is my authority on hog physiology and behavior. See also John C. Hudson, *Making the Corn Belt: A Geographical History of Middle-Western Agriculture* (Bloomington: Indiana University Press, 1994), 80–87, 140, 158.

14. H. H. McCarty and C. W. Thompson, *Meat Packing in Iowa*, Iowa Studies in Business, no. 12 (Iowa City: State University of Iowa, 1933); William Cronon, *Nature's Metropolis: Chicago and the Great West* (New York: W. W. Norton, 1991).

15. McCarty and Thompson, *Meat Packing in Iowa*, 114–20.

16. "Officers Elected for Hausserman Packing Co.," *Chief*, June 18, 1919.

17. "Plans for Meat Packing Plant Are Completed," *Chief*, March 26, 1919.

18. Figures from the U.S. Bureau of Agricultural Economics' Crop Reporting District Farm Commodity Prices, 1910–1925.

19. "Perry Plant Grows in Spite of Depression," *Chief*, January 17, 1922.

20. "Receiver Named for Hausserman Packing Co.," *Chief*, February 7, 1925.

21. "Hausserman Plant Sold by Sheriff," *Chief*, July 8, 1926; "Packing Plant Forms New Company," *Chief*, July 22, 1926; "Perry Packing Plant Shows Big Growth in Nine Years since Its Founding by Charles Hausserman," *Chief*, September 19, 1928; "Perry Packing Co. Improves Plant," *Chief*, June 3, 1929.

22. Editorial, *Chief*, July 11, 1933.

23. "Perry Plant to Butcher Relief for U.S.," *Chief*, August 30, 1934; "Hog Excess to Be Butchered Here," *Chief*, February 7, 1935; Jimmy M. Skaggs, *Prime Cut: Livestock Raising and Meatpacking in the United States, 1607–1983* (College Station: Texas A&M University Press, 1986), 98.

24. Hastie, *History of Perry*, 190; "Swift and Co. to Suspend Hog Processing Here," *Chief*, June 1, 1956.

25. "Swift . . . to Suspend Hog Processing Here."

26. Upton Sinclair, *The Jungle* (New York: Doubleday, 1906). For a historical overview of the packing industry, see Skaggs, *Prime Cut*, or, more briefly, Richard J. Crom, *Economics of the U.S. Meat Industry*, U.S. Department of Agriculture, Economic Research Service Bulletin 545 (Washington D.C.: GPO, 1988), 29–48. For a history of labor relations in the meatpacking industry, see Charles R. Perry and Delwyn H.

Kegley, *Disintegration and Change: Labor Relations in the Meat Packing Industry*, Labor Relations and Public Policy Series, no. 35 (Philadelphia: University of Pennsylvania, 1989).

27. Skaggs, *Prime Cut*, 152.

28. Shelton Stromquist, *Solidarity and Survival: An Oral History of Labor in the Twentieth Century* (Iowa City: University of Iowa Press, 1993), 111–22; Larry D. Engelmann, " 'We Were the Poor People': The Hormel Strike of 1933," *Labor History* 15 (1974): 483–510; Roger Horowitz, " 'It Wasn't a Time to Compromise': The Unionization of Sioux City's Packinghouses, 1937–1942," *Annals of Iowa* 50 (1989/90): 241–69; Wilson J. Warren, "The Welfare Capitalism of John Morrell and Company, 1922–1937," *Annals of Iowa* 47 (1984): 497–517, and "The Heyday of the CIO in Iowa: Ottumwa's Meatpacking Workers, 1937–1954," *Annals of Iowa* 51 (1992): 363–89.

29. Stromquist, *Solidarity*, 156–58, 175–86; Horowitz, "Time to Compromise"; Warren, "Heyday."

30. Skaggs, *Prime Cut*, 166–68; Perry and Kegley, *Disintegration*, 127; Stromquist, *Solidarity*, 189.

31. Perry and Kegley, *Disintegration*, 127–31; Dennis A. Deslippe, " 'We Had an Awful Time with Our Women': Iowa's United Packinghouse Workers of America, 1945–75," *Journal of Women's History* 5 (1993): 12–16.

32. "Hope of New Industry Is Top News in Perry during 1961," *Chief*, December 30, 1961.

33. "Facts You Should Know about IPC," *Chief*, February 20, 1962.

34. "Explain Stock Selling at Public Meeting," *Chief*, February 19, 1962; "Urge Community to Act for New Industry in Perry," *Chief*, October 3, 1961; "At Helm of New Perry Industry," *Chief*, January 6, 1962.

35. "OWA Pork Plant Built for Speedy Kill, Chill and Carcass Shipment," *National Provisioner*, January 19, 1963.

36. Editorial, *Chief*, July 20, 1963.

37. "Iowa Pork Co. and Iowa Beef Packers Plan to Merge," *Chief*, August 30, 1963.

38. Editorials, *Chief*, March 17, 27, October 3, 1963; "Workers Overwhelmingly Support United Packinghouse," *Chief*, December 3, 1964.

39. "Top Officials Enter Packing Strike," *Des Moines Register*, March 23, 1965. For more detail on the conflict between Iowa Beef and UPWA, see Chapter 5.

40. "Perry Strike to Continue," *Chief*, April 6, 1964; "Armour Terminates Contract," *Chief*, May 1, 1965; "Strike Settled at Perry IPC," *Chief*, May 20, 1965.

41. "IBP," *International Directory of Company Histories* (Chicago: St. James Press, 1990), 2:515–16.

42. "Kraft General Foods," ibid., 7:274.

43. *Agreements between Oscar Mayer & Co., Perry, Iowa and Amalgamated Meat Cutters & Butcher Workmen of North America, AFL-CIO District Local Union No. P-1149, October 19, 1970 through October 18, 1973, October 19, 1973 through October 18, 1976, and October 10, 1976 through October 18, 1979; Agreement (Oscar Mayer and United Food and Commercial Workers), October 19, 1979 through October 18, 1982.*

44. Thomas Geohegan, *Which Side Are You On? Trying to Be for Labor When It's Flat on Its Back* (New York: Farrar, Straus and Giroux, 1991); Bennett Harrison and Barry

Bluestone, *The Great U-Turn: Corporate Restructuring and the Polarizing of America* (New York: Basic Books, 1988), 21–52; Nelson, *Farm and Factory*, 187, 197.

45. "Kraft," 7:274.

46. Mark Grey, "Turning the Pork Industry Upside Down: Storm Lake's Hygrade Work Force and the Impact of the 1981 Plant Closure," *Annals of Iowa* 54 (1995): 244–59; "IBP," 2:515.

47. Jane E. Limprecht, *ConAgra Who? $15 Billion and Growing* (Omaha: ConAgra, Inc., 1989), 186–202; Winston Williams, "An Upheaval in Meatpacking," *New York Times*, June 20, 1983; Bill Eftink, "Pac-Man Packers Gobble Up the Competition," *Successful Farming*, March 1989, 6–7; Arnold Garson, "ConAgra: New Giant in Rural America," *Register*, September 18, 1983; Maria L. LaGanga, "Meat Market Slaughter," *Los Angeles Times*, April 22, 1990; Perry and Kegley, *Disintegration*, 90; Mike McGraw, "Why Conglomerates Are Setting Meat Packers Adrift," *Register*, May 10, 1981.

48. Henry Weinstein, "NLRB Says It Will Sue ConAgra for Alleged Discrimination," *Los Angeles Times*, December 9, 1985; "ConAgra in Settlement," *New York Times*, September 7, 1987; Gene Erb, "U.S. Labor Takes Its Lumps," *Register*, August 20, 1989.

49. Limprecht, *ConAgra Who?*, 191.

50. Douglas Constance and William Heffernan, "IBP's Dominance in the Meat Packing Industry: Boxed Beef and Busted Unions" (paper presented at the Food, Agriculture, and Human Values Society meeting, Little Rock, Ark., November 1989); Crom, *Economics of the U.S. Meat Industry*, 39; Michael F. Sheehan, "Predatory Competition, Jobs, and the Supply of Hogs: The Role of State Assistance in the Collapse of the Independent Hog Packing Industry in Iowa" (Iowa City: Fisher, Sheehan and Colton, 1987); Lois Therrien, "ConAgra Turns Up the Heat in the Kitchen," *Business Week*, September 2, 1991, 58–60.

51. Anthony Baldo, "Boxed In," *Financial World*, March 21, 1989, 50–51.

52. The UFCW, with 1.4 million members, is North America's largest private-sector union. Ninety thousand UFCW members, 6 percent of the total, work in the packing or processing of beef or pork.

53. Louis DeFrieze interview, Davenport, Iowa, 1987, Iowa Labor History Oral Project, State Historical Society of Iowa, Iowa City (hereafter cited as ILHOP); Chris Lauritsen interview, Denison, Iowa, July 22, 1987, ILHOP; Stromquist, *Solidarity*, 268–71.

54. "Leaders React Cautiously to Mayer Letter," *Chief*, March 1, 1983; "Oscar Mayer Negotiations Over," *Chief*, April 25, 1983; "Workers Approve Pact," *Chief*, May 3, 1983. According to the old-line packers, the UFCW master contract remuneration, with benefits, came to $17–$18, more than twice the wages of IBP. See Williams, "Upheaval."

55. "Oscar Mayer Union Local Is Ousted," *Chief*, June 1, 1983. Ironically, two years later the UFCW placed the Austin, Minnesota, Hormel Local P-9 in receivership for not accepting wage concessions. See Hardy Green, *On Strike at Hormel: The Struggle for a Democratic Labor Movement* (Philadelphia: Temple University Press, 1990); Peter Rachleff, *Hard-Pressed in the Heartland: The Hormel Strike and the Future of the Labor Move-*

ment (Boston: South End Press, 1993); and Dave Hage, *No Retreat, No Surrender: Labor's War at Hormel* (New York: William Morrow, 1989). For the decline of an Iowa packing local, see Wilson J. Warren, "When 'Ottumwa Went to the Dogs': The Erosion of Morrell-Ottumwa's Militant Unionism, 1954–73," *Annals of Iowa* 54 (1995): 217–43.

56. *Agreements between Oscar Mayer and United Food and Commercial Workers*, October 19, 1979 to October 18, 1982, and April 4, 1986 to April 9, 1989.

57. Lisa Collins and Dale Kasler, "Oscar Mayer Workers Angry; Perry Hopes for White Knight," *Register*, October 8, 1988.

58. Gene Erb and Dale Kasler, "Hundreds of Jobs Saved as IBP Buys Perry Pork Plant," *Register*, December 24, 1988.

59. Norm Brewer, "IBP Worker Safety Plan Called Landmark," *Register*, November 24, 1988; Collins and Kasler, "Oscar Mayer Workers Angry"; Dale Kasler, "After Two Heavy Fines, IBP Begins to Clean Up Its Health and Safety Act," *Register*, September 19, 1988; "Humpels Leave State," *Chief*, May 11, 1989; Joel Novek, Annalee Yassi, and Jerry Spiegel, "Mechanization, the Labor Process, and Injury Risks in the Canadian Meat Packing Industry," *International Journal of Health Services* 20 (1990): 281–96.

60. "Perry Welcomes Plant's Reopening," *Register*, August 16, 1989.

61. "IBP to Reopen Perry Plant, Hire 600 within Year," *Register*, July 7, 1989.

62. IBP, Inc., "Notice of Annual Meeting of Stockholders to Be Held April 22, 1992," 8 (written by Lonnie O. Grigsby); Anne Fitzgerald, "IBP Expands in Iowa," *Register*, April 5, 1995.

63. "IBP May Expand Plant by 175 Jobs," *Register*, June 24, 1993. The Waterloo IBP plant, opened in 1990, produces pepperoni and other pizza toppings.

64. Dale Kasler, "Union Wins Battle at Illinois Plant," *Register*, September 21, 1988.

65. House Subcommittee on Government Operations, *Underreporting of Occupational Injuries and Its Impact on Workers' Safety, Part 3*. 100th Cong., 1st sess., 1987, 29.

66. David Moberg, "Is the UFCW Slaughtering Itself?," In *These Times*, February 8–14, 1989; Aaron Bernstein, "How Osha Helped Organize the Meatpackers," *Business Week*, August 29, 1988, 82.

67. Gene Erb, "Meatpackers Leader Fired," *Register*, January 13, 1989, and "Food Union's New Course Sparks Derision, Applause," *Register*, January 22, 1989.

68. Chris Lauritsen interview, Denison, Iowa, July 22, 1987, ILHOP.

69. Marc Cooper, "The Heartland's Raw Deal," *Nation*, February 3, 1997, 11–17; Dennis Farney, "Price of Progress: A Town in Iowa Finds Big New Plant Destroys Its Old Calm," *Wall Street Journal*, April 3, 1990; Maria LaGanga, "Meat Market Slaughter," *Los Angeles Times*, April 22, 1990; Dale Kasler, "Renegade Past Shadows IBP as It Confronts Powerful Forces," *Register*, September 18, 1988; A. V. Krebs, *The Corporate Reapers: The Book of Agribusiness* (Washington, D.C.: Essential Books, 1992), 362–71; James Flansburg, "The Citizens Challenge IBP," *Register*, October 21, 1989; David Ostendorf, "The Social Costs of Meatpacking Industry," *Register*, June 28, 1990; Editorial, *Register*, October 2, 1988; Charles Isenhart, "Church-Led Coalition Fights Meatpacker," *National Catholic Life Reporter* 24 (April 1, 1988): 22; Editorial, *Register*, April 5, 1994; Anne Fitzgerald, "IBP Accused by USDA of Unfair Pricing," *Register*, August 4, 1995; George Clifford III, "Candidate Pins Blame for Crime on IBP," *Reg-*

ister, June 17, 1994; Citizens against River Pollution, Iowa State University Library Special Collections, T-301.

70. Personal communication, Thomas R. Patterson, Senior Research Analyst, Democratic Research Staff, Iowa House of Representatives, 1995, copy in author's possession; Personal communication, Iowa Department of Economic Development, 1992, copy in author's possession; Dave Nagle, "Iowa Shouldn't Pay Corporate Blackmail," *Register*, April 4, 1990; "Perry Offers to Help Widen Highway," *Register*, August 9, 1989.

71. On ConAgra's Monfort meatpacking division, see Carol Andreas, *Meatpackers and Beef Barons: Company Town in a Global Economy* (Niwot: University Press of Colorado, 1994); "The Monfort Decision: Spencer Residents Speak Out," *Spencer Daily Reporter*, March 25, 1995; and "Spencer Rejects Rezoning Proposal," *Register*, March 29, 1995. On Cargill, see Ralph Nader and William Taylor, *The Big Boys: Power and Position in American Business* (New York: Pantheon, 1986), 292-349; George Gunset, "Behind-the-Scenes Battles Detailed in Cargill, Inc. History," *Register*, April 27, 1992; and Dirck Steimel, "Cargill Reshapes Life in S.E. Iowa," *Register*, June 27, 1993.

72. Dirck Steimel, "IBP to Close Perry Plant," *Register*, January 29, 1994; Denise Pierce, "Closing Announced," *Chief*, February 3, 1994; Steimel, "Perry Scrambles to Keep IBP Plant Up and Running," *Register*, March 13, 1994; Pierce, "IBP Stays in Perry; New Contract Adopted," *Chief*, April 7, 1994; Jerry Perkins, "200 New Jobs for IBP Plant at Perry," *Register*, January 20, 1995; "Business Roundup," *Register*, May 9, 1995.

CHAPTER THREE

1. This incident and an abbreviated discussion of gender in meatpacking are found in Deborah Fink, "Reorganizing Inequality: Gender and Structural Transformation in Iowa Meatpacking," in *Unionizing the Jungles: Labor and Community in the Twentieth-Century Meatpacking Industry*, edited by Shelton Stromquist and Marvin Bergman (Iowa City: University of Iowa Press, 1997), 218-41.

2. For discussions of gender and the working class, see Ava Baron, "Gender and Labor History: Learning from the Past, Looking to the Future," in *Work Engendered: Toward a New History of American Labor*, edited by Ava Baron (Ithaca: Cornell University Press, 1991), 1-46; Elizabeth Faue, "Gender and the Reconstruction of Labor History: An Introduction," *Labor History* 34 (1993): 169-77; Alice Kessler-Harris, "Treating the Male as 'Other': Re-defining the Parameters of Labor History," *Labor History* 24 (1993): 190-204; and Gay L. Gullickson, "Commentary: From the Perspective of a Women's Historian," in *Rethinking Labor History: Essays on Discourse and Class Analysis*, edited by Lenard R. Berlanstein (Urbana: University of Illinois Press, 1993), 200-213. For gender in union organizing, see Diane Balser, *Sisterhood and Solidarity: Feminism and Labor in Modern Times* (Boston: South End Press, 1987); Ruth Milkman, *Gender at Work: The Dynamics of Job Segregation by Sex during World War II* (Urbana: University of Illinois Press, 1987); Michael J. Lewandowski, "Democracy in the Workplace: Working Women in Midwestern Unions, 1943-45," *Prologue* 25 (1993): 156-69; Nancy Gabin, *Feminism in the Labor Movement: Women and the United Auto Workers, 1935-1975* (Ithaca: Cornell University Press, 1990); and Nancy A.

Hewitt, " 'The Voice of Virile Labor': Labor Militancy, Community Solidarity, and Gender Identity among Tampa's Latin Workers, 1880-1921," in Baron, *Work Engendered*, 142-67.

3. Alice Kessler-Harris, *Out to Work: A History of Wage-Earning Women in the United States* (New York: Oxford University Press, 1982).

4. Deborah Fink, *Open Country, Iowa: Rural Women, Tradition and Change* (New York: State University of New York Press, 1986).

5. Karen J. Hossfield, " 'Their Logic against Them': Contradictions in Sex, Race, and Class in Silicon Valley," in *Women Workers and Global Restructuring*, edited by Kathryn Ward (Ithaca: Cornell University Press, 1990), 150-78; Milkman, *Gender at Work*, 100; Alice Kessler-Harris, "A New Agenda for American Labor History: A Gendered Analysis and the Question of Class," in *Perspectives on American Labor History: The Problems of Synthesis*, edited by J. Carroll Moody and Alice Kessler-Harris (Urbana: University of Illinois Press, 1989), 217-34; Dolores Janiewski, "Southern Honor, Southern Dishonor: Managerial Ideology and the Construction of Gender, Race, and Class Relations in Southern Industry," in Baron, *Work Engendered*, 70.

6. Elizabeth Faue, *Community of Suffering and Struggle: Women, Men, and the Labor Movement in Minneapolis, 1915-1945* (Chapel Hill: University of North Carolina Press, 1991), Kessler-Harris, "Treating the Male," 198; Milkman, *Gender at Work*, 40.

7. For the acceptance of gender divisions, see Janiewski, "Southern Honor," 70; Carole Turbin, *Working Women of Collar City: Gender, Class, and Community in Troy, New York, 1864-86* (Urbana: University of Illinois Press, 1992), 212; Cynthia Fuchs Epstein, "Workplace Boundaries: Conceptions and Creations," *Social Research* 56 (1989): 584; and Baron, "Gender," 27. For gender conflict, see Gabin, *Feminism*; Kessler-Harris, "New Agenda," 231; and Sharon Hartman Strom, "Challenging 'Woman's Place': Feminism, the Left and Industrial Unionism in the 1930s," *Feminist Studies* 9 (1983): 359-86.

8. Kessler-Harris, "Treating the Male"; Faue, *Community of Suffering*, 95, 166.

9. David D. Gilmore, *Manhood in the Making: Cultural Concepts of Masculinity* (New Haven: Yale University Press, 1990), 220-31. For a discussion of varying reactions of blue-collar unions to women's issues, see Brigid O'Farrell and Suzanne Moore, "Unions, Hard Hats, and Women Workers," in *Women and Unions: Forging a Partnership*, edited by Dorothy Sue Cobble (Ithaca: ILR Press, 1993), 69-84.

10. Joan C. Scott, *Gender and the Politics of History* (New York: Columbia University Press, 1988), 64.

11. For critiques of the use of gender to imply women, see Faue, "Gender," 170; Baron, "Gender," 20; and Kessler-Harris, "Treating the Male."

12. "Topsy Turvy Marriages Are Tragic, Not Funny" (editorial), *Perry Daily Chief*, November 14, 1936; "To the Hills! The Women Are Coming" (editorial), *Chief*, October 12, 1938.

13. Fink, *Open Country*, 19-35.

14. Ibid.; Strom, "Challenging 'Woman's Place'," 362; Lois Scharf, *To Work and to Wed: Female Employment, Feminism, and the Great Depression* (Westport, Conn.: Greenwood Press, 1980). Studies that have shown the centrality of working-class women's income include Sandra Morgen, "Beyond the Double Day: Work and Family in Working-Class Women's Lives," *Feminist Studies* 16 (1990): 53; Larry S.

Carney and Charlotte B. O'Kelly, "Women's Work and Women's Place in the Japanese Miracle," in Ward, *Women Workers*, 144; Myra Marx Ferree, "Sacrifice, Satisfaction, and Social Change: Employment and the Family," in *My Troubles Are Going to Have Trouble with Me: Everyday Trials and Triumphs of Women Workers*, edited by Karen Brodkin Sacks and Dorothy Remy (New Brunswick: Rutgers University Press, 1984), 61–79; Nancy Folbre, "Women's Informal Market Work in Massachusetts, 1875–1920," *Social Science History* 17 (1993): 135–60; Martha May, "The Historical Problem of the Family Wage: The Ford Motor Company and the Five Dollar Day," in *Unequal Sisters: A Multicultural Reader in U.S. Women's History*, edited by Ellen Carol DuBois and Vicki L. Ruiz (New York: Routledge, 1990), 275–91; and Turbin, *Collar City*, 5.

15. It was not given that families would stay together. By an Iowa law of 1913, children could be removed from the homes of destitute parents and placed in institutions. Examples of such children in Perry include "Do You Want a Nice Healthy Baby Boy?," *Chief*, October 3, 1924; "Wanted: Home for Three Kiddies," *Chief*, March 2, 1928; and "Five Children Sent to Home," *Chief*, December 16, 1913. For a description of children's placement in institutions in the early twentieth century, see Stephanie Coontz, *The Way We Never Were: American Families and the Nostalgia Trap* (New York: Basic Books, 1992).

16. Deborah Fink, *Agrarian Women: Wives and Mothers in Rural Nebraska, 1880–1940* (Chapel Hill: University of North Carolina Press, 1992), 99. For an example of a "Help Wanted, Married" ad, see *Chief*, August 14, 1934.

17. "Chicken Ordinance to Be Enforced," *Chief*, April 14, 1927; "Spring Has Come—So Tie Up Fido and Pen Chickens," *Chief*, April 5, 1941.

18. Data are from 1920 federal manuscript census schedules for Perry.

19. Jeanne Boydston, "To Earn Her Daily Bread: Housework and Antebellum Working-Class Subsistence," *Radical History Review* 35 (1986): 7–25. According to James Barrett, at the turn of the century wives of Chicago packinghouse workers made more money in the home than they could have made in the plants; Barrett, *Work and Community in the Jungle: Chicago's Packinghouse Workers, 1894–1922* (Urbana: University of Illinois Press, 1987), 97.

20. This recollection appears in Deborah Fink, "What Kind of Woman Would Work in Meatpacking, Anyway?: World War II and the Road to Fair Employment," *Great Plains Research* 5 (1995): 241–62.

21. Thomas J. Morain, *Prairie Grass Roots: An Iowa Small Town in the Early Twentieth Century* (Ames: Iowa State University Press, 1988), 155; "Scarlet Women Ordered Out," *Perry Advertiser*, April 6, 1915; "Officers Make Big Booze Raid at Moran," *Chief*, December 29, 1922.

22. Folbre, "Women's Informal Market Work," 135.

23. In the Iowa state census of 1915, 13.9 percent of the labor force was female; in the federal census of 1940, 19.9 percent of the Iowa labor force was female. U.S. Bureau of the Census, *Characteristics of the Population, Part 2: Florida-Iowa*, vol. 2 of *Sixteenth Census of the United States, 1940* (Washington, D.C., 1943), 866.

24. In spite of the tendency for domestic service to be irregularly recorded in the census, as late as the 1940 census, domestic service was the most commonly listed occupation of formally employed Iowa women; see 1940 Census, 869.

25. Harriett Erzinger interview, Ottumwa, Iowa, September 10, 1981, Iowa Labor

History Oral Project, State Historical Society of Iowa, Iowa City (hereafter cited as ILHOP); Louise Mann interview, Sioux City, Iowa, December 10, 1979, ILHOP; Velma Otterman Schrader interview, May 7, 1986, United Packinghouse Workers of America Oral History Project, State Historical Society of Wisconsin, Madison (hereafter cited as UPWAOHP).

26. Jeanette Haymond interview, Cedar Rapids, Iowa, November 9, 1977, ILHOP. Haymond is ambiguous about whether she lost her job or quit the first time she was in the plant.

27. Otterman Schrader interview; Mary St. John interview, Fort Dodge, Iowa, September 13, 1978, ILHOP; Mary Ashlock interview, Mason City, Iowa, November 17, 1981, ILHOP. For discussion of gender and the defense of respectability, see Baron, "Gender," 34.

28. "New Reporting of Women's Wage and Employment Trends," *Woman Worker* 18 (March 1938): 3–6; *Wages and Hours of Labor in the Slaughtering and Meat-Packing Industry*, 1917, U.S. Department of Labor Bulletin 252 (Washington, D.C., 1919); *Wages and Hours of Labor in the Slaughtering and Meat-Packing Industry*, 1927, U.S. Bureau of Labor Statistics Bulletin 472 (Washington, D.C., 1929); Iowa, *Fifteenth Report of the Bureau of Labor Statistics, 1912: Statistics for the State of Iowa for the Biennial Period, 1910–1911* (Des Moines, 1913), 84, 154, 196, 368, 390; Mary Elizabeth Pidgeon, *The Employment of Women in Slaughtering and Meat Packing*, U.S. Department of Labor, Women's Bureau Bulletin no. 88 (Washington, D.C., 1932).

29. U.S. Bureau of the Census, *Occupations, by States*, vol. 4 of *Fifteenth Census of the United States, 1930: Population* (Washington, D.C., 1933), 755; 1940 Census, 867.

30. In Perry, local poultry operations went through a series of names and owners, including Des Moines Valley Produce Company, Priebe and Sons, A. F. Murmann Company, and Pantier Poultry.

31. Gilbert Anderson interview, Fort Dodge, Iowa, April 20, 1981, ILHOP; St. John interview.

32. St. John interview; Anderson interview; *Industrial Survey in Selected Industries in the United States, 1919: Preliminary Report*, U.S. Bureau of Labor Statistics Bulletin 265 (Washington, D.C., 1920), 26.

33. Ashlock interview; Erzinger interview; St. John interview; Jenny Shuck interview, June 2, 1986, UPWAOHP.

34. Richard Lindner interview, Fort Dodge, Iowa, August 18, 1981, ILHOP; Maureen Honey, *Creating Rosie the Riveter: Class, Gender, and Propaganda during World War II* (Amherst: University of Massachusetts Press, 1984), 154.

35. Ethel Jerred interview, Ottumwa, Iowa, October 5, 1981, ILHOP; Faue, *Community of Suffering*, 168–88; Karen Anderson, *Wartime Women: Sex Roles, Family Relations, and the Status of Women during World War II* (Westport, Conn.: Greenwood Press, 1981); Susan Hartmann, *Home Front and Beyond: American Women in the 1940s* (Boston: Twayne, 1982).

36. Jerred interview; Ruth Morrow interview, Ottumwa, Iowa, September 8, 1981, ILHOP.

37. Mary Edwards interview, Sioux City, Iowa, March 23, 1983, ILHOP.

38. Bruce Fehn, "Striking Women: Gender, Race and Class in the United Packing-

house Workers of America (UPWA), 1938-1968" (Ph.D. dissertation, University of Wisconsin, Madison, 1991), 224.

39. Rachel Maerschalk interview, Dubuque, Iowa, September 3, 1980, ILHOP; Mann interview; Jerred interview; St. John interview; Edwards interview; Shuck interview.

40. William C. Pratt, "Interviews with Vida Morrison and James C. Harris," *Prairie Schooner* 60 (1986): 84; Velma Wetzel interview, Cedar Rapids, Iowa, October 12, 1979, ILHOP; Sylvester Ames interview, Waterloo, Iowa, March 1978, ILHOP; John Andon interview, Mason City, Iowa, November 16, 1981, ILHOP; Jerred interview.

41. Otterman Schrader interview. The greater skill associated with men's work, though granted by women as well as men, may in itself have been based on gender ideology; see Patricia Cooper, "The Faces of Gender: Sex Segregation and Work Relations at Philco, 1928-1938," in Baron, *Work Engendered*, 326-27. For a woman's testimony that unequal pay was no problem, see Mann interview; for an opposing interpretation, see Fehn, *Striking Women*, 16, 18, 204-5, 231, 319.

42. Florence Jones interview, Fort Dodge, Iowa, August 12, 1981, ILHOP; Julia Naylor interview, Fort Dodge, Iowa, August 7, 1981, ILHOP; Edwards interview.

43. Fehn, *Striking Women*, and " 'Chickens Come Home to Roost': Industrial Reorganization, Seniority, and Gender Conflict in the United Packinghouse Workers of America, 1956-1966," *Labor History* 34 (1993): 324-41.

44. Dennis A. Deslippe, " 'We Had an Awful Time with Our Women': Iowa's United Packinghouse Workers of America, 1945-75," *Journal of Women's History* 5 (1993): 10-32.

45. Pratt, "Interviews," 79.

46. Ames interview; Jerred interview; Shuck interview; Otterman Schrader interview; St. John interview; Robert Horowitz, " 'It Wasn't a Time to Compromise': The Unionization of Sioux City Packinghouses, 1937-1942," *Annals of Iowa* 40 (1989/90): 252.

47. Mann interview.

48. Otterman Schrader interview; Maerschalk interview; Edwards interview; Ashlock interview.

49. Otterman Schrader interview; Jerred interview; Ashlock interview; Naylor interview.

50. Jerred interview; Ashlock interview; Naylor interview; Haymond interview; Otterman Schrader interview. One of my informants reported that she knew women who were out of work as long as thirteen years after taking pregnancy leave in the 1950s. Women would be called back in the order of their leaving their jobs, but also by seniority. A woman who took pregnancy leave soon after starting work could expect to be out of work a long time. In the 1950s women's departments were shrinking rather than expanding, and part of the mechanism for doing this was not having to call back women after pregnancy leave.

51. U.S. Department of Labor, *Progress toward Equal Pay in the Meat-Packing Industry*, Women's Bureau Bulletin 251 (Washington, D.C., 1953), 15. For an account of women getting paid less than men for the same work under union contract, see Pratt, "Interviews," 83.

52. Jerred interview.

53. For accounts of women losing packing jobs in the 1960s, see Lucille Bremer interview, Waterloo, Iowa, June 2, 1982, ILHOP; Dorven (Arky) Bride interview, Ottumwa, Iowa, January 19, 1983, ILHOP; and Jerred interview.

54. "Civil Rights Act, Title VII, 1964," in *Women's America: Refocussing the Past*, edited by Linda K. Kerber and Jane DeHart Mathews (New York: Oxford University Press, 1982), 445.

55. Quoted in Deslippe, "An Awful Time," 10. Nancy Gabin (*Feminism*) discusses blue-collar feminism in the auto industry in the 1950s. In terms of women contesting the division of labor or men's dominance in union politics, this did not come to the meatpacking industry until the 1960s.

56. Dennis Deslippe, "Organized Labor, National Politics, and Second-Wave Feminism in the United States, 1965–1975," *International Labor and Working Class History* 49 (1996): 143–65, and "An Awful Time"; Fehn, " 'Chickens Come Home to Roost.' "

57. Ruth Morrow interview; Violet Bohaty interview, Ottumwa, Iowa, September 15, 1981, ILHOP; Jerred interview.

58. Nadine Klaner interview, Cedar Rapids, Iowa, August 26, 1982, ILHOP. For another account of harassment of women trying to work under the ABC system, see Morrow interview.

59. Viola Jones interview, Waterloo, Iowa, May 6, 1986, UPWAOHP. Roxanne Conlin, a consistent and public advocate for working women in Iowa, has been a deputy industrial commissioner, an assistant attorney general, a U.S. attorney for the Southern District of Iowa, and a private attorney; see Louise Noun, *More Strong-Minded Women: Iowa Feminists Tell Their Stories* (Ames: Iowa State University Press, 1992), 118–33.

60. Elizabeth "Sue" Smith interview, Ottumwa, Iowa, September 15, 1981, ILHOP; Mickey Lockhart interview, Cedar Rapids, Iowa, October 12, 1979, ILHOP; Erzinger interview; Wetzel interview.

61. "Darlene, Marlene Add Charm to the Pork Plant," *Chief*, October 30, 1962.

62. Charles R. Perry and Delwyn H. Kegley, *Disintegration and Change: Labor Relations in the Meat Packing Industry*, Labor Relations and Public Policy Series, no. 35 (Industrial Research Unit, University of Pennsylvania, 1989), 136–37; "Local UPW Men Strike at Iowa Pork Co.," *Chief*, March 11, 1965.

63. "Officials Declare IBP's Child Care a Unique Success," *Ames Tribune*, April 15, 1992.

64. For deskilling of industrial production, see Harry Braverman, *Labor and Monopoly Capital: The Degradation of Work in the Twentieth Century* (New York: Monthly Review Press, 1974), 124–38.

65. Nick Lamberto, "Beef Strike Spreads to Iowa Plants," *Des Moines Register*, October 21, 1969; Jerry Knight, "Long Iowa Beef Strike Seen," *Des Moines Register*, October 26, 1969. In 1968 the Amalgamated and UPWA had merged to become the Amalgamated, the single packing worker international (see Chapter 2).

66. Knight, "Long Iowa Beef Strike Seen"; "Union Denial of 'Sabotage,' " *Des Moines Register*, October 8, 1969.

67. Knight, "Long Iowa Beef Strike Seen."

68. Lamberto, "Beef Strike Spreads."

69. Ronald E. Miller, "An Analysis of the Wage System at Iowa Beef Processors, Inc." (M.A. thesis, University of Iowa, 1976), 46.

70. Ibid., 62.

71. Ibid., 183.

72. Ibid., 252.

73. But see Fehn, *Striking Women*, for an alternate interpretation.

74. Nadine Klaner, who worked at the Wilson plant in Cedar Rapids in the 1970s, corrected the interviewer who told her only white-collar women supported the ERA; see Klaner interview.

75. Other workers' perceptions that federal law forced plants to hire women in the 1970s are found in Freda Admire interview, Cherokee, Iowa, March 31, 1983, ILHOP; Gaylen Klinker interview, Cherokee, Iowa, March 25, 1983, ILHOP; Wallace Taylor interview, Storm Lake, Iowa, November 18, 1982, ILHOP; and Tom Thoma interview, Cherokee, Iowa, March 25, 1983, ILHOP.

76. For women's continuing problems with knives, see Klaner interview.

77. Jerred interview.

78. *Chief*, April 27, 1989.

79. Jerred interview; Haymond interview; Otterman Schrader interview; Wetzel interview; Ashlock interview; Bohaty interview.

80. Miller, "Analysis of the Wage System," 190.

81. I am assuming that she meant all women on the kill floor; there were women with graded jobs on cut.

82. *Agreement between IBP, Inc. and United Food & Commercial Workers, International Union AFL-CIO, CLC, on Behalf of Its Local Union No. 1149, Perry, Iowa, October 22, 1990 through June 27, 1993*, 2.

83. Under union procedures followed after IBP opened, stewards were appointed rather than elected. Although Ardie and a few other women became union stewards, they did not become powerful union members, nor did they contest actions of higher union officers.

84. When OSHA officials appeared to check the ammonia leak, they found nothing. A plant worker told me that his supervisor had given him advance notice of the OSHA inspection. The OSHA office denied notifying anyone prior to the inspection, the only exception being the union, which had the right to have a representative present during the inspection.

85. Taylor interview.

86. Ibid.

87. Marshall Wells interview, Fort Dodge, Iowa, July 30, 1981, ILHOP.

88. E. Anthony Rotundo finds the Civil War to have been a major root of this strain of manhood, of which Theodore Roosevelt was a major exponent. See Rotundo, *American Manhood: Transformations in Masculinity from the Revolution to the Modern Era* (New York: Basic Books, 1993), 235–36.

CHAPTER FOUR

1. Cornel West, *Race Matters* (New York: Vintage Books, 1993).

2. Robert R. Dykstra, *Bright Radical Star: Black Freedom and White Supremacy on the Hawkeye Frontier* (Cambridge: Harvard University Press, 1993), 269.

3. Robert J. Neymeyer, "In the Full Light of Day: The Ku Klux Klan in the 1920s in Iowa," *Palimpsest* 76 (1995): 56–63; Leonard Moore, *Citizen Klansman: The Ku Klux Klan in Indiana, 1921–1928* (Chapel Hill: University of North Carolina Press, 1991).

4. Dykstra, *Bright Radical Star*; Susan Stanford Friedman, "Beyond White and Other: Relationality and Narratives of Race in Feminist Discourse," *Signs* 21 (1995): 1–49; David R. Roediger, *The Wages of Whiteness: Race and the Making of the American Working Class* (New York: Verso, 1991).

5. See M. F. Ashley Montagu, *Statement on Race*, 3d ed. (New York: Oxford University Press, 1972), and Evelyn Nakano Glenn, "From Servitude to Service Work: Historical Continuities in the Racial Division of Paid Reproductive Labor," *Signs* 18 (1992): 1–43.

6. I pattern the use of the term black on West, *Race Matters*.

7. Roediger, *Wages of Whiteness*, 4, 134, 146.

8. For a somewhat similar analysis of ethnicity and its significance in shaping the experience of class, see Philippe Bourgois, "Conjugated Oppression: Class and Ethnicity among Guaymi and Kuna Banana Workers," *American Ethnologist* 15 (1988): 328–48.

9. Friedman, "Beyond White and Other," 3.

10. Ibid.; Roediger, *Wages of Whiteness*.

11. These arguments are summarized in Roediger, *Wages of Whiteness*, 9.

12. David Griffith, *Jones's Minimal: Low-Wage Labor in the United States* (Albany: State University of New York Press, 1993).

13. Eric Arnesen, "Following the Color Line of Labor: Black Workers and the Labor Movement before 1930," *Radical History Review* 55 (1993): 53–87; Robert J. Thomas, *Citizenship, Gender, and Work: Social Organization of Industrial Agriculture* (Berkeley: University of California Press, 1985); Thomas Almaguer, "Racial Domination and Class Conflict in Capitalist Agriculture: The Oxnard Sugar Beet Workers' Strike of 1903," *Labor History* 25 (1984): 315–50.

14. Dykstra, *Bright Radical Star*, viii, 26.

15. U.S. Bureau of the Census, *1990 Census of the Population: Social and Economic Characteristics, Iowa* (1900 CP-2-17) (Washington, D.C., 1993), 1, *Characteristics of the Population, Part 2: Florida-Iowa*, vol. 2 of *Sixteenth Census of the Population: 1940*, 849, 866–67, *Composition and Characteristics, Part 1: Alabama-Missouri*, vol. 3 of *Fifteenth Census of the United States, 1930*, 747, and *Historical Statistics of the United States, Colonial Times to 1970*, pt. 2, 27.

16. U.S. Bureau of the Census, *1990 Iowa Census*, 1, 35, 39, 42; *1940 Census*, 849; *1930 Census*, 747.

17. U.S. Bureau of the Census, *1990 Iowa Census*, 1, 35, 39, 42.

18. Data are from the 1910 and 1920 federal census manuscripts for Dallas County, Iowa.

19. Eugene N. Hastie, *History of Perry, Iowa* (Fort Dodge, Iowa: Walterick Printing Co., 1962); Federal census manuscript for Dallas County, 1910; William J. Peterson, *The Story of Iowa: The Progress of an American State*, vol. 1 (New York: Lewis Historical Publishing, 1952), 357; Dorothy Schwieder, *Iowa: The Middle Land* (Ames: Iowa State University Press, 1996), 36–39.

20. Iowa Census, 1925, 745–47; Schwieder, *Iowa*, 192–94; Zaragosa Vargas, *Proletarians of the North: A History of Mexican Industrial Workers in Detroit and the Midwest, 1917–1933* (Berkeley: University of California Press, 1993), 24–41. See also Mark Reisler, *By the Sweat of Their Brow: Mexican Immigrant Labor in the United States, 1900–1940* (Westport, Conn.: Greenwood Press, 1976), 3–2, and Victor S. Clark, *Mexican Labor in the United States*, U.S. Bureau of Labor Bulletin 17 (Washington, D.C., 1908), 478–79.

21. Sebastian Alvarez interview, Fort Madison, Iowa, May 12, 1994, Iowa State Historical Society Archives, Iowa City; "Mexican Contract Workers Came, Worked and Settled," *Fort Madison Daily Democrat*, May 1, 1987; "Fiesta Time Down in Old Fort Madison," *Des Moines Sunday Register*, November 5, 1972. For a short history of "Hyde Park," the 1920s settlement of Mexican railroad workers in Valley Junction, west of Des Moines, see "Mexicans in West Des Moines Struggle to Gain Acceptance," *Des Moines Tribune*, April 9, 1976.

22. Dorothy Schwieder, Joseph Hraba, and Elmer Schwieder, *Buxton: Work and Racial Equality in a Coal Mining Community* (Ames: Iowa State University Press, 1987), 185.

23. "Colored Men in Gun Play," *Perry Daily Chief*, July 24, 1912; "Colored Folks Must Move Out," *Chief*, January 5, 1916.

24. Mendez history, Fort Madison, n.d., copy in author's possession; Alvarez interview; Juan Vasquez interview, Davenport, Iowa, May 9, 1994, Iowa State Historical Society Archives, Iowa City.

25. "Court Gathers in the Fines," *Chief*, December 20, 1913.

26. "Colored People Barred," *Chief*, May 11, 1913; "Form African A.M.E. Church," *Chief*, November 25, 1913.

27. In Buxton the Consolidated Coal Company placed miners' houses on quarter-acre tracts so that the mining families could plant large gardens and fruit trees. Miners' households also kept milk cows, hogs, and poultry. Buxton's black households were largely self-sufficient in food; see Schwieder, Hraba, and Schwieder, *Buxton*, 115.

28. Federal census manuscript for Dallas County, 1920.

29. Dorothy Schwieder, *Black Diamonds: Life and Work in Iowa's Coal Mining Communities, 1895–1925* (Ames: Iowa State University Press, 1983), 168–70.

30. "Many Perry Cases Decided," *Chief*, April 14, 1915; "Officers Make Big Booze Raid at Moran," *Chief*, December 29, 1922; "Fine Negro Woman on Liquor Charge," *Chief*, May 14, 1927; "Intoxication Brings Fine for Negro," *Chief*, September 27, 1927.

31. Editorial, *Chief*, July 20, 1918.

32. Black residents remember Buxton as an island of ethnic harmony, but this camp, laid out in 1900, disappeared before World War I; see Schwieder, Hraba, Schwieder, *Buxton*, 6, 185; "Colored Man Made to Kiss Flag," *Chief*, April 11, 1917; "A Permanent Loyalty Committee Formed," *Chief*, April 16, 1917; "No More German

in Perry Schools," *Chief*, March 9, 1918; "Yellow Paint on Pro-German Buildings," *Chief*, August 20, 1918; "Patriotic Meeting at Round House," *Chief*, September 27, 1918; "Bouton Laborer Killed after a Bloody Fight," *Chief*, March 29, 1919.

33. Neymeyer, "Full Light of Day," 63; Leonore Goodenow, "My Encounters with the Ku Klux Klan," *Palimpsest* 76 (1995): 52–55. Klan news appeared regularly in the *Perry Daily Chief* through the 1920s and early 1930s—for example, "Huge Crowd Hears Rev. Tom Roberts Uphold the Ku Klux Klan in an Open Air Meeting" (July 28, 1923) and "Klan Ceremony Brings Biggest Crowd in History" (June 2, 1924). A personal account of 1930s ethnic prejudice in Fort Dodge is found in Mary St. John interview, Fort Dodge, Iowa, September 13, 1978, Iowa Labor History Oral Project, State Historical Society of Iowa, Iowa City (hereafter cited as ILHOP).

34. "Convocation of Iowa Klansmen Here Sunday," *Chief*, July 19, 1933. Thomas J. Morain, in his study of Jefferson, Iowa, also notes that the Iowa Klan, in spite of itself, had a humorous side; see Morain, *Prairie Grass Roots: An Iowa Small Town in the Early Twentieth Century* (Ames: Iowa State University Press, 1988), 48–49.

35. Newspaper reports confirming black persons' memories of community cohesion in Perry include "Colored People Plan Barbecue," *Perry Advertiser*, July 28, 1915; "Colored League Announces Labor Day Celebration," *Chief*, August 18, 1928; and "A.M.E. Zion Church Room for Children," *Chief*, July 6, 1939.

36. Incidences of violence came up frequently in interviews done for this study. There were also reports in newspapers, although this does not, of course, indicate that violence was necessarily more prevalent within minority households. Perry examples include "Negro Must Answer a Grave Charge," *Chief*, January 31, 1917; "Two Chickens Disrupt Community," *Chief*, March 15, 1917; "Negro Lovers Quarrel Cause of Neighborhood Fight," *Chief*, February 13, 1929.

37. Alvarez interview.

38. Mary and Alvin Edwards interview, July 1, 1986, United Packinghouse Workers of America Oral History Project, State Historical Society of Wisconsin, Madison (hereafter cited as UPWAOHP); Jenny Shuck interview, June 2, 1986, UPWAOHP; Jeanette Haymond interview, February 24, 1986, UPWAOHP; Velma Otterman Schrader interview, May 7, 1986, UPWAOHP; Jarvis Hiles interview, Estherville, Iowa, November 11, 1982, ILHOP; Bill Silag, "Introduction: The Social Response to Industrialism in Sioux City," *Annals of Iowa* 50 (1989/90): 119–29; Scott Sorensen and B. Paul Chicoine, *Sioux City: A Pictorial History* (Norfolk, Va.: Donning Co., 1982), 121.

39. Bruce Nolan, ILHOP interview, quoted in Shelton Stromquist, *Solidarity and Survival: An Oral History of Iowa Labor in the Twentieth Century* (Iowa City: University of Iowa Press, 1993), 85.

40. Shuck interview; Mary and Alvin Edwards interview; Jack and Stella Melsha interview, April 16, 1986, UPWAOHP; Viola Jones interview, Waterloo, Iowa, May 6, 1986, UPWAOHP; Lucille Bremer interview, UPWAOHP, May 6, 1986; Earl DuPey interview, Fort Dodge, Iowa, September 7, 1978, ILHOP.

41. Marshall Wells interview, Fort Dodge, Iowa, July 30, 1981, ILHOP.

42. "The UPWA Story," United Packinghouse, Food and Allied Workers, AFL-CIO, Chicago, 1961, State Historical Society of Iowa Archives, Iowa City, Z125, box 1.

43. Bruce Fehn, " 'The Only Hope We Had': United Packinghouse Workers, Local 46 and the Struggle for Racial Equality in Waterloo, Iowa, 1948–1960," *Annals of Iowa* 54 (1995): 185–216, reprinted in *Unionizing the Jungles: Labor and Community in the Twentieth-Century Meatpacking Industry*, edited by Shelton Stromquist and Marvin Bergman (Iowa City: University of Iowa Press, 1997), 159–87; Roger Horowitz, " 'It Wasn't a Time to Compromise': Unionization of Sioux City Packinghouses, 1937–1942," *Annals of Iowa* 50 (1989/90): 241–68.

44. UPWA Local 46 Newsletter, September 2, 1952, and UPWA Local 46 Statistics, July 20, 1959, Iowa State Historical Society Archives, Iowa City, Z125, box 1.

45. Clinton A. Ruby interview, Fort Dodge, Iowa, August 7, 1981, ILHOP.

46. Anna Mae Weems interview, May 9, 1986, UPWAOHP.

47. Weems interview; Fehn, "Only Hope We Had."

48. Mary and Alvin Edwards interview; Bremer interview; Wells interview; Horowitz, "Wasn't a Time to Compromise," 245; Wilson J. Warren, "The Heyday of the CIO in Iowa: Ottumwa's Meatpacking Workers, 1937–1954," *Annals of Iowa* 51 (1992): 363–89, and "When 'Ottumwa Went to the Dogs': The Erosion of Morrell-Ottumwa's Militant Unionism, 1954–73," *Annals of Iowa* 54 (1995): 217–43; 1989/90: 245); Svend Godfredson, "Unionism in Packing," [1947?], Iowa State Historical Society Archives, Iowa City, Z125, box 1.

49. Fehn, "Only Hope We Had"; Wilson J. Warren, "The Limits of Social Democratic Unionism in Midwestern Meatpacking Communities: Patterns of Internal Strife, 1948–1955," in *Unionizing the Jungles: Labor and Community in the Twentieth-Century Meatpacking Industry*, edited by Shelton Stromquist and Marvin Bergman (Iowa City: University of Iowa Press, 1997), 128–58; Roger Horowitz, " 'This Community of Our Union': Shop Floor Power and Social Unionism in the Postwar UPWA," in *Unionizing the Jungles*, 96–127; Wilson J. Warren, "When 'Ottumwa Went to the Dogs.' "

50. Juli Probasco, "Blacks Treated Well," *Chief*, March 30, 1983.

51. Vasquez interview.

52. For another discussion of racism in rural Iowa, see Osha Gray Davidson, *Broken Heartland: The Rise of America's Rural Ghetto* (New York: Random House, 1990), 120–23.

53. "Beef Strike Spreads to Iowa Plants," *Des Moines Register*, October 21, 1969; William Petroski, "Woman Claims IBP Misled Her about Position," *Register*, November 27, 1988; Michael Wagner, "Refugees Seizing Iowa Opportunity," *Register*, October 9, 1988; Janet E. Benson, "The Effects of Packinghouse Work on Southeast Asian Refugee Families," in *Newcomers in the Workplace: Immigrants and the Restructuring of the U.S. Economy*, edited by Louise Lamphere, Alex Stepick, and Guillermo Grenier (Philadelphia: Temple University Press, 1994), 99–126; Mark A. Grey, "Pork, Poultry, and Newcomers in Storm Lake, Iowa," in *Any Way You Cut It: Meat Processing and Small-Town America*, edited by Donald D. Stull, Michael J. Broadway, and David Griffith (Lawrence: University Press of Kansas, 1995), 109–27; Ron DeRochie interview, Sioux City, Iowa, July 20, 1987, ILHOP.

54. Davidson, *Broken Heartland*, 125–32; Lourdes Gouveia and Donald D. Stull, "Dances with Cows: Beefpacking's Impact on Garden City, Kansas, and Lexington, Nebraska" (85–109), David Griffith, "*Hay Trabajo*: Poultry Processing, Rural

Industrialization, and the Latinization of Low-Wage Labor" (129-52), and Robert Hackenberg and Gary Kukulka, "Industries, Immigrants, and Illness in the New Midwest" (187-212), all in Stull, Broadway, and Griffith, *Any Way You Cut It*; Benson, "Effects of Packinghouse Work"; Michael Broadway, "Beef Stew: Cattle, Immigrants, and Established Residents in a Kansas Beefpacking Town," in Lamphere, Stepick, and Grenier, *Newcomers*, 25-43.

55. *Code of Iowa*, chap. 91E.

56. Juli Probasco, "Burke Learns to Walk Again," *Chief*, March 31, 1983.

57. "IBP Gives Locals Tour," *Chief*, March 16, 1989.

58. Household information on Laotian and Vietnamese American packinghouse workers in Kansas is found in Benson, "Effects of Packinghouse Work," and Janet E. Benson, "Staying Alive: Economic Strategies among Immigrant Packing Plant Workers in Three Southwest Kansas Communities," *Kansas Quarterly* 25 (1994): 107-20.

59. *Agreements between Oscar Mayer & Co., Perry, Iowa and Amalgamated Meat Cutters & Butcher Workmen of North America, AFL-CIO District Local Union No. P-1149, October 19, 1970 through October 18, 1973, October 19, 1973 through October 18, 1976, and October 10, 1976 through October 18, 1979; Agreement (Oscar Mayer and United Food and Commercial Workers), October 19, 1979 through October 18, 1982*, 2.

60. Vargas, *Proletarians*, 8-10, 205-6; Héctor L. Delgado, *New Immigrants, Old Unions: Organizing Undocumented Workers in Los Angeles* (Philadelphia: Temple University Press, 1993), 68; Tamara Ooms, "Mexican Women Immigrants in Marshalltown, Iowa: The Complexity of Needs Assessment" (senior thesis, Grinnell College, 1994).

61. In 1991 testers demonstrated racial discrimination in access to Perry housing; see Juli D. Probasco, "Test Results Indicate Bias," *Chief*, September 19, 1991.

62. On transnational communities, see Griffith, *Jones's Minimal*, 27.

63. Delgado, *New Immigrants*, 79, 87.

CHAPTER FIVE

1. Senate Subcommittee on Agriculture, Nutrition, and Forestry, *Economic Concentration in the Meatpacking Industry*, 102d Cong., 1st sess., 20 July 1991, 233.

2. Thomas Jefferson, "Notes on Virginia," in *The Life and Selected Writings of Thomas Jefferson*, edited by Adrienne Koch and William Peden (New York: Modern Library, 1944), 280-81.

3. For a discussion of Jefferson's evolving viewpoint, see A. Whitney Griswold, "The Agrarian Democracy of Thomas Jefferson," *American Political Science Review* 40 (1946): 657-81. For a modern agrarian review of Jefferson's views, see Wendell Berry, *The Unsettling of America* (San Francisco: Sierra Club Books, 1977), 143-44.

4. Liberty Hyde Bailey, *The Holy Earth* (New York: Charles Scribner's Sons, 1915), 137; Osha Gray Davidson, *Broken Heartland: The Rise of America's Rural Ghetto* (New York: Doubleday, 1990), 170.

5. Discussions of rural class among farmers include Howard Newby and Frederick H. Buttel, "Toward a Critical Rural Sociology," in *The Rural Sociology of the Advanced Societies*, edited by Buttel and Newby (Montclair, N.J.: Allanheld, Osmun,

1980), 1–35; Patrick H. Mooney, *My Own Boss?: Class, Rationality, and the Family Farm* (Boulder, Colo.: Westview Press, 1986); Marty Strange, *Family Farming: A New Economic Vision* (Lincoln: University of Nebraska Press, 1988); and "Class in the Countryside," in H-Rural, 25 January–3 February, 1996, available from H-Rural@msu.edu. On rural towns, see Thomas J. Morain, *Prairie Grass Roots: An Iowa Small Town in the Early Twentieth Century* (Ames: Iowa State University Press, 1988), and Lewis Atherton, *Main Street on the Middle Border* (Chicago: Quadrangle Books, 1954). For studies of rural labor, see David Griffith, *Jones's Minimal: Low-Wage Labor in the United States* (Albany: State University of New York Press, 1993); David Griffith and Ed Kissam, *Working Poor: Farmworkers in the United States* (Philadelphia: Temple University Press, 1995); and Donald D. Stull, Michael J. Broadway, and David Griffith, eds., *Any Way You Cut It: Meat Processing and Small-Town America* (Lawrence: University Press of Kansas, 1995).

6. Dorothy Schwieder, Joseph Hraba, and Elmer Schwieder, *Buxton: Work and Racial Equality in a Coal Mining Community* (Ames: Iowa State University Press, 1987); Elizabeth Corey, *Bachelor Bess: The Homesteading Letters of Elizabeth Corey, 1909–1919*, edited by Philip L. Berber (Iowa City: University of Iowa Press, 1990); Howard Lamar, "From Bondage to Contract: Ethnic Labor in the American West, 1600–1890," in *The Countryside in the Age of Capitalist Transformation: Essays in the Social History of Rural America*, edited by Steven Hahn and Jonathan Prude (Chapel Hill: University of North Carolina Press, 1985), 293–324; Herbert Quick, *Vandemark's Folly* (New York: A. L. Burt, 1922).

7. Catherine McNicol Stock, *Main Street in Crisis: The Great Depression and the Old Middle Class on the Great Plains* (Chapel Hill: University of North Carolina Press, 1992), 13, 48.

8. Curtis Harnack, *We Have All Gone Away* (Garden City, N.Y.: Doubleday, 1973; Ames: Iowa State University Press, 1981), 92.

9. Alice Kessler-Harris, "Treating the Male as 'Other': Re-defining the Parameters of Labor History," *Labor Studies* 34 (1993): 190–204; Richard Sennett and Jonathan Cobb, *The Hidden Injuries of Class* (New York: Random House, 1973).

10. Davidson, *Broken Heartland*, 13–46.

11. Marc W. Steinberg, "The Dialogue of Struggle: The Contest over Ideological Boundaries in the Case of London Silk Weavers in the Early Nineteenth Century," *Social Science History* 18 (1994): 511.

12. Ibid., 506–15. See also Aihwa Ong, "The Gender and Labor Politics of Postmodernity," *Annual Review of Anthropology* 20 (1991): 279–309.

13. June C. Nash, *From Tank Town to High Tech: The Clash of Community and Industrial Cycles* (Albany: State University of New York Press, 1989); Griffith, *Jones's Minimal*.

14. Interestingly, pre–World War I writings of the local press were often socialist and pacifist in tone compared with the turn taken during and after World War I. See, for example, "Omaha Strikers Come to Perry," *Perry Advertiser*, January 16, 1912; "Socialists Name County Ticket," *Advertiser*, March 25, 1912; and "The Candidates and Labor," *Perry Daily Chief and Advertiser*, September 5, 1916.

15. See, for example, "A Mrs. MacVicar Talks Socialism on Perry Streets," *Chief*, July 15, 1922; "Horrors of Russian Famine Brought to Perry People," *Chief*, October 25, 1923; "Embattled Women Lead Male IWW Pickets in Fight," *Chief*, Octo-

ber 22, 1927; "Communists Led Newton Strike!" *Chief*, 15 August 1938; "Armour Strike at Fargo Settled," *Chief*, November 4, 1939; "Sabotage Charge in Labor Trials," *Chief*, April 26, 1940; "Labor Trouble in Perry," *Chief*, April 29, 1941; Editorial, *Chief*, December 16, 1942; and "Workers at Rath Accept Proposal," *Chief*, August 4, 1956.

16. "Labor Day—An Editorial," *Chief*, September 5, 1927.

17. "Eugene V. Debs," *Chief*, October 23, 1926.

18. "Fascist Party to Realize Dream of Mussolini," *Chief*, March 21, 1926.

19. "Labor Day—1935," *Chief*, September 2, 1935; "Landon's Labor Views," *Chief*, August 1, 1936; "Why Farmers Won't Join with Labor," *Chief*, October 19, 1937 (reprinted from *Business Week*); "A Lesson to Labor in City Elections," *Chief*, November 23, 1937.

20. Willis Thornton, "A Divided Labor Movement Looks Ahead to Critical Months," *Chief*, September 2, 1938; "One Union Divisible by Its Friends," *Chief*, August 13, 1938; "Murderer Admits Labor Slaying in Minneapolis," *Chief*, May 26, 1938; "Labor Department Aided Communism Dies Report Says," *Chief*, January 3, 1939; "Disorder Breaks Out in Sioux City," *Chief*, October 19, 1938; "Officers Arrest Swift Pickets," October 20, 1938; "Two Strikes Cost State $75,000," *Chief*, December 1, 1938; "Morrell Union Out on Strike," *Chief*, August 24, 1939; "Violence Threat in Iowa Strike," *Chief*, August 29, 1939.

21. Carol Johnson interview, Storm Lake, Iowa, November 17, 1982, Iowa Labor History Oral Project, State Historical Society of Iowa, Iowa City (hereafter cited as ILHOP); Bohumir (Bum) Keeler interview, Estherville, Iowa, November 11, 1982, ILHOP; Mary Ashlock interview, Mason City, Iowa, November 17, 1981, ILHOP.

22. Jarvis Hiles interview, Estherville, Iowa, November 11, 1982, ILHOP.

23. Willys Stearns interview, Estherville, Iowa, November 10, 1982, ILHOP.

24. Nadine Klaner interview, Cedar Rapids, Iowa, August 26, 1982, ILHOP.

25. Velma Otterman Schrader interview, Waterloo, Iowa, May 7, 1986, United Packinghouse Workers of America Oral History Project, Wisconsin State Historical Society, Madison (hereafter cited as UPWAOHP).

26. Wilson J. Warren, "The Heyday of the CIO in Iowa: Ottumwa's Meatpacking Workers, 1937–1954," *Annals of Iowa* 51 (1992): 373–89; Jeanette Haymond interview, Cedar Rapids, Iowa, November 9, 1977, ILHOP.

27. After a merger in 1979, the packing union was the United Food and Commercial Workers (UFCW); see Chapter 2.

28. Gaylen Klinker interview, Cherokee, Iowa, March 25, 1983, ILHOP.

29. Daniel Nelson, *Farm and Factory: Workers in the Midwest, 1880–1990* (Bloomington: Indiana University Press, 1995), 137. See Ron DeRochie interview, Sioux City, Iowa, July 20, 1987, ILHOP; Merlyn Wee interview, Estherville, Iowa, November 12, 1982, ILHOP; Jan Bednarczyk interview, Cherokee, Iowa, March 31, 1983, ILHOP; Leo Zinnel interview, Estherville, Iowa, November 11, 1982, ILHOP; Paul Larsen interview, Cedar Rapids, Iowa, July 15, 1981, ILHOP; and Haymond interview.

30. Warren, "Heyday," 365; Barney Hassel interview, Estherville, Iowa, November 11, 1978, ILHOP.

31. Hassel interview.

32. Warren, "Heyday."

33. Ethel Minor, "Why Continue My Education," *Chief*, June 16, 1923.

34. Sebastian Alvarez interview, Fort Madison, Iowa, May 12, 1994, and Juan Vasquez interview, Davenport, Iowa, May 9, 1994, Iowa State Historical Society Archives, Iowa City. Alvarez, an exceptional athlete, stood out as the first Mexican student to graduate from high school. Vasquez describes an early and continuing love of books that did not translate into a high school diploma or a sense of intellectual potential. For the general phenomenon of class selection in public schools, see Jonathan Kozol, *Savage Inequalities: Children in America's Schools* (New York: Crown, 1991).

35. Fidel Alvarez interview, Fort Madison, Iowa, February 3, 1990, ILHOP.

36. Although I have uncovered no memory of a meatpacking local in Perry in the 1940s, newspaper accounts indicate that some forty Perry members of the UPWA went out during the strike of 1946, but they did not close the plant; see "Packinghouse Worker Strike Is Called," *Chief*, January 2, 1946, and "Picket Lines Removed at Meat Plants," *Des Moines Register*, January 27, 1946. Accounts of the 1946 and 1948 strikes in other Iowa packing plants can be found in Shelton Stromquist, *Solidarity and Survival: An Oral History of Iowa Labor in the Twentieth Century* (Iowa City: University of Iowa Press, 1993), 175–86; David Brody, *The Butcher Workmen: A Study of Unionization* (Cambridge: Harvard University Press, 1964), 229–47; and Charles R. Perry and Delwyn H. Kegley, *Disintegration and Change: Labor Relations in the Meat Packing Industry*, Labor Relations and Public Policy Series, no. 35 (Philadelphia: University of Pennsylvania, 1989), 126–27.

37. "Urge Community to Act for New Industry in Perry," *Chief*, October 3, 1961; "Hope of New Industry Is Top News in Perry during 1961," *Chief*, December 30, 1961; "Many Sharp Exchanges at Union Talk," *Chief*, March 26, 1963.

38. Editorial, *Chief*, March 15, 1963.

39. Editorial, *Chief*, March 30, 1963.

40. "File Charges in Union Election," *Chief*, April 8, 1961; "Object to Newspaper Editorials," *Chief*, August 26, 1983.

41. "IPC Workers Reaffirm Original Labor Stand," *Chief*, September 26, 1963; "NLRB Wants New Election," *Chief*, September 25, 1964.

42. Editorials, *Chief*, October 3, 1961, March 27, 1963; "No IPC Decision on Possibility of Appeal," *Chief*, December 3, 1964; "140 Walk Out at Iowa Pork," *Chief*, January 19, 1965; "Local UPW Union Men Strike at Iowa Pork Co.," *Chief*, March 11, 1965.

43. "Perry Merchants Complaint on Tactics of UPWA Solicitors Here," *Chief*, March 19, 1965; "Opens Commissary for Strikers," *Chief*, April 2, 1965.

44. Harold E. Hughes, *The Man from Ida Grove: A Senator's Personal Story* (Lincoln, Va.: Chosen Books, 1979), 198.

45. Ros Jensen, "Beef Plant Picketing Curbed," *Register*, March 7, 1965; Nick Lamberto, "Hughes Acts in Beef Strike," *Register*, March 17, 1965; Jack Gillard, "Strike Talks Deadlocked," *Register*, April 4, 1965; "Ratify Pact at Iowa Beef in Fort Dodge," *Register*, April 6, 1965; "Fire At IPC," *Chief*, April 12, 1965; "Iowa Pork Co. Strike Is Settled," *Chief*, May 20, 1965.

46. "Progress Is Shifting Gears for Perry's Second Hundred Years," *Chief*, June 28, 1969; Arlene Klinker interview, Cherokee, Iowa, March 31, 1983, ILHOP.

47. Roy Clabaugh interview, Estherville, Iowa, November 11, 1982, ILHOP.

48. Wee interview.

49. Dean Hanson interview, Estherville, Iowa, November 11, 1982, ILHOP. See also Arleen Klinker interview; Julia Naylor interview, Fort Dodge, Iowa, August 7, 1981, ILHOP; Clem Kilby interview, Charles City, Iowa, June 18, 1982, ILHOP; and Anna Mae Weems interview, Waterloo, Iowa, May 9, 1986, UPWAOHP.

50. Velma Otterman Schrader interview, Waterloo, Iowa, May 7, 1986, UPWAOHP; Alvin Edwards interview, Sioux City, Iowa, July 1, 1986, UPWAOHP; Stromquist, Solidarity, 175-86; Nick Lamberto, "Hughes Acts"; "Curbing Strike Violence" (editorial), Register, March 18, 1965; "200 Invade Denison, Hit Beef Plant," Register, November 9, 1969; "Iowa Beef Picket Shot," Register, November 22, 1969; Jerry Knight, "Secret Role of Wounded Girl Is Bared," Register, October 25, 1969; "IBP," International Directory of Company Histories (Chicago: St. James Press, 1990), 2:515-16.

51. See also "Indict Perry Union Leader," Register, November 22, 1966.

52. Dick Sturgeon interview, Sioux City, Iowa, March 18, 1983, ILHOP.

53. Lucille Bremer and Viola Jones interviews, Waterloo, Iowa, May 6, 1986, UPWAOHP; Ethel Jerred interview, Ottumwa, Iowa, October 5, 1981, ILHOP; Willys Stearns interview, Estherville, Iowa, November 10, 1982, ILHOP; John Andon interview, Mason City, Iowa, November 16, 1981, ILHOP; Clabaugh interview.

54. Dissatisfaction with union policies and union leadership cannot be adequately assessed on the basis of oral history projects sponsored by unions if the oral history subjects are identified by union leaders. Although instances of silencing and intimidation have arisen in the course of my study, my research—like the oral labor history projects—was not designed to expose a lack of democracy in the meatpacking unions.

55. I took notes during this interview rather than taping it.

56. Iowa Postwar Rehabilitation Commission, Report Presented to the Governor of Iowa and the Iowa 51st General Assembly (Des Moines, 1945); Iowa Development Commission, Iowa . . . Land of Industrial Opportunity (Des Moines, 1950).

57. Iowa Development Commission, Iowa; Kate Rousmaniere, "The Muscatine Button Workers' Strike of 1911-12: An Iowa Community in Conflict," Annals of Iowa 46 (1982): 243-62.

58. Iowa Development Commission, Iowa, C8.

59. Ibid., C11.

60. Personal communication, Thomas R. Patterson, Senior Research Analyst, Democratic Research Staff, Iowa House of Representatives, 1995, copy in author's possession.

61. William Ryberg, Jonathan Roos, and Jay P. Wagner, "Ipsco Chooses Iowa for Steel Mill," Register, March 23, 1994; Veronica Fowler and Holli Hartman, "Marshalltown Keeps Lennox Plant," Register, May 8, 1993; Pete Anderson, "Job Development: What Is Fair for Iowans?," Register, February 11, 1994; Veronica Fowler, "Think Tank Issues Development Guidelines," Register, April 6, 1994.

62. William Coffey, "The Role of Producer Services in Modern Production Systems: Implications for Rural Development," in Rural America and the Changing Structure of Manufacturing: Spatial Implications of New Technology and Organization, edited by G. Andrew Bernat Jr. and Martha Frederick, Agricultural and Rural Economy Divi-

sion, Economic Research Service, U.S. Department of Agriculture, ERS Staff Report No. AGES 9319 (1993), 69–94; Amy K. Glasmeier, Jeffry Thompson, and Amy Kays, "Trade Policy, Corporate Strategy and Future Industrial Restructuring: The Impact of Globalization on Rural Manufacturing," in Bernat and Frederick, *Rural America*, 95–106; Christina E. Gringeri, *Getting By: Women Homeworkers and Rural Economic Development* (Lawrence: University Press of Kansas, 1994); Thomas A. Heberlein, "Is Rural Better?," *As You Sow: Social Issues in Agriculture* (University of Wisconsin, Madison, April 1992). News stories on Iowa rural development and wages include Dale Kasler, "Rural Iowa May Lose Out in Search for Cheap Labor," *Register*, February 20, 1996; Veronica Fowler, "Repeated Trips to DEBA Trough Trouble Officials," *Register*, June 17, 1994; and Melinda Voss, "Downwardly Mobile—and No Improvement in Sight," *Register*, September 25, 1994.

63. "Jobs Don't Guarantee Wages That Provide Good Quality of Life," *Register*, April 7, 1996.

64. For a discussion of the way that the middle-class residents of an Iowa town negotiated the changes of the 1990s, see Nancy Naples, "Contradictions in Agrarian Ideology: Restructuring Gender, Race-Ethnicity, and Class in Rural Iowa," *Rural Sociology* 59 (1994): 110–35.

EPILOGUE

1. "Church Extends Welcome Hand," *Perry Daily Chief*, August 17, 1995. For employment of East Africans elsewhere in rural Iowa, see Deborah Fisch, "Somalians Ask for Consideration," *O'Brien County Bell*, June 22, 1995.

2. Appearing as I write is Thomas O'Donnell, "Man and Daughter Slain in Storm Lake," *Des Moines Register*, April 11, 1996.

3. Robert A. Hackenberg, "Conclusion: Joe Hill Died for Your Sins: Empowering Minority Workers in the New Industrial Labor Force," in *Any Way You Cut It: Meat Processing and Small-Town America*, edited by Donald D. Stull, Michael J. Broadway, and David Griffith (Lawrence: University Press of Kansas, 1995), 254.

4. Upton Sinclair, *The Jungle* (New York: Penguin, 1985), 45–47.

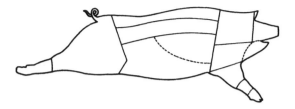

INDEX